Patterns and Profiles of Promising Learners From Poverty

Patterns and Profiles of
Promising
Learners
From Poverty

Edited by
Joyce L. Van Tassel-Baska, Ed.D.

Prufrock Press Inc.
Waco, Texas

a service publication of

NATIONAL ASSOCIATION FOR
Gifted Children

Library of Congress Cataloging-in-Publication Data

Patterns and profiles of promising learners from poverty / edited by Joyce L. VanTassel-Baska.
   p. cm. — (The critical issues in equity and excellence in gifted education series)
Includes bibliographical references.
ISBN-13: 978-1-59363-396-7 (pbk.)
ISBN-10: 1-59363-396-3
1. Gifted children—Education—United States. 2. Children with social disabilities—Education—United States. 3. Poor children—Education—United States. I. VanTassel-Baska, Joyce. II. National Association for Gifted Children (U.S.)
LC3993.9.P375 2009
371.95086'942—dc22
                2009029159

At the time of this book's publication, all facts and figures cited are the most current available. All telephone numbers, addresses, and Web site URLs are accurate and active. All publications, organizations, Web sites, and other resources exist as described in the book, and all have been verified. The authors and Prufrock Press Inc. make no warranty or guarantee concerning the information and materials given out by organizations or content found at Web sites, and we are not responsible for any changes that occur after this book's publication. If you find an error, please contact Prufrock Press Inc.

Prufrock Press Inc.
P.O. Box 8813
Waco, TX 76714-8813
Phone: (800) 998-2208
Fax: (800) 240-0333
http://www.prufrock.com

Contents

List of Tables

List of Figures

Introduction:
An Overview of *Patterns and Profiles of Promising Learners From Poverty*

Joyce VanTassel-Baska

Patterns and Profiles of Promising Learners From Poverty represents a labor of love. It is the last volume in the series on equity and excellence that I have edited during the past 4 years. It also represents one of our most critical issues as a field. How do we ensure that children of poverty have the opportunity to participate in gifted programs? How do we prepare them to be ready for such program participation? Can equity and excellence become twin realities in American education?

This book posits that poverty is the overarching variable that leads to underrepresentation in gifted programs, not race or ethnicity, nor gender. It is a culture all its own, with rules and mores for conduct by its members, at least among the working poor. It causes untold grief among its brightest members who have the desire, but not the means, to break its bonds. It stunts growth at critical periods of development and renders children vulnerable to lives of underachievement in school and life. Even as early as the 1940s, as we saw the results of the Terman study C group, we knew the power of low incomes in depressing achievement and happiness in all aspects of life (Terman & Oden, 1940).

Poverty is a family circumstance that affects more than 24 million children per year (Gross & Capuzzi, 2000; Hodgkinson,

2002). It knows no racial boundaries, as more Caucasian children are poor than all minority groups combined, even though more than half of all African American and Hispanic American families also reside in poverty. It knows no geographic boundaries either, as rural poverty is as extensive as that in urban areas, just less concentrated. It knows no gender bias, as both adult men and women experience poverty every day, many in homeless conditions. Single parent mothers, however, as a subgroup of women, are far more likely to experience poverty. Being poor also is a status, despite the American dream, that all but perhaps 5% of Americans are likely to remain in due to the insidious relationship of educational attainment and job accessibility. Sennett and Cobb (1972) confirmed the difficulty in moving up from the lower class in our society, suggesting that social mores, one's neighborhood, parental education and career, and the prevalence of divorce and child-bearing all collude to make upward mobility unlikely. Intergenerational poverty is common as well, particularly among African Americans, where the single parent rate constitutes more than half of the population.

Students from impoverished backgrounds are at greater risk for a host of social-emotional problems, including lower levels of motivation, when compared to children who do not come from such backgrounds (Beirne-Smith, Patton, & Ittenbach, 1994). Oftentimes, the risks for social-emotional problems come from related special challenges for students living in poverty, including higher rates of disabilities, teenage mothers, absent fathers, lower motivational levels, parents without resources, health problems, concerns about safety and daily survival, and increased risk of homelessness (Beirne-Smith et al., 1994; Stormont, 2000).

The chapters in this book represent a vision of poverty that is based in an understanding of the cultural and social identity issues of the minority poor as well as the particular aspects of the poor from urban and rural areas, and aspects of the perceptions that poor children, their parents, and their teachers hold about the value of gifted programs in the context of their learning preferences and habits. A chapter on curriculum delineates prototypical models that can address characterological needs. There also are chapters that address the support networks necessary to assure that these children are accepted and nurtured within the gifted program context through professional development and local and state policies that facilitate rather than impede their progress.

The Kitano chapter, Chapter 2, focuses on the impact of culture and its role in shaping children of poverty. It lays out the cultural pattern found among several minority groups and suggests that students from these cultures manifest their competence in different ways, many times alien to classroom norms and patterns for traditional achievement. Using Rogoff's (2003) sociocultural perspective, she posits that the instructional context for culturally diverse learners matters as much as their individual characteristics in being successful. Kitano suggests that teachers need to provide a supportive environment for culturally diverse learners, including acknowledging their cultural strengths and sharing them with others as well as working on the transference of culturally based competence to school-based expectations for competence. She highlights differences between home and school cultures of these learners to emphasize the gap that teachers must bridge while maintaining high expectations for performance. She ends the chapter with a set of questions for teachers on how they are addressing cultural diversity in their classrooms.

Chapter 3, the Worrell chapter, lays out the research on social identity, especially among African Americans. He posits that two theories are central in understanding the construct of social identity: sense of belonging and stereotype threat. These theories allow us to understand the individual need to connect to groups and how group perception of one's own culture can negatively impact upward mobility, especially in respect to advanced educational access and attainment. His central thesis is that African American students disproportionately experience psychosocial stressors that interfere with academic achievement due to several factors that include oppositional defiant behaviors born of being involuntary minorities in America, misconceptions of ability as innate, and fear of letting down one's race. Worrell advocates for providing stronger social support networks in university-based gifted programs and providing counseling that is targeted on these identity issues in order to keep potentially gifted learners from non-mainstream cultures on a positive educational path.

The Stambaugh chapter, Chapter 4, delineates the central issues in working with the rural poor, including geographic isolation, and given fewer students, the less frequent presence of gifted learners and extra resources to serve them. Moreover, there is a real tendency for rural educators to overlook gifted students and neglect a service delivery for them, because most education occurs in regular classroom settings and gifted education often is viewed with suspicion as an elitist enterprise by rural educators and parents. She analyzes existing national datasets that confirm the prevalence of rural poverty and lays out alternative identification protocols and intervention approaches that may be successful in finding and serving the rural poor, including acceleration and grouping. She also highlights findings from the reform literature on the leadership needs for rural Title I schools, all efforts that would support the needs of the gifted at the systems level.

Chapter 5, the Olszewski-Kubilius chapter, frames the issues of poverty in work she has conducted in the Chicago area, most recently her work with Project Excite in Evanston, IL, a small city north of Chicago. Her central thesis is that these students need support from multiple agencies over time in order to access the same benefits as their more advantaged peers. Support for academic preparation, especially in core areas like reading and math, is necessary along with the social supports so crucial to nurturing such students to perform at high levels. The author skillfully lays out the model for enhancing the success of these learners—value-added education during the academic year and in the summer, counseling for psychosocial and academic issues that emerge, work with families, and importing role models in the form of tutors and mentors who can guide their development at crucial points of schooling such as middle school and entrance to college.

The MacFarlane and Feng chapter, Chapter 6, examines case study material on low-income African American students. Data from parents, teachers, and students themselves all attest to the support from both family and school in helping these learners attain a high level of competence. Concerns for the peer group left behind appears to be a major issue with these learners as is their isolation, with such children often being the only African American children in gifted classes. Nevertheless, the portrait that emerges is that of children of fortitude and internal strength, forged from family belief systems that sustain their involvement in educational upward mobility.

The Swanson chapter on Caucasian low-income learners, Chapter 7, uses the case study material collected for a series of 37 vignettes of children of poverty from different ethnic groups to forge a portrait of promising development in these young lives, captured during their middle school years after being in gifted programs for 3 years or more. Swanson zeroes in on the supportive nature of families and teachers, the role of gifted programs in providing self-confidence and important communication skills, and the resilience of these learners in handling high-level schoolwork in the context of social and emotional turmoil.

Chapter 8, the Swanson chapter on high nonverbal and low verbal profile students, provides a glimpse into the lives of students who traditionally have been underrepresented in gifted programs because of their ability profile. In a state where nonverbal ability is a major part of the identification protocol, these students emerged as eligible candidates for programs, and the results shared by Swanson support both the right and the struggle of these students to be in gifted programs, even though they, like the other underrepresented populations featured in this volume, suffer from areas of weakness in academic preparation and functional skill level. In the case of these students, the lack of high verbal skills handicaps them in gifted program environments that focus strongly on verbal curriculum. However, their creative abilities and outside interests keep them grounded and able to persevere.

The VanTassel-Baska chapter on curriculum, Chapter 9, delineates important types of interventions for students in poverty and of minority status, sharing the literature on what has worked with these students in special programs both in school and outside of traditional school settings. Drawing on the research conducted at The College of William and Mary on successful curriculum in Title I schools, she posits the importance of key components in planning and developing new curricula for these populations as well as highlighting extant curriculum that addresses core areas of need by tapping into constructivist approaches to learning. She describes the Integrated Curriculum Model as a framework for designing research-based curriculum that is responsive to these students and shares some prototypical examples of curriculum that may be employed in all school settings that are consonant with underrepresented population characteristics and needs. The chapter concludes with guidelines for practitioners in implementing such differentiated and adapted curriculum.

Supportive teachers are a crucial component of ensuring that students of poverty are successful in their efforts to excel. Chapter 10, the Swanson chapter on teacher preparation to work effectively with these learners, emphasizes the social, cultural, and academic areas that teachers must understand and develop skills in if they are to facilitate talent development among these underrepresented populations. She highlights the new teacher education standards and their major emphasis on these kinds of learners, suggesting the use of case studies and vignettes to help teachers see the complexity of these young lives. She also offers guidelines for school administrators to develop such cultural competence in teachers and challenges educators to undertake the effort required to prepare teachers for the role of talent developers with low-income learners.

Just as teachers matter at the classroom level in providing social support to low-income learners, the support structure at the district and state level also matters in providing access to programs and services. The Lord chapter, Chapter 11, emphasizes the importance of policy development as a crucial part of sustaining efforts to help underrepresented populations at state and local levels. He lays out a case study from his own experience as a state director of gifted programs where collaborative policy development was forged to ensure that students from poverty would have a greater chance of being identified and served effectively. He notes the difficulty in anticipating the impact of changing policy on statewide services and the need to evaluate such impacts thoughtfully. He also provides a template for other educators to follow in creating and implementing supportive policies on behalf of these learners.

Chapter 12, the final chapter, presents a model for examining the need for interlocking systems of support for working with promising learners from poverty. At the national level of support, these learners require policy resources in the form of social and intellectual capital to reach their potential. At state and local levels, they require the support of home, school, and community systems to sustain them over time in reflecting on and learning from experience. Finally, students of poverty require systems of interventions that will catalyze their abilities and predispositions into talent development areas. These interventions will necessitate an emphasis on affective and conative areas like motivation and passion as well as cognitive areas like higher level thinking and problem solving. The model is informed by the literature on students from poverty and is further informed by the major ideas and findings from the chapters of this book.

The audience for this book is school practitioners and parents who struggle daily with viewing the potential of low-income students but who often feel powerless to do anything about it. It is my sincere hope that this book will empower and inspire all of us to do more for these students in and out of school. Several recent reports have documented the importance of establishing a social agenda nationally to focus on low-income students of promise (VanTassel-Baska & Stambaugh, 2007; Wyner, Bridgeland, & DiIulio 2007). The agenda laid out for action by VanTassel-Baska and Stambaugh included the following points:

- Educators in gifted education need to be more proactive in collaborating with local, state, and national organizations and foundations that focus on students of poverty in order to maximize efforts, including joint research studies, reports, conferences, and service provisions.
- Model policies for use at state and local levels need to be developed to ensure equitable practices for identification and service of promising learners in poverty.
- Exemplary program models, pre-K–16, that posit a systematic approach to identification and services for promising learners in poverty need to be developed and disseminated to state and local education constituencies.
- More sophisticated research related to promising learners in poverty needs to be conducted. School districts need to

recruit a more diverse population of educators, including educators from low-income schools and those from various minority groups, and train them to work effectively with promising students of poverty.

- An emphasis on family education and involvement is critical to the enterprise of talent development in these learners. (pp. 86–87)

Such an agenda can only be successful if the audience for this book chooses to activate it in the settings of home, school, or agency. If each of us only focused on one child in poverty for the next 3 years and followed the suggestions provided in the wisdom of these chapters, real lives would be improved immeasurably. The circumstance to be born into certain families who have scant resources is not a choice that children have; helping them survive and thrive in educational settings beyond those circumstances is a choice we all have and can achieve.

References

Beirne-Smith, M., Patton, J., & Ittenbach, R. (1994). *Mental retardation* (4th ed.). Columbus, OH: Macmillan.

Gross, D. A., & Capuzzi, D. (2000). Defining youth at risk. In D. Capuzzi & D. A. Gross (Eds.), *Youth at risk: Prevention resources for counselors, teachers and parents* (pp. 3–21). Alexandria, VA: American Counseling Association.

Hodgkinson, H. (2002). Demography and democracy. *Journal of Teacher Education, 53,* 102–105.

Rogoff, B. (2003). *The cultural nature of human development.* Oxford, UK: Oxford University Press.

Sennett, R., & Cobb, J. (1972). *The hidden injuries of class.* New York: Knopf.

Stormont, M. (2000). Early child risk factors for externalizing and internalizing behavior at a five year follow-forward assessment. *Journal of Early Intervention, 23,* 180–190.

Terman, L., & Oden, M. (1940). Status of the California gifted group at the end of sixteen years. In G. M. Whipple & G. D. Stoddard (Eds.), *Intelligence: Its nature and nurture, 39th yearbook of the National Society for the Study of Education* (pp. 67–74). Bloomington, IL: Public School Publishing Co.

VanTassel-Baska, J., & Stambaugh, T. (2007). *Overlooked gems: A national perspective on low-income promising learners.* Washington, DC: National Association for Gifted Children.

Wyner, J. S., Bridgeland, J. M., & DiIulio, J. J., Jr. (2007). *Achievementrap: How America is failing millions of high-achieving students from low-income families.* Landsdowne, VA: Jack Kent Cooke Foundation.

The Role of Culture in Shaping Expectations for Gifted Students

Margie K. Kitano

Over the years, the academic community has debated the relative contributions of race and class to student outcomes. During the 1960s and 1970s, the writings of William Wilson and Milton Gordon stimulated a sometimes acrimonious debate about the relative importance of race and social class in determining behavior and values (Banks, 1988). These authors argued that social class takes precedence, with Black middle-class individuals having more in common with White middle-class peers than with Blacks in lower classes. However, accumulating data demonstrate clearly that economic status accounts for only a portion of variance in achievement (Magnuson & Duncan, 2006). African American, Latino, and Native American students exhibit lower average achievement test scores than White and Asian students across economic levels (College Board, 1999), and all economic segments of these three groups are underrepresented at the highest levels of achievement (Miller, 2004).

Recent research points to the complexity of interactions among the individual's characteristics (e.g., culture, class, nativity, primary language) and features of the social environment (e.g., expectations, bias, curriculum, instructional approach) in determining achievement. Explanations for differences in performance are shifting from a focus on the learner alone to a focus on the learner in interaction with a social and cultural context (Rogoff, 2003). Using a sociocultural framework, this chapter examines the role of culture in the performance of gifted students and instructional strategies that can support culturally diverse gifted students' expression of their high performance capability.

Sociocultural Framework

More than 35 years ago, Cole and Bruner (1971) synthesized anthropological and cross-cultural psychology research, arguing against cultural deficit perspectives. Their work demonstrated that

> those groups ordinarily diagnosed as culturally deprived have the same underlying competence as those in the mainstream of the dominant culture, the differences in performance being accounted for by the situations and contexts in which the competence is expressed. (p. 868)

One illustration of this argument offered by Cole and Bruner (1971) compared Yale sophomores and nonliterate Kpelle rice farmers on estimation tasks. The Yale sophomores outperformed the Kpelle rice farmers in estimating distance, while the rice farmers displayed greater accuracy than the sophomores in estimating volume of rice. Both groups possessed competence in estimation skills but manifested that competence in different situations. Closer to home, Cole and Bruner cited Labov's (1970) work similarly demonstrating the integral contribution of situation and context in the linguistic performance of an 8-year-old African American male student. The child's monosyllabic linguistic output in a standardized test situation stood in stark contrast to the same child's fluent dialogue with the same interviewer in the boy's apartment, accompanied by one of the boy's friends, on the floor with potato chips, discussing "taboo" subjects in dialect. Labov argued that typical test situations can elicit defensive behavior from a child who reasonably expects that talking openly exposes himself to harm and thus cannot measure competence.

Cole and Bruner (1971) concluded that cultural differences reside more in differences in the situations to which different cultural groups apply their skills than to differences in the skills possessed by the groups in question.

Based on accumulating cross-cultural research and the works of Bronfenbrenner and Vygotsky, the sociocultural perspective (Rogoff, 2003) views an individual's cognitive development and processes as inseparable from the instructional environment. They are not attributable solely to the individual, but to the individual in action with the specific social and cultural context (Rueda & Moll, 1994). In this perspective, the student's prior experiences (e.g., culturally based knowledge and practices, ways of interacting, expectations) and the specific classroom environment (e.g., instructional approach, task demands, expectations) together influence cognition. This framework considers the effects of the instructional context and focuses attention on analysis of activities within which students are learning, thinking, and engaged (or not) because learning, thinking, and engagement are features of the student in the activity (Rueda & Moll, 1994).

Implications for the Gifted and Talented

The sociocultural approach has implications for how we conceptualize and identify giftedness and how we can support the performance of gifted and talented students from culturally and linguistically diverse backgrounds.

Conceptualizing Giftedness

High performance capability is present in all cultures but manifested in different ways consistent with the experiences and values of the individual within his or her culture. In this country, schools typically define giftedness operationally as exceptionally high performance in a particular social and cultural context: the standardized test situation. We can infer a capacity under these conditions at least as high as the observed performance. However, we cannot infer an individual's capacity from low performance occurring in this context, any more than we can accurately judge the linguistic capacity of Labov's (1970) 8-year-old in the formal test situation. One factor inhibiting expression of capacity may be a student's difficulty transferring his or her competence to the test situation. For example, a student may have limited experience or familiarity with the type of questioning, such as requests for information out of context (e.g., "What is a ruby?"). Fear of confirming negative stereotypes (Steele, 2003) or discomfort based on prior experience with similar situations also may hinder the expression of capacity in the test situation. Performance on tests of academic achievement additionally is influenced by the quality of schooling afforded the student in prior years.

Giftedness, conceptualized as exceptionally high performance capability, is a characteristic of the individual as defined by the particular culture. Its expression in performance is located in the student acting in a particular social and cultural activity. Standardized assessment measures performance, not necessarily capacity, within this context and favors those who have greatest experience with the social and cultural requirements of the situation. Sternberg (2007) warned:

> By testing children for giftedness outside their cultural context, we may fail to identify children who, by virtue of their cultural context, are gifted. We also may identify as gifted those children who are not so outstanding, considering their background. (p. 164)

It is important to note that culturally and linguistically diverse students range broadly in the extent to which they are acculturated to school expectations and standardized test situations. Some students from culturally and linguistically diverse (CLD) backgrounds begin school with values, beliefs, and behaviors consistent with school expectations or readily adapt to these expectations. This chapter addresses instructional strategies for those students who, due to cultural and linguistic backgrounds and experiences within the larger community, may find mainstream classrooms unfamiliar and alienating places.

Supporting Gifted Performance in the Classroom

From a sociocultural perspective, students from cultur-ally diverse backgrounds possess the same competence as their mainstream peers but may express or apply their competence under different conditions. The teacher's primary challenges and goals are:

1. supporting students' transfer of their competence—high-level thinking, problem solving, creativity—to the school context;
2. enhancing students' flexibility and fluency in demon-strating their cognitive competence across different cultural contexts, including home, community, and school; and
3. capitalizing on students' cultural strengths and encour-aging them to share their strengths with others.

Facilitating culturally and linguistically diverse students' transfer of their underlying cognitive competence from home to school contexts begins with teachers assuming that their students possess high performance capability.

High Expectations

Supporting CLD students' transfer of high-level thinking from familiar to unfamiliar contexts begins with recognizing students' underlying cognitive abilities. Experts consistently exhort teachers to have high expectations for CLD students. Although most teachers would say they hold high expecta-tions for all students, the research does suggest that cultural bias continues to be an issue in identifying gifted CLD stu-dents. Studies examining referral and placement recommen-dations have reported that teachers are more likely to refer White than Latino (Peterson & Margolin, 1997) and African American (Elhoweris, Mutua, Alsheikh, & Holloway, 2005) students as gifted despite identical descriptions of academic performance. Cultural groups may vary in their conceptual-izations of giftedness, and these differences may influence recognition of giftedness in students and their affirmation in the classroom (Peterson, 1999).

Gifted students recognize teachers' levels of expectations. In one study (Harmon, 2002), gifted African American students described ineffective teachers as communicating low expectations of African American students and behaving in ways that appeared disrespectful and prejudicial. They lacked understanding of these students' needs and did not respond to name calling and harassment. The students described effective teachers—both Black and White—as holding high expectations and being respectful of all students, understanding students' culture, implementing multicultural curriculum, explaining concepts in accessible ways, using cooperative learning, discussing coping skills for dealing with racism, providing a disciplined classroom, and not tolerating name-calling and harassment. Additional studies have documented negative stereotyping of African American families (Harry, Klingner, & Hart, 2005) and failure to recognize family and student strengths, including gifted potential.

Teachers' lower expectations for CLD gifted students may result in part from observing some students' below-grade-level performance on basic skills such as reading and writing in English. School districts using nonverbal intelligence tests may identify some students as gifted who are underachieving academically. In these cases, it is important to distinguish between cognitive capacity and processes (high-level thinking, problem solving, categorizing, synthesizing, etc.) and current level of school-related knowledge and skills (subject matter, reading, writing). The latter may be depressed by limited educational opportunity. These children benefit from activities that engage high-level thinking and support for acquisition of basic knowledge and skills. Addressing needs for both challenging curricula and basic skill development may require increased class time through longer hours, afterschool programs, and Saturday and summer classes.

Although cultural sensitivity as well as high expectations appear important to effective teaching of CLD students, more critical is translating these positive attributes into challenging and meaningful curriculum. Evidence exists that self-reported sociocultural awareness, self-understanding, and cultural responsiveness do not distinguish effective from ineffective urban teachers (Sachs, 2004). More likely, effective teachers apply their cultural understandings in supporting students' transfer of their high abilities to the school context.

Supporting Students' Transfer of Competence to School Contexts

Rogoff (2003) noted that enabling culturally diverse students to transfer high-level thinking skills from a familiar to unfamiliar context is a challenging task. She cited as an example Carol Lee's (1995) successful work with low-income African American students in applying their high-level analytic skills, demonstrated in signifying, to literary analysis. Signifying, playing the dozens, and capping are types of verbal repartee (e.g., "Your momma . . . ") requiring high-level analogical thinking, speed, humor, and creativity. Lee developed a curriculum designed to engage African American high school students from low-income backgrounds in bringing these skills to bear on analysis of African American fiction.

Lee (1995, 2006) reported that students in classes using the curriculum demonstrated gains compared to controls in interpreting complex implied relationships in inferential reading. Instruction included small-group discussion and analysis of the communicative functions of signifying and its various structural forms. Students generated a list of strategies they unconsciously employed in interpreting the unstated, intended meanings of signifying dialogues. Teachers coached the students—some who saw no relationship between their own discourse and the characters' speech and who did not believe signifying an appropriate focus in school—through scaffolding and repeated practice in applying these strategies to familiar and unfamiliar fiction. Lee described proficiency in signifying as requiring complex problem-solving skills highly similar to those needed for literary interpretation: thinking analogically and recognizing use of irony, metaphor, symbolism, and unusual verbal inventions and unapparent similarities between objects or events. Her work demonstrated how the same skills can be generalized to African American texts (e.g., Hurston's *Their Eyes Were Watching God*) as well as Shakespearian dialogue.

Lee's (1995, 2006) curriculum involved recognizing students' high-level thinking skills in nonschool contexts, engaging students in analyzing and making explicit their thinking strategies, using instructional techniques supporting social construction of meaning, coaching students in applying their identified strategies to more familiar texts, and scaffolding to enable students to generalize their skills to less familiar texts.

Additional ethnographic research has suggested that teachers can enhance transfer of underlying abilities to school contexts by incorporating familiar participation structures or content. Wills, Lintz, and Mehan (2004) concluded from their review of ethnographic research on multicultural teaching that connecting instruction and content is important in enhancing the learning of culturally and linguistically diverse students. They first posited that incorporating social participation structures familiar to students increases their access to new content. Typically, the social participation structure of classrooms involves individual recitation, with teachers calling on individual students who respond and receive public acknowledgement of response accuracy. Recitation often involves teachers asking questions with known answers (e.g., "Where is your nose?") and/or questions out of context (e.g., "What is the state flower?"). Wills et al. suggested that evidence from ethnographic studies supports the use of teaching strategies that simulate or incorporate the conversational patterns used by students and their families and communities in everyday life. They provided evidence, for example, that instruction emphasizing cooperation and group praise rather than individual competition can enhance Native American students' engagement in learning. Similarly, they noted that engaging students in instructional conversations rather than recitation may support the performance of Puerto Rican students. The authors described a third study suggesting that use of culturally familiar speech events such as rhythmic language, rapid intonation, repetition, alliteration, call and response, variation in pace, and creative language play improved reading scores of African American students from low-income backgrounds.

Wills et al.'s (2004) second hypothesis was that incorporating familiar content supports students' motivation to try new ways of learning. Among the examples they cited was a teacher at a Navajo reservation school generating student enthusiasm for inquiry by showing them scenes from the community and asking them to identify needs, group and categorize needs, and make generalizations about the community. In another example, Haitian junior high school students conducted a study identifying preferred water fountains in the building and analyzing the water in preferred and nonpreferred fountains. In both of these studies, teachers chose content that drew upon students' prior knowledge from everyday experiences to actively solve new problems, disproving stereotypes of these students' passivity in learning.

Consistent with the propositions of Wills et al. (2004), a recent study by Kanu (2006) demonstrated that integrating native cultural knowledge and perspectives, resources, and instructional methods into a high school social studies class produced greater gains among Native students on social studies exam scores, higher level thinking, and self-esteem compared to a traditional social studies curriculum. These examples are consistent with findings in studies on strategies that support learning of gifted CLD students, including bridging current functioning level and cultural experience to enriched curriculum emphasizing higher order skills and inquiry techniques (VanTassel-Baska, 2007).

Additional Strategies for Facilitating Transfer

Culturally sensitive and creative teachers recognize the underlying abilities of CLD students and create learning contexts that foster transfer of these abilities to the classroom. Teachers can maximize gifted students' expression of their cognitive capacity by creating a social and cultural context most likely to elicit transfer. In addition to explicit instruction in transferring cognitive competence to the classroom, teachers can use strategies consistent with students' preferred and familiar approaches to learning and work with students' motivational sets.

Recognizing Differences in Values, Beliefs, and Behaviors

Individuals from different cultural backgrounds exhibit a wide variety of values, beliefs, and behaviors both across and

Case Example: Pairing Familiar Content With New Approaches to Learning

Mr. Rojas engages his fourth-grade classroom of English language learners in their first Socratic discussion. As part of biography study, the students read and compared several biographies of the Mexican mural artist, Diego Rivera. For the Socratic discussion, they are using Rivera's painting, *La Piñata*, as text. Mr. Rojas begins by asking students to describe what is happening in the painting. Students eagerly identify the setting as a birthday party, interpreting the various characters' emotions (frustrated, excited, happy, sad) based on incidents they recall from their own experiences. Mr. Rojas asks students to reflect on all elements in the painting. Students note the unusual contents of the piñata (e.g., onions). The teacher segues to a question about the message the artist intends to convey, requesting evidence from the painting and biographies. Helena points to the piñata's contents, the background colors, and range of emotions depicted on faces to support her opinion that Rivera's message is "Life is both happy and sad." Discussion turns to incidents in the artist's biography. Mr. Rojas asks if anyone has a different idea about the painter's theme that he or she can support with evidence.

within distinct cultural groups. From a sociocultural perspective, students whose culturally derived values, beliefs, and behaviors clash with those of the school would be more likely to have difficulty transferring their abilities to the school context. Rogoff (2003) offered numerous examples from a wide range of cultures on different values regarding important school expectations such as competition; speed; individual performance (singling out individuals for praise or reprimand, public evaluation of individual performance); categorizing taxonomically; and direct, elaborated oral communication. Rogoff cited, for example, Navajo parent complaints about singling out their children when a high school counselor posted photos of students with high grades on a high-achiever bulletin board. In this case, promoting individual accomplishment conflicted with the community ethic of contributing to the group.

Additional research has suggested that instructional strategies inconsistent with student cultural experiences can impede student learning. Although students of East Asian descent vary widely in their cultural behaviors, some tend toward verbal sparseness, having families that encourage thoughtfulness and discourage recounting what the listener can infer (Nisbett, 2003). Kim (2002) investigated the effects of requiring Asian American students to explain aloud their reasoning as they solved complex logic problems. Verbalizing aloud did not affect the performance of European Americans but undermined the performance of their Asian counterparts. Kim concluded that talking interfered with East Asian Americans' performance because they rely less on language in their thinking than do European Americans.

Readers interested in gaining cultural knowledge on specific groups would enjoy Lynch and Hanson's (2004) excellent edited text for service providers with chapters on a variety of groups, including European Americans. Readings specific to gifted students include Ford (2003) on African Americans, Kitano and DiJiosia (2002) and Plucker (1996) on Asian Americans, Diaz (1999) on Latinos, Foley and Skenandore (2003) on Native Americans, and Granada (2003) on bilingual students.

Cultural understanding of specific groups can enable teachers to create learning environments more likely to support CLD students' expression of high-level thinking skills (as well as understand family concerns). A general strategy across cultural groups is to analyze task demands in relation to cultural expectations and strengths. Areas where individuals from diverse cultural backgrounds are likely to experience conflict with mainstream school culture are outlined in Table 2.1 (derived from Lynch & Hanson, 2004; Nisbett, 2003; Rogoff 2003; Shade, 1989).

Enhancing Flexibility

To succeed at home and in the community, school, and world of work, students whose home and school cultures differ in expected values and behaviors must develop a repertoire of approaches to problem solving and become fluent and flexible in distinguishing the appropriate approach for the setting

Table 2.1
Some Dimensions of Difference
Between Home and School Cultures

Home/Community Culture(s)	School Culture
• Conceptualizes in images, models, and webs—preferring to view the whole	• Focuses on parts, details, and steps that make up the whole
• Better at learning characterized by freedom of movement and physical activity	• Better at learning characterized by sitting, reading, and listening
• Prefers creative, intuitive thinking using trial-and-error	• Prefers cause-and-effect thinking
• Responds to questions and learns facts embedded in a meaningful context	• Accustomed to answering questions out of context and with known answers and learning facts in isolation
• Prefers natural pacing (task will be completed in the time it takes)	• Prefers pacing as scheduled (task will be completed according to timeline)
• Prefers group work, uncomfortable with being singled out	• Prefers individual work, expects to be singled out
• Oriented to people and relationships	• Oriented to tasks, objects, and ideas
• More reliant on nonverbal communication	• More reliant on verbal communication
• Communicates indirectly (e.g., via stories)	• Communicates directly (e.g., through facts)
• Says less, makes less eye contact, and is more comfortable with pauses and silences	• Talks more, speaks more rapidly, makes eye contact, and is uncomfortable with silence
• Motivated to advance the group	• Motivated to advance the individual
• More comfortable with cooperation and sharing	• More comfortable with competition and acquiring
• Expects equity in turn-taking	• Accustomed to interrupting
• Need for racial trust	• Does not consider race an issue
• Success defined as well-roundedness (in school, social relationships, family, and community)	• Success defined as achievement

(Rogoff, 2003). They need to determine which strategy to apply on a given test or other cognitive activity. For example, a student may avoid eye contact with one's father to show respect at home and establish eye contact with the teacher at school to express engagement and attention. Another may need to wait respectfully to express a viewpoint at home and interrupt to make a point at school. Students who exhibit traditional reticence in competitive discussions will benefit from developing extemporaneous speaking skills required by college and the workplace. Teachers can help students understand the need for these skills and scaffold by encouraging journaling and reading aloud from their journals or expanding discussions from dyads to increasingly larger groups. From a sociocultural perspective, teachers can facilitate students' flexibility by identifying cultural discontinuities and making the connections explicit. The goal would be to support students in becoming fluently bicultural, able to negotiate a variety of settings (Trueba, 2002).

Case Example:
Building a Repertoire of Approaches

Ms. Aguilar teaches a second-grade cluster class composed of general education and gifted students who are English language learners. The students have finished reading a book describing what Tomás sees as he sits on park bench in the city: cars, buses, and taxis driving down a busy street flanked by apartments, stores, restaurants, a school, hospital, and office buildings. Birds perch on lampposts, and pedestrians wait at traffic lights with their dogs. Ms. Aguilar asks the students to recall what Tomás has seen, categorize similar items, provide a rationale for their categories, and draw a generalization. The first five students who share their work identify various categories based on functional relationships to people ("The apartment and car go together because they are both used by people"). The sixth student, Beatriz, has grouped the apartments, stores, restaurants, school, hospital, and office buildings together because they are "all buildings"—a category based on typology. The teacher asks the students if they can form other categories based on types as Beatriz did rather than use by people. They immediately identify automobiles, animals, and public furniture as separate categories.

Understanding Motivational Sets

Evidence is accumulating that the legacy of discrimination faced by African American and Latino students—especially high achievers motivated to succeed (Steele, 2003)—renders them susceptible to stereotype threat. Stereotype threat refers to concern that one's performance will be judged on the basis of commonly held stereotypes about intellectual ability. Studies indicate that stereotype threat can affect the performance of primary-age through college students. McKown and Weinstein (2003) investigated stereotype threat among 202 African American, Asian American, Latino, and White children ages 6 to 10 attending general and gifted and talented programs. Findings demonstrated that African American and Latino children as young as 6, though more typically by age 8 or 9, are aware of broadly held racial stereotypes. Moreover, for children who are aware of such stereotypes, classroom-type test situations that even subtly activate negative stereotypes can diminish performance on academic tasks. Anxiety about confirming negative stereotypes may lead to reduced effort. McKown and Weinstein concluded that "children from academically stigmatized ethnic groups show earlier and greater awareness of broadly held stereotypes" than do children from nonstigmatized groups (p. 511). Their finding that age and verbal ability are related to increased likelihood of awareness of broadly held stereotypes suggests that gifted CLD students may develop stereotype consciousness at earlier ages and be more susceptible to stereotype threat.

Just as negative stereotypes can impair performance, positive stereotypes can facilitate performance. Research on kindergarten through middle school Chinese, Japanese, and Korean American children (Ambady, Shih, Kim, & Pittinsky, 2001) suggested that gender and ethnic stereotypes can have positive and negative effects on academic performance of children as young as age 5. Stereotypes of male superiority in mathematics negatively affected younger and older girls' performance on a mathematics test, while stereotypes of Asian superiority in mathematics significantly facilitated performance. Primary and middle school boys scored higher than controls when gender and ethnic stereotypes were activated.

These studies suggest that stereotypes can begin to affect the academic performance of CLD children at early ages. On the positive side, they also suggest that teachers can enhance performance by challenging stereotypes; using nonbiased assessments, such as curriculum-based assessments; and explicitly describing the assessments as unbiased, if they indeed are: "This test will help me assess what you've learned about the solar system. Girls and boys from all backgrounds do equally well on this test."

Capitalizing on Cultural Strengths

John Ogbu's (1994) work on voluntary and involuntary minorities has significantly influenced educators' understanding of the dilemma of giftedness among African American students pressured to develop "oppositional identities" to avoid the label of "acting White." Ogbu's theory explains low achievement in terms of social oppression and adoption of the view that school achievement is a "White" characteristic inconsistent with African American identity. Yet other scholars argue that education and achievement were historically central to African American identity (Perry, 2003). Trueba (2002) called for a theory better able to account for the success of people of color who experienced social oppression and poverty and who succeeded in education and later life—one that acknowledges the individual's ability to adopt multiple identities rather than maintain a single identity (e.g., an oppositional one) that mitigates against achievement:

> as demographics change, those individuals who can best function in a diverse society will have a large cultural capital and greater ability to function effectively. The mastery of different languages, the ability to cross racial and ethnic boundaries, and a general resiliency associated with the ability to endure hardships and overcome obstacles will clearly be recognized as a new cultural capital that will be crucial for success in a modern diversified society, not a handicap. The hypothesis is that oppression and abuse can also generate precisely the opposite—resilience and cultural capital to succeed. (p. 7)

Harry et al.'s (2005) ethnographic study of school personnel interactions with low-income African American students
and their families vividly illustrated the negative effects of edu-
cator stereotypes, including failure to recognize gifted potential.
These authors argued that applying a strength-based paradigm
to educational practice and research will encourage practitioners to recognize the positive qualities that CLD families provide and better identify and serve students with exceptional
needs and strengths. Recent literature has demonstrated the
positive potential of changing the paradigm to one that views
cultural and linguistic diversity as a strength rather than as a risk
factor. For English language learners in particular, conceptualizing exceptional capacity for dual language proficiency as a gift
could increase identification and support affective development
as well as academic achievement.

In a study of The National Research Center on the Gifted
and Talented, Valdes (2002) examined the high-level thinking skills of 25 high-school-age Latino students who served
as interpreters for their families. More than half (13) were
described as at risk for academic failure, with test scores suggesting low-level functioning in both Spanish and English. Yet
on a simulated interpretation task, these students performed
complex skills under stressful conditions, including transmit-
ting essential meanings, using a variety of strategies to select
and compress original utterances and to convey the tone and
stance of the original, keeping up with flow of information,
and simultaneously attending to content and social context.
Valdes argued that bilingual youth exhibit traits normally considered characteristic of children with superior ability as measured by IQ.

Kettler, Shiu, and Johnsen (2006) investigated the effects of
a middle school program honoring primary-language Spanish
speakers' ability to communicate in their native language as
an academic skill. Eighth-grade students from low-income
backgrounds whose home language was Spanish received the
opportunity to participate in Advanced Placement (AP) Spanish
classes. Kettler et al. found that these students outperformed
high school students on the AP Spanish Language exam.
Additionally, students participating in the program reported a

greater sense of belonging in school, self-confidence, self-efficacy, and academic aspirations than did students in comparison groups. They were more likely to select close friends who valued school achievement and to plan for additional AP courses. Over 3 years of program implementation, 79% earned qualifying scores on the AP exam.

The studies by Harry et al. (2005), Valdes (2002), and Kettler et al. (2006) proceeded by assuming, recognizing, and capitalizing on the strengths of culturally and linguistically diverse students. Shifting the paradigm to assume underlying abilities sets the stage for holding higher expectations and creating learning environments in which students express their abilities in performance.

Summary and Recommendations

Sociocultural theory assumes that students from all cultural backgrounds have the same underlying abilities expressed in ways that are influenced by culture and experience. Assessment and instructional contexts inconsistent with students' cultural expectations or contrary to their experiences may mask students' giftedness and achievement potential. As educators, we can support CLD students' achievement by assuming students' high potential and facilitating transfer of their abilities to the classroom. We can begin with familiar content to engage students in high-level thinking and introduce challenging content through familiar approaches to interacting and learning. We can consider cultural values, beliefs, and behaviors as well as experience-based motivational sets in adapting instructional interactions. We can support long-term success by helping students expand their range of approaches to learning and flexibly apply problem-solving strategies appropriate to the context. We can adopt a strengths-based framework that views cultural and language diversity as an entrée rather than a barrier to success. Questions listed in Figure 2.1 can be used to assess the consistency of our teaching strategies with a sociocultural framework.

Enhancing Expression of Competence in the School Context

❏ Is the performance of my CLD students higher than grade-level expectancies and commensurate with potential in their area(s) of talent?

❏ Do I assume students arrive with high-level thinking abilities that, with scaffolding and coaching as needed, they can apply to rigorous content?

❏ Do I incorporate familiar and meaningful content when increasing task demands for new ways of thinking? Do I incorporate familiar thinking processes and participation structures when expecting mastery of challenging new content?

❏ If careful assessment suggests my CLD students lack some prerequisite knowledge or skills, am I providing the scaffolding and extended time needed to acquire these?

Enhancing Fluency and Flexibility Across Contexts

❏ Do I explicitly identify school and workplace expectations regarding approaches to learning?

❏ Do I enable students to increase their repertoire of approaches to learning and flexibly apply strategies appropriate to the setting and task at hand?

Capitalizing on Cultural Strengths

❏ Do I recognize students' cultural strengths?

❏ Do I find ways for students to apply their strengths in and beyond the classroom?

❏ Do I find ways for students to share their strengths with others?

Figure 2.1. Checklist of questions to assess teaching strategies.

References

Ambady, N., Shih, M., Kim, A., & Pittinsky, T. L. (2001). Stereotype susceptibility in children: Effects of identity activation on quantitative performance. *Psychological Science, 12,* 385–390.

Banks, J. A. (1988). Ethnicity, class, cognitive, and motivational styles: Research and teaching implications. *The Journal of Negro Education, 57,* 452–466.

Cole, M., & Bruner, J. S. (1971). Cultural differences and inferences about psychological processes. *American Psychologist, 26,* 867–876.

College Board. (1999). *Reaching the top: A report of the National Task Force on Minority High Achievement.* New York: College Board Publications.

Diaz, E. (1999). Hispanic Americans: USA. In A. Y. Baldwin & W. Vialle (Eds.), *The many faces of giftedness: Lifting the masks* (pp. 23–44). Belmont, CA: Wadsworth.

Elhoweris, H., Mutua, K., Alsheikh, N., & Holloway, P. (2005). Effects of children's ethnicity on teachers' referral and recommendation decisions in gifted and talented programs. *Remedial and Special Education, 26,* 25–31.

Foley, K., & Skenandore, O. (2003). Gifted education for the Native American student. In J. A Castellano (Ed.), *Special populations in gifted education* (pp. 113–122). Boston: Allyn & Bacon.

Ford, D. Y. (2003). Equity and excellence: Culturally diverse students in gifted education. In N. Colangelo & G. A. Davis (Eds.), *Handbook of gifted education* (3rd ed., pp. 506–520). Boston: Allyn & Bacon.

Granada, J. (2003) Casting a wider net: Linking bilingual and gifted education. In J. A Castellano (Ed.), *Special populations in gifted education* (pp. 1–16). Boston: Allyn & Bacon.

Harmon, D. (2002). They won't teach me: The voices of gifted African American inner-city students. *Roeper Review, 24,* 68–75.

Harry, B., Klingner, J. K., & Hart, J. (2005). African American families under fire: Ethnographic views of family strengths. *Remedial and Special Education, 26,* 101–112.

Kanu, Y. (2006). Getting them through the college pipeline: Critical elements of instruction influencing school success among Native Canadian high school students. *Journal of Advanced Academics, 18,* 116–145.

Kettler, T., Shiu, A., & Johnsen, S. K. (2006). AP as an intervention for middle school Hispanic students. *Gifted Child Today, 29*(1), 39–46.

Kim, H. (2002). Speech and silence: A cultural analysis of the effect of talking on psychology. *Dissertation Abstracts International: Section B: The Sciences and Engineering, 62*(9-B), 4275.

Kitano, M. K., & DiJiosia, M. (2002). Are Asian and Pacific Americans over-represented in programs for the gifted? *Roeper Review, 24,* 76–80.

Labov, W. (1970). The logical non-standard English. In F. Williams (Ed.), *Language and poverty* (pp. 153–173). Chicago: Markham Press.

Lee, C. D. (1995). Signifying as a scaffold for literary interpretation. *Journal of Black Psychology, 21,* 357–381.

Lee, C. D. (2006). "Every good-bye ain't gone": Analyzing the cultural underpinnings of classroom talk. *International Journal of Qualitative Studies in Education, 19,* 305–327.

Lynch, E. W., & Hanson, M. J. (2004). *Developing cross-cultural competence: A guide for working with children and their families* (3rd ed.). Baltimore: Brookes.

Magnuson, K. A., & Duncan, G. J. (2006). The role of family socioeconomic resources in the Black-White test score gap among young children. *Developmental Review, 26,* 365–399.

McKown, C., & Weinstein, R. (2003). The development and consequences of stereotype consciousness in middle childhood. *Child Development, 74,* 498–515.

Miller, L. S. (2004). *Promoting sustained growth in the representation of African Americans, Latinos, and Native Americans among top students in the United Sates at all levels of the education system* (Research Monograph 04190). Storrs: University of Connecticut, The National Research Center on the Gifted and Talented.

Nisbett, R. (2003). *The geography of thought: How Asians and Westerners think differently and why.* New York: Free Press.

Ogbu, J. U. (1994). Understanding cultural diversity and learning. *Journal for the Education of the Gifted, 17,* 355–383.

Perry, T. (2003). Up from the parched earth: Toward a theory of African-American achievement. In T. Perry, C. Steele, & A. Hilliard, III, *Young, gifted, and Black: Promoting high achievement among African-American students* (pp. 1–108). Boston: Beacon Press.

Peterson, J. S. (1999). Gifted—Through whose cultural lens? An application of the postpositivistic mode of inquiry. *Journal for the Education of the Gifted, 22,* 354–383.

Peterson, J. S., & Margolin, L. (1997). Naming gifted children: An example of unintended reproduction. *Journal for the Education of the Gifted, 21,* 82–100.

Plucker, J. A. (1996). Gifted Asian-American students: Identification, curricular, and counseling concerns. *Journal for the Education of the Gifted, 19,* 315–343.

Rogoff, B. (2003). *The cultural nature of human development.* Oxford, England: Oxford University Press.

Rueda, R., & Moll, L. C. (1994). A sociocultural perspective on motivation. In H. F. O'Neil, Jr., & M. Drillings (Eds.), *Motivation theory and research* (pp. 117–137). Hillsdale, NJ: Lawrence Erlbaum.

Sachs, S. K. (2004). Evaluation of teacher attributes as predictors of success in urban schools. *Journal of Teacher Education, 55,* 177–187.

Shade, B. J. R. (1989). *Culture, style, and the educative process.* Springfield, IL: Charles C. Thomas.

Steele, C. (2003). Stereotype threat and African-American student achievement. In T. Perry, C. Steele, & A. Hilliard, III, *Young, gifted, and Black: Promoting high achievement among African-American students* (pp. 109–130). Boston: Beacon Press.

Sternberg, R. J. (2007). Cultural concepts of giftedness. *Roeper Review,* *29,* 160–165.

Trueba, H. T. (2002). Multiple ethnic, racial, and cultural identities in action: From marginality to a new cultural capital in modern society. *Journal of Latinos and Education, 1,* 7–28.

Valdes, G. (2002). *Understanding the special giftedness of young interpreters.* Storrs: University of Connecticut, The National Research Center on the Gifted and Talented. (ERIC Document Reproduction Service No. ED478268)

VanTassel-Baska, J. (2007, April). *Working with children of color and poverty.* Paper presented at the Council for Exceptional Children Symposium, Louisville, KY.

Wills, J. S., Lintz, A., & Mehan, H. (2004). Ethnographic studies of multicultural education in U.S. classrooms and schools. In A. Banks & C. A. M. Banks (Eds.), *Handbook of research on multicultural education* (2nd ed., pp. 163–183). San Francisco: Jossey-Bass.

Psychosocial Stressors in the Development of Gifted Learners With Atypical Profiles

Frank C. Worrell

Although a literature search using the four keywords, "social," "emotional," "gifted," and "talented" yields more than 3,000 references, a search replacing "social" and "emotional" with the term, "psychosocial stressors," yields only three works, a dissertation study on depression in gifted children (Davis, 1996), a journal article on therapy with families including a child with the gifted label (Moon & Hall, 1998), and a book chapter on counseling gifted children (Moon, 2002). Although searches are inevitably limited by the keywords assigned to articles and books, the results of these two searches suggest that there is a lot more information on the social and emotional lives of students classified as gifted and talented (see Cross, 2002; Neihart, Reis, Robinson, & Moon, 2002) than there is on specific psychosocial stressors in this population, at least at first glance. Of course, stressors are a part of daily life for all individuals, and can result from catastrophes, significant life events, or daily hassles (Myers, 2004). Severe and prolonged stress can overwhelm a person's ability to cope. Individuals who live in poverty and who are discriminated against experience more stress on average than their affluent and nonstigmatized counterparts. The literature also has established that severe or prolonged stress can have a negative impact on brain development with implications for learning and academic achievement (De Bellis, Hooper, & Sapia, 2005; Noble, Tottenham, & Casey, 2005; Pardon & Marsden, 2008).

However, as stress is dependent on an individual's appraisal and interpretation of events (Lazarus, 1998), stressors that are perceived as challenges that can be overcome often result in increased motivation and improved performance (Myers, 2004). In this chapter, the focus is not on the catastrophic or major life event categories, but on the less severe stressors that students face as they interact with their families, their schools, and their communities, a perspective more in keeping with Eriksonian (1950, 1968) notions of psychosocial. However, before discussing the psychosocial stressors faced by gifted learners with atypical profiles, it is important to define the key terms in the title to delimit the groups under discussion and to articulate some assumptions inherent in this paper. I then discuss potential psychosocial stressors, drawing primarily from the literatures on motivation and cultural identity attitudes. Finally, I provide some examples of things that have been done at the University of California, Berkeley's (UC Berkeley) Academic Talent Development Program (ATDP), with which I am affiliated.

Who Achieves the Label "Gifted"?

It is an understatement to say that there are multiple definitions of giftedness in the literature (see Coleman & Cross, 2005; Marland, 1972; Matthews & Foster, 2005; Renzulli, 1986; Sternberg & Davidson, 1986, 2005). In a session sponsored by the Special Interest Group, Research on Giftedness and Talent at the 2007 convention of the American Educational Research Association, each of the four groups of authors used a different procedure for identifying the gifted students they were presenting on, with identification procedures ranging from self-nomination via the Web to precocious abilities as a preschooler and the more traditional use of test scores. Research also has highlighted developmental slippage—that is, being classified as gifted at one age and losing the label as one gets older (Simonton, 1998)—and what Coleman and Cross (2005) called *ex post facto giftedness*, or attaining the gifted label on the basis of extraordinary accomplishments as an adult.

It is for this reason that who is gifted is probably less important than who gets classified as gifted. Therefore, I suggest that the term *gifted* applies to any child or adolescent who has been given that label, or has been accepted into a program for gifted and talented students in a public school or other setting, including university summer programs, special schools for the visual and performing arts, and elite sports programs. Thus, although related to innate potential, being gifted is not simply biological endowment; rather, it is a classification that a student attains on the basis of above-average performance or the potential for such, as determined by the appropriate gatekeepers using a variety of indicators. This classification includes students who are chosen on the basis of IQ, achievement tests, nomination procedures, rating scales, performance, potential, or some combination thereof. Although this definition may seem overly broad, it is perhaps a more accurate representation of the current state of affairs, in that it acknowledges the psychological importance of labeling and reflects the notion that giftedness is relative to a comparison group.

This definition also should make evident that there is no clear delineation between the gifted and the nongifted. Therefore, all of the psychosocial stressors that apply to learners more generally apply to students with the label gifted. What psychological characteristics related to giftedness separate a student with an IQ of 128 from one with an IQ of 132? Can we distinguish in the classroom on the basis of behaviors the five students who are just above the particular cut-off that we used for classification from the five students who just missed making the cut-off? Are the issues for a student who is a mathematical prodigy the same as the issues for a student who is a musical prodigy because they both happen to be classified as gifted? My answers to these three questions are "I am not sure that there are any," "No," and "Maybe." Thus, Moon's (2002) claim that gifted learners "have unique social and emotional issues related to their giftedness" (p. 213) may be true; however, the field does not yet have the data to make this claim.

This definition of giftedness also acknowledges that psychosocial stressors may result from being classified as gifted and the expectations that come with the classification. Some students will handle being gifted with equanimity—that is, they will perceive it as a challenge that they can live up to—whereas others may find the label overwhelming, resulting in increased stress and poor coping. Their responses will depend on their individual temperaments, the socialization processes that they have experienced, and the responses to their particular gifts by those with whom they come into regular contact.

Stress in Gifted Populations

There are several assumptions in this paper that need to be acknowledged explicitly. The first assumption is that there is a group of learners who can be reliably described as gifted. A natural extension of the first assumption is that most gifted learners have a certain profile and that there are a few who achieve the label whose profiles are such that they are atypical. A third assumption is that there are stressors that affect only gifted learners with atypical profiles, and these stressors are important enough to warrant the attention of educators and researchers.

As indicated previously, stressors that are perceived as manageable can lead to superior performance (Myers, 2004). Moreover, students who are labeled gifted by almost any definition are students who are functioning at higher levels than their peers (at least in one domain), and are therefore more likely to be able to cope with the stressors in that domain. Terman's seminal studies of the gifted (1924, 1925; Terman & Oden, 1947, 1959; see also Burks, Jensen, & Terman, 1930; Cox, 1926) are relevant in this discussion. Terman's participants were chosen on the basis of IQ scores greater than 130, a fairly restrictive and limited criterion. However, his conclusions about this group went far beyond academic and intellectual ability. In addition to noting that the parents of the children had more education "than the average person of their generation in the United States" (Terman & Oden, 1959, p. 6), these authors described their participants as follows:

> The proportion of gifted subjects rated superior to unselected children of corresponding age averaged 89 percent for 4 intellectual traits, 82 percent for 4 voli-

tional traits, 67 percent for 3 emotional traits, 65 percent for 2 aesthetic traits, 64 percent for 4 moral traits, 61 percent for 2 physical traits, and 57 percent for 5 social traits. (Terman & Oden, 1959, p. 16)

Terman and Oden (1959) went on to note that 35 years later, "the superior child, with few exceptions, becomes the able adult, superior in nearly every aspect to the generality" (p. 143).

The important point here is that there is no reason to believe that typical gifted learners will be more vulnerable to psychosocial stressors than their peers—indeed, the literature suggests that they are likely to be less vulnerable. It also is likely that atypical students will have high, if not comparable, achievement profiles to their more typical peers, especially if they have been chosen using the same processes as these peers. Thus, atypical gifted learners are perhaps more likely to experience psychosocial stressors due to their atypicality (rather than their giftedness), based on the ways in which they perceive themselves and in which their groups are perceived by society. Moreover, it also is likely that the stressors related to being atypical will apply to atypical learners in other areas who are not gifted. My goal in this chapter, then, is not to provide any definitive statements about the specific psychosocial stressors that atypical students with the gifted and talented label face, but rather to suggest some of the issues that educators and researchers should pay more attention to with regard to students who are atypical in gifted programs.

Who Are the Gifted With Atypical Profiles?

The answer to the question opening this section should be easily obtainable by asking what the typical learner classified as gifted looks like. Ironically, the research literature provides an answer to this by telling us who the typical gifted learner is not. In general, members of marginalized minority groups (i.e., African Americans, American Indians, Latinos), English language learners, and individuals from low socioeconomic backgrounds are least likely to be labeled gifted or attend talent development programs (Baldwin, 1985; Barkan & Bernal,

1991; Ford, 1995, 1998; Matthews & Matthews, 2004; Richert, 1987; Robinson, Bradley & Stanley, 1990; Terman, 1925; Worrell, 2003, 2007b; Worrell, Szarko, & Gabelko, 2001). The corollary to this is that typical gifted students are from middle-class and wealthier families, and are of Asian or White racial/ethnic backgrounds, as can be seen in many descriptions of gifted and talented samples in the literature (e.g., Lee & Olszewski-Kubilius, 2006; Rinn, 2006; Terman, 1924, 1925; Worrell, 2007a). However, Kitano and DiJiosia (2002) also reminded us that the label Asian American subsumes many subgroups, some of whom typically are classified as gifted (e.g., Chinese, East Indian, Japanese, and Korean Americans) and some of whom are not (e.g., Filipino, Hmong, and Vietnamese Americans). This diversity also is present in Hispanic American groups (Lopez, Lopez, Suarez-Morales, & Castro, 2005).

Another common method of identifying typical gifted students is by their characteristics. Although identifying gifted children by gifted characteristics is grossly unreliable, which is not surprising given the wealth of definitions, many books and the World Wide Web have turned the search for gifted characteristics into a cottage industry. If you Google "characteristics of the gifted," you will obtain more than one million entries. Whatever the limitations of Web-based research, these lists of proposed characteristics are in the public domain and easily accessible. To the extent that teachers, parents, and educators accept lists of gifted characteristics as true, children will experience stress in trying to live up to these lists.

Although the atypical gifted include youth from stigmatized ethnic and racial groups, youth from low-income families, English language learners, and twice-exceptional students, I will only focus on the first two groups in this chapter, given the limitations of space. I also will be using academic giftedness as my primary focus, although it is probable that some of my comments will apply to all of the groups and to other domains as well.

Psychosocial Stressors

Up to this point, I have argued for a broad definition of giftedness that is tied to classification as gifted by acceptance into a program. I also have suggested that certain demographic groups (e.g., the poor, marginalized minorities, English language learners) are the individuals who are atypical gifted learners. I now will argue that psychosocial stress manifests itself for these groups in terms of their academic or achievement identities, which represent complex interactions of their personal identities (e.g., self-concept, motivation, self-efficacy, achievement orientation) and their collective identities or reference group orientations (e.g., socioeconomic status, race, ethnicity).

There is an emerging consensus that academic achievement is affected by both sets of variables (McKown & Weinstein, 2002; Worrell 2007a), in part because academic identity is based on one's personal history and one's social context. In this chapter, I will discuss a sense of belonging and conceptions of ability as major psychosocial stressors for atypical gifted students, also drawing from the literature on collective identity processes (e.g., cultural ecological theory, stereotype threat, and status-based rejection sensitivity). Although these processes affect individuals from poor backgrounds as well as individuals who are marginalized minorities, much of the research on these topics has focused on racial and ethnic minority students. Of course, there is a substantial overlap between marginalized minority and low-income groups. More than 33% of African American children live in poverty (Worrell, 2005), and figures are comparable for some Hispanic American groups (e.g., Mexican Americans, Puerto Ricans; Federal Interagency Forum on Child and Family Statistics, 2002). Although this chapter will not focus on English language learners, it is worth noting that classification as gifted differs across Hispanic and Asian American groups with comparable rates of second language learners, suggesting that this variable requires more scrutiny by researchers.

Belongingness

The importance of a sense of belonging is increasingly acknowledged as an important variable in school achievement (Goodenow & Grady, 1993; Roeser, Midgley, & Urdan, 1996), although this variable more typically has been studied in students who are at risk for dropping out. Indeed, many comprehensive high schools have been divided into smaller schools to allow students and teachers to have more personal relationships with each other. One result of being labeled gifted is having to enter and become a part of another academic community. In the public school system, this may mean getting different assignments from classmates, leaving your regular classroom for a pull-out program, or being assigned to other classes (e.g., honors or Advanced Placement courses) with other students with the same label. In other cases, it may mean attending a special school during the school year or going to classes in the summer when many of one's peers from school are doing other things. Thus, one immediate concern for atypical gifted students is being put into a community where there are few others like them. Unlike sports teams and orchestras, which generally have shared goals that facilitate social integration, typical gifted programs often are based on competitive goal structures with limited numbers of winners. If programs do not actively build in activities to increase a sense of belonging, atypical members of the community may feel a tremendous sense of isolation.

One of the most gifted African Americans that I know indicated that after graduating from an Ivy League college, he began attending a prestigious law school where he was always being reminded by his peers that he had probably gotten into the school as a result of affirmative action. This young man observed that his undergraduate degree from one of the most selective institutions in the country and his other qualifications for law school—99th percentile on the LSAT and GMAT and a history of academic awards—did not provide a sufficient psychological buffer against these attacks. Consequently, he perceived his law school as a hostile environment. Indeed, he stopped attending classes for some time and had to take an additional year to complete his degree. Two theories that speak to the issue of belongingness include status-based rejection sensitivity (Mendoza-Denton, Downey, Purdie, Davis, & Pietrzak, 2002) and cultural ecological theory (Ogbu, 2004; Ogbu & Simons, 1998).

Rejection Sensitivity

Research on status-based rejection sensitivity being conducted with students at selective colleges (Mendoza-Denton et al., 2002; Mendoza-Denton, Page-Gould, & Pietrzak, 2006; Pietrzak, 2004) has implications for one's sense of belonging in institutions and programs such as gifted programs where one's group is not present in large numbers:

> Whether one is a disabled person entering the workplace, a woman entering the U.S. military, or an African American student entering a predominantly White university, a history of rejecting experiences based on status characteristics can lead to doubts about one's acceptance by members of these social institutions. (Mendoza-Denton et al., 2002, p. 896)

Basically, Mendoza-Denton and his colleagues (Mendoza-Denton et al., 2002; Mendoza-Denton et al., 2006) have proposed that being a member of a devalued group can lead people to expect and to perceive rejection on the basis of their group membership, which in turn has implications for bonding with the institution or program and for achieving in that program. They found that Black college students who were high in race-based rejection sensitivity had fewer White friends after their first year of college, reported greater anxiety about requesting assistance from professors and less frequent attendance at review sessions, and had significantly lower achievement, even after controlling for previous ability. In a sense, these students were in self-imposed exile while attending the institution.

Although the research on status-based rejection sensitivity has been conducted with college students, there are studies that suggest children and adolescents can experience similar concerns. In 1979, Weinstein and Middlestadt reported that students in the elementary grades differentiate between teachers' behaviors with high-achieving versus low-achieving students. In a more recent study including academically talented students, McKown and Weinstein (2003) found that more than 60% of 8-, 9-, and 10-year-olds recognized negative group stereotypes, with more African American and Latino children being aware of the group stigma than their Asian American and White counterparts at each age level.

To date, studies of status-based rejection involving low-income youth are studies of low-income minority youth, confounding our ability to disentangle the impact of racial/ethnic minority group membership and socioeconomic status (SES). However, there are a few studies whose results are suggestive with regard to poverty. Arunkumar (2000) found that being different in SES from peers was related to higher feelings of dissonance about school. Isakson and Jarvis (1999) reported that peer support was predictive of perceived sense of school membership, and as noted above, atypical youth do not have their established peer networks in gifted programs. It is not difficult to infer a lower sense of belonging in low-income and minority students entering gifted programs where they are not only statistical minorities, but also where their presence often results in expressions of surprise on the part of other program attendees. A lower sense of belonging is one hypothesis about why retention of atypical students in gifted programs is a problem (Ford, 1998).

Cultural Ecological Theory

Ogbu's (1992, 2003, 2004; Ogbu & Simons, 1998) cultural ecological theory also has implications for racial and ethnic minority students' sense of belonging, specifically with regard to academic institutions. Ogbu (2004) contended that oppressed minority status (e.g., discrimination, subordination, and mistreatment of the group) can trigger responses by minority group members "in opposition to their understanding of who the dominant group members are" (p. 5) and in opposition to institutions of the dominant group such as schools. Therefore, one interpretation of Black students' success in school is "assimilation, a one way acculturation or a subtractive process, that takes away their Black identity" (Ogbu, 2004, p. 20).

For ethnic and racial minority students who belong to groups with oppositional frames of reference to the mainstream, being good at school or being identified as gifted may place them on the horns of a personal and social dilemma. Although they care about doing well and are successful academically, they also may be worried about betraying their group, and may be receiving equally mixed messages from friends and family. This dilemma is eloquently portrayed in the movie, *Akeelah and the Bee* (Fishburne & Atchison, 2006), when Akeelah is initially derided by her peers and family members for daring to dream of being a contestant in the national spelling bee. Similarly, one of my doctoral students from South-Central Los Angeles told me that as an undergraduate, he downplayed his university experiences when he went home because it quickly became clear to him that his academic success was not viewed positively by all of his relatives and friends. As Graham (2004) so elegantly put it, ethnic minority children may well think about high academic achievement in this way: "I can, but do I want to?" (p. 125). Both of these examples confound poverty and minority status, as noted before, and highlight the need for studies aimed at disentangling the effects of these two variables.

Conceptions of Ability

Dweck (1999, 2001; also see Cain & Dweck, 1989) has been writing about children's theories of intelligence for several years. She argues that some people believe that intelligence is fixed and therefore, unchangeable, whereas others see intelligence as malleable.

> The belief in fixed intelligence leads even the most able students to worry about how smart they are, to think they're dumb when they fail, to dislike and avoid effort, and to show impaired performance when they face academic difficulty. . . . The belief that intelligence can be developed makes students want to do just that: It leads them to value learning over looking smart, to enjoy effort and challenges, and to thrive in the face of difficulty. (Dweck, 2002, p. 39)

A belief in intelligence as fixed results in interpreting failure and high effort as signs of low intelligence. On the other hand, exceptional attainment typically requires sustained and extraordinary effort (Worrell, 2003).

Consider then, the psychosocial stress that arises when atypical gifted students are called upon to perform in a gifted program for the first time. It generally will be necessary for these students to exert more effort than they have done in their regular classes, and the returns may not be as readily evident, at least in the short term. How do these students interpret their relative decline in performance? Moreover, segregation of schools by race and income continues to be high and many Black, Latino, and low-income students continue to live primarily in segregated neighborhoods and attend segregated schools (Edelman & Jones, 2004; Iceland, Sharpe, & Steinmetz, 2003; Logan, Oakley, Smith, Stowell, & Stults, 2001; Massey, 2000), which often are less competitive. The drop in academic self-concept upon entering a more selective environment is well-established (see work on the Big-Fish-Little-Pond effect; Marsh & Hau, 2003; Marsh & Parker, 1984; Werts & Watley, 1969). It is probable that these students will think that the fault lies in themselves, especially if they hold entity theories of intelligence.

Stereotype Threat

Falling squarely in the conceptions of intelligence realm is a phenomenon known as stereotype threat (Steele, 1997), which refers to the anxiety felt by members of groups who are negatively stereotyped in society, especially when they are in situations that may confirm the group stereotype. Thus, groups about whom there are pervasive stereotypes about low intelligence in the population, such as African Americans (Steele, 2003; Steele & Aronson, 1995, 1998), Latinos (Gonzales, Blanton, & Williams, 2002; McKown & Weinstein, 2003; Schmader & Johns, 2003), and low-income individuals (Croizet & Claire, 1998; Harrison, Stevens, Monty, & Coakley, 2006), are especially vulnerable to stereotype threat. These groups also happen to be ones that are the atypical members of gifted programs. Stereotype threat typically is activated in situations where students' performance will be judged (e.g., examinations, tests), and it can be made salient by teachers' comments or the instructions accompanying a task. It also may be activated simply because the situation involves evaluation. The anxiety and other psychosocial stress that is produced by the activation of stereotype threat results in decreased performance on the part of the group in whom the stereotype is activated.

Stereotype threat effects have been demonstrated across all racial/ethnic and socioeconomic groups, all education levels from elementary school to college, and in a variety of performance areas (e.g., Aronson, 2002; McKown & Weinstein, 2003; Shih, Pittinsky, & Ambady, 1999; Stone, Lynch, Sjomeling, & Darley, 1999). Thus, it is not necessary to be a member of a group that is underrepresented in gifted and talented programs to be susceptible. However, Aronson pointed out that some individuals are more vulnerable than others to stereotype threat. Risk factors include being a member of a stigmatized group, having an in-group only attachment to a stigmatized group, caring a lot about achievement, and having a fixed theory of intelligence. As atypical gifted students are doing well enough to earn the gifted label, it follows that they care about achieving. Thus, they are potentially vulnerable to stereotype threat.

Stereotype Threat and SES

Researchers of stereotype threat have been able to examine this phenomenon in socioeconomic groups independent of race and ethnicity. For example, Croizet and Claire (1998) classified 128 French undergraduates into low- and high-income groups on the basis of school records. Low-SES students performed more poorly than their low- and high-SES counterparts when their SES was made salient and they believed that the tasks were diagnostic of their intellectual ability. High-SES students were not affected, nor were low-SES students who were not anxious about being evaluated on the basis of their group. Harrison et al. (2006) reported similar findings using undergraduate students in northern California and three SES levels: low, middle, and high. In this study, stereotype threat had an impact on the low-SES group, but not on middle- or high-SES groups.

Stereotype Threat and Race-Ethnicity

There are numerous studies that address the impact of stereotype threat in racial and ethnic minority students, albeit not with students identified as gifted. Oyserman, Kemmelmeier, Fryberg, Brosh, and Hart-Johnson (2003) interviewed 94 African American, American Indian, and Latino urban eighth graders to ascertain their racial-ethnic self-schemas. On the basis of the interviews, they classified the students into three groups: aschematic (15%; individual rather than collective identities), in-group only (59%), and dual (15%; accepting in-group membership but also seeking connections to the broader society). It should be noted that the in-group only racial-ethnic schema postulated to be vulnerable by Aronson (2002) constituted the largest group in the study. Oyserman et al. found that the dual schema group had higher grades than the aschematic and in-group schema only students, and the dual group's grades increased across the year in comparison to the other groups.

Oyserman et al. (2003) replicated these findings in a second study with a group of 65 junior high and high school American Indian students attending rural and reservation schools. Sixty-eight percent of this group was classified as in-group only, with 15% each classified in the aschematic and dual categories. In Study 2, the researchers manipulated stereotype threat experimentally by asking students what it meant to be a member of their race or ethnic group before (high salience) or after (low salience) having them complete a mathematics task. They reported that students who had dual racial-ethnic schemas persisted longer on the mathematics task, particularly in the high salience condition when stereotype threat was highest, suggesting that having a dual schema helps to protect against stereotype threat. However, the small numbers in the aschematic and dual schema groups limit the conclusions that can be drawn from these studies.

Other Cultural Identity Research

Even as Oyserman et al. (2003) have been examining racial and ethnic identity qualitatively, other researchers have been examining these variables from a quantitative perspective. In

2006, Worrell, Vandiver, Schaefer, Cross, and Fhagen-Smith argued that (a) there were generalizable profiles of racial identity attitudes in the population and (b) these profiles had meaningful relationships with other important variables (e.g., educational achievement, psychological well-being). Using the Cross Racial Identity Scale (Vandiver et al., 2000), a measure of Black racial identity attitudes with scores validated in adolescents and adults, Worrell et al. found four clusters of racial identity attitudes that generalized across the three samples. One of these identities was an in-group only identity, two were aschematic, and one reflected a negative perception of the in-group. A dual identity also emerged but only in two of the three samples.

In another quantitative study, this time with Black middle and high school students, Worrell and Gardner-Kitt (2006) found two canonical variates. The first, labeled Black Racial-Ethnic Identification, consisted of negative attitudes toward Americans, Whites, and members of other ethnic groups, and positive attitudes toward Blacks, and reflected an in-group only orientation. The second variate, which was labeled Grounded Multiculturalism, reflected a dual orientation and consisted of positive attitudes toward Blacks and toward other ethnic groups. Thus, Oyserman et al.'s (2003) findings with regard to racial-ethnic schemas have been replicated in quantitative examinations of adolescents and college students. Although the impact of these identity profiles on academic performance is not yet known, current evidence suggests that many of these students are likely to experience debilitating anxiety in circumstances where they are being evaluated. Additional research also has indicated that minority students are more susceptible to teacher expectation effects (Lee & Harber, 2005; McKown & Weinstein, 2002).

Countering Psychosocial Stressors

In the last few pages, I have argued that many of the psychosocial stressors that face atypical gifted students involve challenges to their sense of academic identity. These challenges come from a low sense of belonging in the competitive environments of gifted and talented programs or from fixed conceptions of ability, and these stressors are supported in part by the stereotypes and treatment of low-income and minority populations in this country. Are there things that can be done to mitigate some of these stressors?

An Intervention Response to Psychosocial Stressors

In 1981, UC Berkeley established a gifted program. In 1989, the name was changed to the Academic Talent Development Program (ATDP) to reflect a change in philosophy from gifted-ness as biological to giftedness as talent development in an aca-demic community (Sosniak & Gabelko, 2008). The program serves more than 2,000 students every summer from kinder-garten to grade 11 in a variety of enrichment and acceleration classes. On average, only 33% of the students are identified as gifted and talented in their home schools.

At ATDP, the idea of belonging is something to which the program pays considerable attention. About 60% of the more than 1,000 students who attend the program's secondary divi-sion indicate that there is at least one other person from their home school attending the program—this is a standard question on the end-of-program evaluation—and friends often take the same class or take classes on the same day. The program allows students to reference each other's applications when applying, and teachers are instructed to work on building community early in the program. The program also provides academic sup-ports using counselor assistance, study labs, and drop-in tutor-ing, programs that are available to all students. Social support also is provided in terms of a weekly newsletter that students can contribute to, which also has clues for a weekly treasure hunt on the Berkeley campus.

It is important to recognize that social support does not nec-essarily depend on having individuals who are of the same ethnic or racial group, but rather is based on commonality of interests. The program learned an important lesson about stereotyping several years ago. In an effort to attract more underrepresented students, some atypical students were told to have friends who were like them apply the next year. Students brought friends who shared the same interests rather than the same socioeco-nomic or ethnic/racial background (Gabelko & Sosniak, 2002), reminding everyone involved that the community that ATDP is building is an academic one based on domain-specific interests and not on demographic characteristics.

Data collection also is an integral part of our program evaluation as well as research agenda at ATDP. For example, data have indicated that ATDP is not immune to the Big-Fish-Little Pond effect (Marsh & Hau, 2003). Every year, we ask students to rate themselves compared to students in their home schools and their ATDP classes on a 5-point Likert scale. The findings have been consistent for several years. Students rate themselves between 4 and 5 at their home schools, and between 3 and 4 in their ATDP classes, yielding an effect size in the large range— Cohen's d was .91 for the 2006 summer. Thus, ATDP is always asking questions of its students and families about psychosocial variables. For example, the program has collected data on intrinsic and extrinsic motivation of the students, as well as the goal orientation of the instructors (mastery versus performance) in the classrooms (Murphy & Worrell, 2001), and we recently have collected other data on motivational variables. Findings indicated that the students were much more intrinsically motivated, and that the students perceived the teachers as stressing mastery rather than performance goals. Data on perfectionism indicated that adaptive perfectionism scores were substantially higher than maladaptive perfectionism scores (Vandiver & Worrell, 2002).

In a recent study (Worrell, 2007a), I examined the relationship between attitudes toward one's own group (Ethnic Identity) and attitudes toward other groups (Other Group Orientation), and academic achievement in four groups (African Americans, Asian Americans, Latinos, Whites). To the extent that Ethnic Identity attitudes reflect an in-group only focus, one would expect to find a negative relationship with academic achievement, with the reverse relationship for Other Group Orientation. The results indicated that for African American students, Ethnic Identity did have a negative relationship with GPA, and Other Group Orientation a positive relationship with GPA, both with medium effect sizes. However, that finding was only for school GPA. The relationships with program GPA were both positive and negligible (i.e., with small effect sizes).

These findings suggest that the nature of the messages that these students receive in the program differ from the messages that they receive in school, even though these students are much less typical in the program than they are in their school settings. Of course, this conclusion is tentative and needs to be explored further, but it suggests that gifted programs may have the potential to reduce some of the typical stressors that atypical gifted students experience in public schools, and by extension, assist the public schools in reducing these stressors in their settings.

Conclusion

In this chapter, I have argued that our knowledge base about psychosocial stressors in gifted learners is limited not only from a lack of research in the area, but also from a lack of definitional clarity. I also have identified some of the stressors that I believe students from low-income and minority students classified as gifted face on a regular basis. My basic contention is this: We should be paying attention to the types of issues that all learners face when studying learners with the gifted and talented label, and we should let the data inform us about meaningful differences between those classified as gifted and those who are not.

To illustrate this point, consider the following. In 2002, Covington and Dray described three groups of undergraduate students based on their goal orientation patterns. One group was described as success-oriented students who were focused on mastery goals and intrinsically motivated. The second group was described as failure-avoidant students who were focused on performance goals and extrinsically motivated. The third group, labeled overstrivers, were driven by both mastery and performance goals. Covington and Dray found all three types of students in the undergraduate population at Berkeley. Although all three groups have attained academic success (i.e., admission into a competitive college), it is probable that the psychosocial stressors that the groups experience are different. It is incumbent on researchers to find out if the success-oriented have better long-term psychosocial outcomes than the failure-avoidant and the overstrivers. In other words, are some pathways to academic success better than others?

Given our concern with equity, much of our literature focuses on the underrepresentation of certain groups in gifted programs and ways to correct that underrepresentation by using broader identification measures and increasing retention. What we do not discuss are the potential costs that come with placement of students in programs where they feel unwelcome and underprepared. Aronson and Steele (2005) reminded us that "competence is much more fragile—and malleable—than we tend to think" (p. 436). This statement may be particularly meaningful in the context of students whose sense of self is tied to how they and others perceive their competence, and may be particularly applicable in dealing with atypical gifted learners.

As researchers and educators of the gifted and talented, we must ensure that our atypical participants experience challenges that are manageable and motivating, and not challenges that are perceived as insurmountable and debilitating. To achieve this goal, our field must ensure that atypical students in gifted programs receive the academic, emotional, and social supports that protect their academic identities. They must be allowed to belong in these environments as much as any of the other students without feeling that they need to sacrifice or hide their cultural heritage. Ethical practice demands that we be as concerned about doing no harm as we are about doing good.

References

Aronson, J. (2002). Stereotype threat: Contending and coping with unnerving expectations. In J. Aronson (Ed.), *Improving academic achievement: Impact of psychological factors on education* (pp. 279–301). San Francisco: Elsevier Science.

Aronson, J., & Steele, C. M. (2005). Stereotypes and the fragility of academic competence, motivation, and self-concept. In A. J. Elliot & C. S. Dweck (Eds.), *Handbook of competence and motivation* (pp. 436–456). New York: The Guilford Press.

Arunkumar, R. (2000). Living in the interface of different cultures: Adolescents' experiences of cultural dissonance between home and school. *Dissertation Abstracts International Section A: Humanities and Social Sciences, 61*(2-A), 491.

Baldwin, A. Y. (1985). Programs for the gifted and talented: Issues concerning minority populations. In F. D. Horowitz & M. O'Brien

(Eds.), *The gifted and talented: Developmental perspectives* (pp. 223–249). Washington, DC: American Psychological Association.

Barkan, J. H., & Bernal, E. M. (1991). Gifted education for bilingual and limited English proficient students. *Gifted Child Quarterly, 35,* 144–147.

Burks, B. S., Jensen, D. W., & Terman, L. M. (1930). *Genetic studies of genius. III. The promise of youth.* Stanford, CA: Stanford University Press.

Cain, K. M., & Dweck, C. S. (1989). The development of children's conceptions of intelligence: A theoretical framework. In R. J. Sternberg (Ed.), *Advances in the psychology of human intelligence* (Vol. 5, pp. 47–82). Hillsdale, NJ: Lawrence Erlbaum.

Coleman, L. J., & Cross, T. L. (2005). *Being gifted in school: An introduction to development, guidance, and teaching* (2nd ed.). Waco, TX: Prufrock Press.

Covington, M. V., & Dray, E. (2002). The developmental course of achievement motivation: A need-based approach. In A. Wigfield & J. S. Eccles (Eds.), *Development of achievement motivation* (pp. 33–56). San Francisco: Elsevier Science.

Croizet, J., & Claire, T. (1998). Extending the concept of stereotype threat to social class: The intellectual underperformance of students from low socioeconomic backgrounds. *Personality and Social Psychology Bulletin, 24,* 588–594.

Cross, T. L. (2002). *On the social and emotional lives of gifted children: Issues and factors in their psychological development* (2nd ed.). Waco, TX: Prufrock Press.

Cox, C. M. (1926). *Genetic studies of genius. II. The early mental traits of three hundred geniuses.* Stanford, CA: Stanford University Press.

Davis, S. D. (1996). A study of depression and self-esteem in moderately gifted and nongifted children. *Dissertation Abstracts International Section A: Humanities and Social Sciences, 56*(10-A), 3886.

De Bellis, M. D., Hooper, S. R., & Sapia, J. L. (2005). Early trauma exposure and the brain. In J. J. Vasterling & C. R. Brewin (Eds.), *Neuropsychology of PTSD: Biological, cognitive, and clinical perspectives* (pp. 153–177). New York: Guilford.

Dweck, C. S. (1999). *Self-theories and goals: Their role in motivation, personality, and development.* Philadelphia: Taylor and Francis.

Dweck, C. S. (2001). The development of ability conceptions. In A. Wigfield & J. Eccles (Eds.), *The development of achievement motivation* (pp. 37–60). San Francisco: Academic Press.

Dweck, C. S. (2002). Messages that motivate: How praise molds students' beliefs, motivation, and performance (in surprising ways). In

J. Aronson (Ed.), *Improving academic achievement: Impact of psychological factors on education* (pp. 37–60). San Francisco: Academic Press.

Edelman, M. W., & Jones, J. M. (2004). Separate and unequal: America's children, race, and poverty. *Future of Children, 14,* 134–137.

Erikson, E. H. (1950). *Childhood and society.* New York: W. W. Norton.

Erikson, E. H. (1968). *Identity, youth, and crisis.* New York: W. W. Norton.

Federal Interagency Forum on Child and Family Statistics. (2002). *America's children: Key national indicators of well-being, 2002.* Washington, DC: U.S. Government Printing Office.

Ford, D. Y. (1995). Desegregating gifted education: A need unmet. *Journal of Negro Education, 64,* 52–62.

Ford, D. Y. (1998). The underrepresentation of minority students in gifted education: Problems and promises in recruitment and retention. *The Journal of Special Education, 32,* 4–14.

Fishburne, L. (Producer), & Atchison, D. (Writer/Director). (2006). *Akeelah and the bee* [Motion picture]. United States: Lionsgate.

Gabelko, N. H., & Sosniak, L. A. (2002). "Someone just like me": When academic engagement trumps race, class, and gender. *Phi Delta Kappan, 83,* 400–405.

Gonzales, P. M., Blanton, H., & Williams, K. J. (2002). The effects of stereotype threat and double-minority status on the test performance of Latino women. *Personality and Social Psychology Bulletin, 28,* 659–670.

Goodenow, C., & Grady, K. E. (1993). The relationship of school belonging and friends' values to academic motivation among urban adolescent students. *Journal of Experimental Education, 62,* 60–71.

Graham, S. (2004). "I can, but do I want to?" Achievement values in ethnic minority children and adolescents. In G. Philogène (Ed.), *Racial identity in context: The legacy of Kenneth B. Clark. Decade of behavior* (pp. 125–147). Washington, DC: American Psychological Association.

Harrison, L. A., Stevens, C. M., Monty, A. N., & Coakley, C. A. (2006). The consequences of stereotype threat on the academic performance of White and non-White lower income college students. *Social Psychology of Education, 9,* 341–357.

Iceland, J., Sharpe, C., & Steinmetz, E. (2003, May). *Class differences in African American residential patterns in U.S. metropolitan areas: 1990–2000.* Paper presented at the annual meeting of the Population Association of America, Minneapolis, MN.

Isakson, K., & Jarvis, P. (1999). The adjustment of adolescents during transition into high school: A short-term longitudinal study. *Journal of Youth and Adolescence, 28,* 1–26.

Kitano, M. K., & DiJiosia, M. (2002). Are Asian and Pacific Americans overrepresented in programs for the gifted? *Roeper Review, 24,* 76–80.

Lazarus, R. S. (1998). *Fifty years of the research and theory of R. S. Lazarus: An analysis of historical and perennial issues.* Mahwah, NJ: Lawrence Erlbaum.

Lee, J., & Harber, K. D. (2005). Teacher expectations and self-fulfilling prophecies: Knowns and unknowns, resolved and unresolved controversies. *Personality and Social Psychology Review, 9,* 131–155.

Lee, S., & Olszewski-Kubilius, P. (2006). Comparison between Talent Search students qualifying via scores on standardized tests and via parent nomination. *Roeper Review, 28,* 157–166.

Logan, J. R., Oakley, D., Smith, P., Stowell, J., & Stults, B. (2001). *Separating the children.* Albany, NY: Lewis Mumford Center for Comparative Urban and Regional Research.

Lopez, C., Lopez, L., Suarez-Morales, L., & Castro, F. G. (2005). Cultural variation within Hispanic American families. In C. L. Frisby & C. R. Reynolds (Eds.), *Comprehensive handbook of multicultural school psychology* (pp. 234–264). Hoboken, NJ: Wiley.

Marland, S. P., Jr., (1972). *Education of the gifted and talented: Vol. 1. Report to the Congress of the United States by the U.S. Commissioner of Education.* Washington, DC: U.S. Government Printing Office. (ERIC Document Reproduction Service No. ED056243)

Marsh, H. W., & Hau, K. (2003). Big-Fish-Little-Pond Effect on academic self-concept: A cross-cultural (26 country) test of the negative effects of academically selective schools. *American Psychologist, 58,* 364–376.

Marsh, H. W., & Parker, J. (1984). Determinants of student self-concept: Is it better to be a relatively large fish in a small pond even if you don't learn to swim as well? *Journal of Personality & Social Psychology, 47,* 213–231.

Massey, D. S. (2000). The residential segregation of Blacks, Hispanics, and Asians, 1970–1990. In G. D. Jaynes (Ed.), *Immigration and race: New challenges for American democracy* (pp. 44–73). New Haven, CT: Yale University Press.

Matthews, D. J., & Foster, J. F. (2005). *Being smart about gifted children: A guidebook for parents and educators.* Scottsdale, AZ: Great Potential Press.

Matthews, P. H., & Matthews, M. S. (2004). Heritage language instruction and giftedness in language minority students: Pathways toward success. *Journal of Secondary Gifted Education, 15,* 50–55.

McKown, C., & Weinstein, R. S. (2002). Modeling the role of child ethnicity and gender in children's differential response to teacher expectations. *Journal of Applied Social Psychology, 32,* 159–184.

McKown, C., & Weinstein, R. S. (2003). The development and consequences of stereotype consciousness in middle childhood. *Child Development, 74,* 498–515.

Mendoza-Denton, R., Downey, G., Purdie, V. J., Davis, A., & Pietrzak, J. (2002). Sensitivity to status-based rejection: Implications for African American students' college experiences. *Journal of Personality and Social Psychology, 83,* 896–918.

Mendoza-Denton, R., Page-Gould, E., & Pietrzak, J. (2006). Mechanisms for coping with status-based rejection expectations. In S. Levin & C. van Laar (Eds.), *Stigma and group inequality: Social psychological perspectives. The Claremont Symposium on Applied Social Psychology* (pp. 151–169). Mahwah, NJ: Lawrence Erlbaum.

Moon, S. M. (2002). Counseling needs and strategies. In M. Neihart, S. M. Reis, N. M. Robinson, & S. M. Moon (Eds.), *The social and emotional development of gifted children: What do we know?* (pp. 213–222). Waco, TX: Prufrock Press.

Moon, S. M., & Hall, A. S. (1998). Family therapy with intellectually and creatively gifted children. *Journal of Marital & Family Therapy, 24,* 59–80.

Murphy, C. P., & Worrell, F. C. (2001, April). *Motivation, goal orientation, and acceptability of cheating in gifted students.* Paper presented at the annual meeting of the American Educational Research Association, Seattle.

Myers, D. G. (2004). *Psychology* (7th ed.). New York: Worth.

Neihart, M., Reis, S. M., Robinson, N. M., & Moon, S. M. (Eds.). (2002). *The social and emotional development of gifted children: What do we know?* Waco, TX: Prufrock Press.

Noble, K. G., Tottenham, N., & Casey, B. J. (2005). Neuroscience perspectives on disparities in school readiness and cognitive achievement. *Future of Children, 15,* 71–89.

Ogbu, J. U. (1992). Understanding cultural diversity and learning. *Educational Researcher, 21*(8), 5–14.

Ogbu, J. U. (2003). *Black American students in an affluent suburb: A study of academic disengagement.* Mahwah, NJ: Lawrence Erlbaum.

Ogbu, J. U. (2004). Collective identity and the burden of "acting White" in Black history, community, and education. *The Urban Review, 36,* 1–35.

Ogbu, J. U., & Simons, H. D. (1998). Voluntary and involuntary minorities: A cultural-ecological theory of school performance with some implications for education. *Anthropology and Education Quarterly, 29,* 155–188.

Oyserman, D., Kemmelmeier, M., Fryberg, S., Brosh, H., & Hart-Johnson, T. (2003). Racial-ethnic self-schemas. *Social Psychology Quarterly, 66,* 333–347.

Pardon, M. C., & Marsden, C. A. (2008). The long-term impact of stress on brain function: From adaptation to mental diseases. *Neuroscience and Biobehavioral Reviews, 32,* 1071–1072.

Pietrzak, J. (2004). Race-based rejection sensitivity and ethnic identity: Interactive effects on institutional affiliation and well being. *Dissertation Abstracts International Section B: The Sciences and Engineering, 64*(12-B), 6379.

Renzulli, J. S. (1986). The three-ring conception of giftedness: A developmental model for creative productivity. In R. J. Sternberg & J. E. Davidson (Eds.), *Serving gifted and talented students: A resource for school personnel* (pp. 285–300). Austin, TX: Pro-Ed.

Richert, E. S. (1987). Rampant problems and promising practices in the identification of disadvantaged gifted students. *Gifted Child Quarterly, 31,* 149–154.

Rinn, A. N. (2006). Effects of a summer program on the social self-concepts of gifted adolescents. *Journal of Secondary Gifted Education, 17,* 65–75.

Robinson, A., Bradley, R. H., & Stanley, T. D. (1990). Opportunity to achieve: Identifying mathematically gifted Black students. *Contemporary Educational Psychology, 15,* 1–12.

Roeser, R. W., Midgley, C., & Urdan, T. C. (1996). Perceptions of the school psychological environment and early adolescents' psychological and behavioral functioning in school: The mediating role of goals and belonging. *Journal of Educational Psychology, 88,* 408–422.

Schmader, T., & Johns, M. (2003). Converging evidence that stereotype threat reduces working memory capacity. *Journal of Personality and Social Psychology, 85,* 440–452.

Shih, M., Pittinsky, T. L., & Ambady, N. (1999). Stereotype susceptibility: Identity salience and shifts in quantitative performance. *Psychological Science, 10,* 80–83.

Simonton, D. K. (1998). Gifted child, genius adult: Three life-span developmental perspectives. In R. C. Friedman & K. B. Rogers (Eds.), *Talent in context: Historical and social perspectives on giftedness* (pp. 151–175). Washington, DC: American Psychological Association.

Sosniak, L. A., & Gabelko, N. H. (2008). *Every child's right: Academic talent development by choice, not chance.* New York: Teachers College Press.

Steele, C. M. (1997). A threat in the air. How stereotypes shape intellectual identity and performance. *American Psychologist, 52,* 613–629.

Steele, C. M. (2003). Stereotype threat and African-American student achievement. In T. Perry, C. Steele, & A. G. Hilliard, III (Eds.), *Young, gifted, and Black: Promoting high achievement among African-American students* (pp. 109–130). Boston: Beacon Press.

Steele, C. M., & Aronson, J. (1995). Stereotype threat and the intellectual test performance of African Americans. *Journal of Personality and Social Psychology, 69,* 797–811.

Steele, C. M., & Aronson, J. (1998). Stereotype threat and the test performance of academically successful African Americans. In C. Jencks & M. Phillips (Eds.), *The Black-White test score gap* (pp. 401–427). Washington, DC: Brookings Institution.

Sternberg, R. J., & Davidson, J. E. (Eds.).(1986). *Conceptions of giftedness.* New York: Cambridge University Press.

Sternberg, R. J., & Davidson, J. E. (Eds.). (2005). *Conceptions of giftedness* (2nd ed.). New York: Cambridge University Press.

Stone, J., Lynch, C. I., Sjomeling, M., & Darley, J. M. (1999). Stereotype threat effects on Black and White athletic performance. *Journal of Personality and Social Psychology, 77,* 1213–1227.

Terman, L. M. (1924). The conservation of talent. *School and Society, 19,* 359–364.

Terman, L. M. (1925). *Genetic studies of genius. Mental and physical traits of a thousand gifted children.* Stanford, CA: Stanford University Press.

Terman, L. M., & Oden, M. H. (1947). *Genetic studies of genius. IV. The gifted child grows up.* Stanford, CA: Stanford University Press.

Terman, L. M., & Oden, M. H. (1959). *Genetic studies of genius. V. The gifted group at midlife.* Stanford, CA: Stanford University Press.

Vandiver, B. J., Cross, W. E., Jr., Fhagen-Smith, P. E., Worrell, F. C., Swim, J. K., & Caldwell, L. D. (2000). *The Cross Racial Identity Scale.* State College, PA: Authors.

Vandiver, B. J., & Worrell, F. C. (2002). The reliability and validity of scores on the Almost Perfect Scale-Revised with academically talented middle school students. *Journal of Secondary Gifted Education, 13,* 108–119.

Weinstein, R. S., & Middlestadt, S. E. (1979). Student perceptions of teacher interactions with male high and low achievers. *Journal of Educational Psychology, 71,* 421–431.

Werts, C. E., & Watley, D. J. (1969). A student's dilemma: Big fish-little pond or little fish-big pond. *Journal of Counseling Psychology, 16,* 14–19.

Worrell, F. C. (2003). Why are there so few African Americans in gifted programs? In C. C. Yeakey & R. D. Henderson (Eds.), *Surmounting the odds: Education, opportunity, and society in the new millennium* (pp. 423–454). Greenwich, CT: Information Age.

Worrell, F. C. (2005). Cultural variation within American families of African descent. In C. L. Frisby & C. R. Reynolds (Eds.), *Comprehensive handbook of multicultural school psychology* (pp. 137–172). Hoboken, NJ: Wiley.

Worrell, F. C. (2007a). Ethnic identity, academic achievement, and global self-concept in four groups of academically talented adolescents. *Gifted Child Quarterly, 51,* 23–38.

Worrell, F. C. (2007b). Identifying and including low-income learners in programs for the gifted and talented: Multiple complexities. In J. VanTassel-Baska & T. Stambaugh (Eds.), *Overlooked gems: A national perspective on low-income promising learners. Conference proceedings from the National Leadership Conference on Low-Income Learners* (pp. 47–51). Washington, DC: National Association for Gifted Children.

Worrell, F. C., & Gardner-Kitt, D. L. (2006). The relationship between racial and ethnic identity in Black adolescents: The Cross Racial Identity Scale (CRIS) and the Multigroup Ethnic Identity Measure (MEIM). *Identity: An International Journal of Theory and Research, 6,* 293–315.

Worrell, F. C., Szarko, J. E., & Gabelko, N. H. (2001). Multi-year persistence of nontraditional students in an academic talent development program. *Journal of Secondary Gifted Education, 12,* 80–89.

Worrell, F. C., Vandiver, B. J., Schaefer, B. A., Cross, W. E., Jr., & Fhagen-Smith, P. E. (2006). Generalizing nigrescence profiles: A cluster analysis of Cross Racial Identity Scale (CRIS) scores in three independent samples. *The Counseling Psychologist, 34,* 519–547.

The Education of Promising Students in Rural Areas: What Do We Know and What Can We Do?

Tamra Stambaugh

Rural Schools: In Search of a Definition

The needs and issues of students in rural areas, especially those who are gifted, have been overlooked in the literature for several decades (Cramond, 2005). Recently, however, there has been a rise in the number of publications focusing on rural education research, although the numbers of articles are still small and highlight regular education and struggling students more than students who are gifted (see citations in Provasnik et al., 2007). Still, little can be generalized about this special population because a collective definition is not available. Researchers have adopted varying definitions of "rural" when conducting studies. Colangelo, Assouline, and New (1999) lamented the lack of a consistent definition when implementing a national survey on the status of gifted education in rural settings. Likewise, the Census Bureau, in conjunction with the National Center for Education Statistics (NCES; 2007), recognized the lack of a common definition after attempting to generalize research findings among rural schools. A common federal definition of "rural" has now been adopted.

Prior to 2007, between one fifth to one half of school districts in America were labeled as rural, depending on how rural was defined (NCES, 1994). For example, some reports labeled rural communities as those with less than 25,000 persons while other reports considered rural communities as those with 2,500 persons or less. The new definition removes the population constraint and labels rural communities in varying degrees of proximity to an urban area. There are three degrees of rural: fringe, distant, and remote. Fringe rural areas are those within a 5 mile radius of an urban area, distant rural areas are between 5 and 25 miles of an urban area, and remote rural areas are those territories more than 25 miles from an urban area. (For a more detailed explanation of each of these, see Office of Management and Budget, 2000.) Under the new definition, 50% of all U.S. school districts, both private and public, are located in a rural area, with the highest concentration of rural schools being in the Midwestern and Southern portions of the United States. Of those districts labeled as rural, 33% of those are public schools that enroll approximately 25% of America's students (Provasnik et al., 2007).

The State of Education in Rural Schools

Even though a considerable part of America remains rural, much of the focus in educational research continues to center on urban education. Perhaps this has occurred due to the over-shadowing issues in urban communities such as crime, lower test scores, and homelessness as broadcast through various media sources as affecting a largely concentrated population. Because urban areas have a higher concentration of residents, those who reside there are more likely to drive policy, research, and resource allocation decisions within state and local gov-ernments, most favoring cities instead of rural communities. Moreover, there is an increased national focus on minor-ity issues even as the majority of students in rural schools are White, while more students in urban areas are of varying ethnic backgrounds (Provasnik et al., 2007).

A recent federal report on the state of rural education described the unique challenges of rural schools and how they differ from urban locales in many ways including (1) the allo-cation of resources and money; (2) teacher preparation and pay; and (3) educational attainment and parental expectations (Provasnik et al., 2007). Belief systems between rural and urban residents also differ (Spicker, Southern, & Davis, 1987). Each of these is explained in more detail.

First, the allocation of educational resources between rural and urban states is inequitable, favoring urban populations, even after being controlled for population differences. Predominately rural states (e.g., those states with more than 65% of the state population living in small towns) are more likely to report unequal distributions of school funding among districts within a state. This impacts the procurement of appropriate physical facilities for housing students in schools (Colangelo et al., 1999). Little has changed in the past 5 years. Federal reports from 2003–2004 (published in 2007) suggested that rural districts rely more heavily on state and federal aid to sustain their existence, whereas urban and suburban school districts receive a larger percentage of money from local revenue sources (Provasnik et al., 2007). Likewise, rural school district personnel, especially those in rural fringe districts, rely more heavily on federal money designated for schools of poverty than do those from urban and suburban areas (Provasnik et al., 2007).

There also are differences in the levels of teacher education, experience, salaries, and qualifications when comparing rural and urban districts. Teachers in rural settings are less likely to hold a master's degree than those in urban and suburban schools. Moreover, a higher percentage of teachers in rural areas teach vocational and technical courses than their urban and suburban counterparts (Provasnik et al., 2007). Teachers in rural schools are more experienced in terms of years of teaching, yet they receive significantly lower salaries, and are less qualified to teach specialized advanced content when compared to their urban counterparts (Colangelo et al., 1999; Provasnik et al., 2007).

Students from rural areas also face unique challenges. They are less likely to obtain a 4-year or advanced degree (Colangelo et al., 1999; Provasnik et al., 2007). This may be due in part to parental expectations and belief systems of those who live in rural areas. Provasnik and colleagues examined parental expectations of high school students and found that parents in rural areas were more likely to expect their children to attain a high school diploma, vocational degree, or an associate degree whereas those from urban and suburban areas are more likely to emphasize the attainment of a 4-year degree or beyond.

Moreover, rural communities typically are more conservative and view the school as a conduit for the teaching of moral and ethical values above all else (Spicker et al., 1987). In many rural communities, especially those of high poverty, local community connections and established relationships among individuals are emphasized over financial gain, lucrative job offers, and educational endeavors (Spicker et al., 1987). Community members fear that advanced education may expose students to a broader world and encourage the most intelligent students to move away from the area (Jones & Southern, 2004). When students from a rural community decide to leave their geographic location to attend college, they are less likely than their suburban counterparts to return to their rural hometown because of lower earning potential and fewer opportunities for employment (Jones & Southern, 2004).

Rural Schools and Poverty

"Poverty is the single strongest and most persistent threat to high student achievement," especially for students in many rural communities (Rural School and Community Trust [RSCT], 2005, p. 6). Of the school-age children who live in rural communities (those with less than 25,000 persons), approximately half qualify for free or reduced lunch (RSCT, 2005). In addition, rural schools are more likely than their urban and suburban counterparts to receive Federal Impact Aid, which is awarded to high-poverty schools throughout the nation (Provasnik et al., 2007). Remote rural areas have the highest percentage of students in poverty, consistent with statistics on inner-city urban schools; moreover, students in rural areas of poverty drop out of high school at higher percentages than their urban and suburban counterparts (Provasnik et al., 2007).

In her book, *Worlds Apart: Why Poverty Persists in Rural America,* Duncan (1999) explained findings from her ethnographic study of life in three rural towns: one in the South, one in the Midwest, and one in the Northeast. All areas were remote, but the Southern and Midwestern areas reported higher poverty than the Northeast, even though all faced similar struggles. Through narratives and qualitative comparisons among the three geographic locations, Duncan concluded that the impoverished areas of the Midwest and South were divided into strict social stratification classes of the "haves" and "have nots." In these areas the lower class groups are blamed for their impoverished situations, held back by upper class politics, and hold internal belief systems that reiterate a continued life of poverty without a vision for higher education or professional endeavors, summarizing that "those good things don't happen to us." She explains that the "*haves*" could afford private schools and that the public educational systems are in a constant state of decline due to decreasing enrollment of middle- and upper class groups. In contrast, the rural areas in the Northeast integrate the "haves" and "have nots" into all aspects of society and provide opportunities for those who desire to break the cycle of poverty. The families bond together to maintain strong public school systems for all classes and celebrate diverse perspectives. There is more trust among community members and less "blaming" for situations. Teachers and community members provide mentorship options and create systems for parents who want to provide "a better life" for their children. Duncan argued for strong schools, access to rigorous courses, high expectations, and caring, capable teachers as a great equalizer for change in these impoverished rural communities.

Rural Schools and Gifted Students

For children who live in rural communities and also are gifted, additional obstacles may be encountered. In many instances, there is community resistance to gifted programs because these programs are viewed as elitist and inequitable (Spicker et al., 1987). Although there are positive aspects for gifted students living in rural communities, such as less competition for involvement in select activities, smaller class sizes, and more opportunity for adult-student interactions (Colangelo et al., 1999; Spicker et al., 1987), there may be fewer opportunities for academic growth, fewer professional role models with advanced academic degrees, limited exposure to advanced materials, and less access to extracurricular academic activities. In high school, rural students are less likely to have access to Advanced Placement (AP) courses and International Baccalaureate (IB) programs, when compared to their urban and suburban counterparts (Provasnik et al., 2007). Moreover, parents in rural areas (as compared to their urban and suburban counterparts) are more likely to take their children to athletic events than to visit museums, zoos, libraries, or aquariums (Provasnik et al., 2007). It is unknown whether this is due to a belief system difference of those in rural areas or simply a geographic issue of access and availability.

The quality of curriculum, instruction, and opportunities for talent development are limited in rural areas, especially those with high poverty rates. Howley, Pendarvis, and Gholson (2005) examined rural gifted students' perceptions of mathematics instruction in a high-poverty school district. These students reported that their courses contained repetitious material and repetitive practice of lower level, basic skills. They felt there was little opportunity for advanced instruction in the regular classroom, and they had to seek assistance from parents and teachers of gifted students to provide advanced options.

This lack of rigorous coursework in impoverished rural schools is echoed in other studies as well. Gentry, Rizza, and Gable (2001) compared urban, suburban, and rural gifted students' attitudes toward school and reported that the rural students found school to be more mundane and less challenging than their suburban and urban counterparts, especially at the middle school level. A national survey on the status of gifted education in rural schools captured pertinent quotes to support this theme of lower level coursework. As one teacher of gifted students reiterated: "It is my experience that without competition and resources, gifted students in rural areas can coast by until college" (Colangelo et al., 1999, p. 55).

Geographic isolation, fewer professional occupations, and transportation costs further inhibit talent development opportunities. Because schools and communities in rural areas are more sparsely populated and may be geographically isolated, gifted students feel that they "stick out" or do not have enough similar peers. Their teachers report that there are fewer opportunities for mentorships, enrichment, or postsecondary opportunities, as colleges are too far away and there is limited access to a myriad of professional role models (Colangelo et al., 1999).

Gifted Education in Rural Schools: What Works?

The discussion of issues in rural schools is more prevalent in the literature than are interventions that work with gifted rural students. Some studies included rural schools in a larger sample. However, the data were not disaggregated by locale, and therefore one could not assume that the study intervention was effective with rural students, especially because in most studies the sample size of participating rural school districts was only a miniscule part of the larger sample. As we examine the interventions, in some instances it was difficult to separate rural and poverty as many studies included rural students of poverty as the sample. Therefore it is unknown whether the intervention is effective for all promising students of poverty or only promising rural students of poverty. Of the studies specific to rural and gifted, three categories emerged and will be discussed in detail: identification, intervention, and reform.

Identification

When considering identification of rural gifted students, one of the first questions one might ask is "do rural gifted students differ from other gifted students to an extent that different identification mechanisms are warranted?" The answer is "it depends." The percentage of students in poverty, the number of minorities and English as a second language (ESL) students within the rural population, as well as the geographic and cultural context of the rural community should be considered when making decisions about identification.

Although studies could not be found that compared differences in urban and rural identification practices or differences in the characteristics of gifted students in both rural and nonrural schools, there are studies available that outline effective practices in identification for rural gifted students as well as characteristics of rural gifted students of poverty. Based on the research available, the following list of recommendations may be generalized to rural populations of gifted students, especially those of poverty.

Use Multiple Measures for Identification

Multiple identification measures are necessary, including both verbal and nonverbal assessments, to accurately identify gifted students, especially those from rural poverty or other disadvantaged situations (Lohman, 2005a, 2005b; Payne, 1996; Slocumb & Payne, 2000; VanTassel-Baska, Johnson, & Avery, 2002). Educators and leaders in gifted education cannot rely on just one assessment tool to identify rural students. Rural gifted students, especially those who are geographically or financially disadvantaged, show their talents in different ways and, therefore, may require multiple assessments to capitalize upon their unique needs. When multiple assessments are used, a larger percentage of rural gifted students are identified, not only by ability (Stephens, Kiger, Karnes, & Whorton, 1999), but in visual and performing arts as well (Clark & Zimmerman, 2001).

Include a Tailored Checklist of Observable Behaviors

A checklist of observable behaviors completed by trained teachers may be used as one of several tools for identifying rural gifted students who differ from other gifted students in terms of geographic constraints and limited resources. District leaders should be wary of adopting one carte-blanche checklist of behaviors that may not appropriately represent some of the nontraditional characteristics of rural gifted students. Instead, teachers should be trained in how to recognize disadvantaged rural gifted students based on their unique characteristics. A checklist of contextual characteristics may be crafted and piloted by district leaders to capitalize on specific characteristics of promising, rural students, highlighting opportunities and behaviors that allow these students to showcase their talents.

Project Spring, a Javits-funded project that examined identification and service options for rural disadvantaged students in Indiana, succinctly outlined differences in characteristics among disadvantaged versus advantaged rural students. The researchers found that when compared to their nondisadvantaged rural counterparts, the disadvantaged, rural gifted students:

- are more passive in the classroom;
- are likely to speak nonstandard English;
- may not complete all assignments;
- are less likely to do well on standardized assessments;
- may have a more uneven profile on assessments (e.g., strong in math but weak in reading);
- have great ideas but poor writing skills, grammar, and handwriting;
- perform better on nonverbal versus verbal assessments; and
- are more likely to demonstrate their abilities through nontraditional or creative outlets outside of school (e.g., 4-H projects, performing arts, auto-mechanics, or rural environmental components; Spicker & Poling, 1993).

District leaders may choose to incorporate these characteristics into professional development trainings for teachers who are responsible for identifying gifted students. A checklist of behaviors also can be created as part of an ongoing screening process for finding gifted rural students who also are of poverty, as long as appropriate reliability and validation procedures are followed for the newly created forms.

Nonverbal Assessments Are Not a Sole Identifier

Nonverbal assessments may serve as one of multiple indicators to identify rural students, especially those of poverty or varying ethnicity groups (Shaunessy, Karnes, & Cobb, 2004; Spicker & Poling, 1993). The research on students of poverty and minority students suggests that nonverbal assessments may be a better indicator of ability than more verbal measures (Naglieri & Ford, 2003, 2005). However, using only nonverbal measures without other sources of data could be detrimental for some rural students, especially those of poverty, and should never be a sole determinant for identification (Lohman, 2005a). Some nonverbal tests have shown more promise with rural students of poverty than others. Shaunessy and colleagues (2004) administered three different nonverbal ability measures to African American students in an impoverished rural school district to compare the differences in student scores on each of the three assessments. They found that the Culture-Fair Intelligence Test and Raven's Standard Progressive Matrices identified more rural, African American students as gifted than the Naglieri Nonverbal Ability Test.

Spicker and Poling (1993) also studied rural students of poverty and found that rural students identified as gifted by alternate means performed significantly lower on verbal measures when compared to traditionally identified gifted students. However, rural student test scores on nonverbal tests of creativity did not differ significantly from the traditional gifted group in the categories of creative writing and nonverbal creativity tasks (Spicker & Poling, 1993).

Use Performance-Based Assessments

Performance-based assessments may be considered as a promising tool for identifying rural students of poverty (Hadaway & Marek-Schroer, 1992; Han & Marvin, 2000; VanTassel-Baska et al., 2002) although limited data exist for rural students. The study with the most empirical data comes from a statewide initiative, Project STAR, in South Carolina. The sample in this group included both rural and urban students. The researchers created performance-based nonverbal and verbal task demands. Preteaching of task archetypes was required to provide a common experience for all students. By using performance-based measures as a criterion for gifted identification, approximately 17% more students from low socioeconomic backgrounds were identified as gifted, when compared to statewide standardized measures of identification (VanTassel-Baska et al., 2002).

Portfolios Can Provide Supporting Evidence of Giftedness

Portfolios provide educators of promising, rural students with information about students' interests, outside class activities, and unique abilities that may not be measured by verbal or nonverbal assessments alone, especially when linked with community activities celebrated in rural areas. Montgomery (2001) used portfolios as a means to identify rural Native American Indian students and found that the use of portfolios as a primary identifier enabled educators to identify 50% more potentially gifted students than ability tests alone. Portfolio assessments for students in rural areas should capitalize on strengths in and outside of the classroom, including agriculture projects, religious activities, art, creative writing, and leadership activities evidenced by participation in various clubs, church functions, or the arts.

Match the Program to the Child

When alternative identification measures are used, programs must be altered to better meet the needs of students who are identified in nontraditional ways. If rural students are identified by alternative means that include nonverbal or creative assessments, districts would be remiss to provide services to these students that focus solely on a verbal curriculum. Instead, the services provided to students who are identified by alternate methods should match the identification procedures in place. This does not imply that verbal activities should be excluded; instead, students may need more scaffolding to enhance their verbal precocity while being exposed to nonverbal and creative opportunities within a subject-specific curriculum.

Interventions

The research specific to interventions with rural gifted students is less definitive than the information on identification. Some studies included rural students as part of a larger group; however, the interventions used were not disaggregated by rural or urban locale, making it difficult to generalize the effects on rural gifted students as opposed to the remainder of the sample in the study. Other interventions, such as the use of technology, also dominated the literature regarding rural gifted but did not provide evidence of effectiveness for this special population, with a few exceptions that will be discussed. Common themes on effective interventions for rural gifted students include: the role of significant others, the use of technology and distance learning, specific curriculum interventions, and instructional/management strategies such as acceleration and grouping.

Role of Significant Others

The most predominant finding in the literature was the importance of significant others as part of the talent development process for rural gifted students, especially those living in poverty. Relationships typically are valued above all else for persons of poverty (Payne, 1996), both rural and urban, making mentorship opportunities a viable option for increasing talent development opportunities for these students. Mentoring can provide mechanisms for rural students of poverty to deal with the consequences of living in poverty, help these students set appropriate goals for the future, and allow them to recognize and enhance their individual talents and skills through the building of relationships with a significant person. Therefore, the opportunity for students who are disadvantaged to work with a mentor provides emotional, professional, and familial benefits. As gifted students work with a mentor, families of these children also learn the skills necessary to develop talent in their children, thus the inclusion of family education in the mentorship process is a critical component (Montgomery, 2001; Olszewski-Kubilius, 2007; VanTassel-Baska & Stambaugh, 2007).

Of the studies perused, the relationship to the mentee varied, but there was always a significant other. In some instances the mentor was a family member, an assigned or serendipitous mentor, a teacher, or a school guidance counselor instrumental in the lives of these students. Hébert (2002) provided an in-depth look at three students living in poverty, two of whom were from rural communities. He described four main themes that significantly impacted the lives of gifted students: educators who were encouraging and held high expectations, the use of a mentoring model when working with these students, involvement in extracurricular activities, and an enriching learning environment.

Another study examined influential factors of mathematics achievement in promising, rural students living in Appalachia regions. The students who were most successful in mathematics had the support of either the teacher of the gifted or a family member (Howley et al., 2005). These students found solace, challenge, and a sense of normalcy when permitted to work with the teacher of the gifted, other gifted students, and family members on arithmetic projects of interest.

Academic Planning

The provision of educational assistance for college planning is another effective approach for students in rural settings, especially those of poverty or first-generation college-bound students (Cross & Burney, 2005; Montgomery, 2001). Lessons learned from the research suggest that high school guidance counselors should be provided professional development regarding (a) hindrances that inhibit rural students from attending college, (b) opportunities beyond the community offerings for promising students to learn about various career options that may not be evident in small communities, (c) how to be admitted to premiere colleges across the United States, and (d) how to aid students in the transition from a rural community to a college setting.

In addition, guidance counselors of students in rural areas should develop plans for helping gifted students access advanced courses in nontraditional ways (e.g., online learning) so that they have the same opportunities for rigorous coursework as students in urban settings. If courses are available, students of rural poverty often are either denied access to these classes in high school due to their lack of appropriate verbal and writing skills (Payne, 1996) or choose not to take advanced courses due to increased workloads that conflict with family time or the potential for a lower grade, as external awards are important (Cross & Burney, 2005). Because many students of poverty consider short-term versus long-term financial gains when making decisions about whether or not to enter college, guidance counselors need to make students aware of the long-term earning benefits for different career paths and help these students find cooperative work and school opportunities (Cross & Burney, 2005).

Because several careers are dependent on exposure to advanced courses in math and science, high school guidance counselors must ensure that rural gifted students have access to the most rigorous courses in these subject areas, even if it means attendance at a local community college or enrollment in online coursework. Otherwise, these students may not be as competitive for selective colleges that offer advanced degrees in these subject areas.

Cross and Burney (2005) provided professional development opportunities to middle and high school guidance counselors employed in rural areas of poverty. As they worked with these counselors, three themes emerged regarding the unique issues of providing academic counseling to rural students of poverty. First, teachers and students found that the provision of rigorous coursework takes too much time. Students and parents of poverty did not understand the reasons for needing to work as hard in school and complained that the homework got in the way of extracurricular activities or afterschool jobs. Parents also felt that schoolwork should be completed during school time as there were other things to do at home and there was little time for parental monitoring of homework. Teachers also complained that AP courses take too much preparation. In rural schools many secondary teachers are overtaxed with planning several different courses while also coaching or leading extracurricular activities.

Second, the school climate and culture has a major effect on student achievement. The authors explained that in less populated schools, such as those in rural communities, a few students can impact the culture, creating either one of achievement or a lack thereof. There also were distinct gender differences suggesting that it is not permissable for boys to achieve in school or work hard on school-related tasks.

The final theme that emerged was of the need for understanding and combating generational poverty. Counselors found it necessary to provide unique program options for first-generation college students and their families. Students needed exposure to college campus life prior to applying to colleges. Parents needed guidance and support in allowing their children to leave home to preview campuses. In addition, parents needed help with financial matters and the juggling of family responsibilities during their child's time away, as many of these students helped with younger siblings or major chores around the house.

Technology and Distance Learning

Technology options are listed throughout the literature as a way for rural students to gain access to opportunities that may not be available in their community. However, little empirical data exists on the effectiveness of technology and student achievement. In rural communities where geographic location may hinder availability to more rigorous coursework or opportunities to enroll in a variety of course offerings, technology may be a viable option, if available (VanTassel-Baska & Stambaugh, 2006). However, "teaching children with exceptional needs requires specialized skills, materials, and technology—three things not available in all [rural] schools" (RSCT, 2005, p. 9). Due to the lack of resources available in some rural schools, students may not have access to appropriate technology or advanced equipment needed for high-level experimentation, especially in technical content areas such as the sciences. Some schools in rural communities may have limited Internet access or may not be able to keep up with the ever-changing demands of technology necessary to maintain ongoing opportunities (Colangelo, Assouline, Baldus, & New, 2003).

When relying on technology as a service-provision option for rural schools in impoverished areas, access must be provided during the school day. The United States Department of Education (NCES, 2003) reported that more than half of families with household incomes of $35,000 or less rely on the school for their sole Internet usage. When access can be provided during the school day, some success has been found in using technology with gifted rural students who are deaf (Belcastro, 2004), have motor impairments of the hand (Belcastro, 2005), need more access to rigorous Advanced Placement courses (Cross & Burney, 2005), or have geographic limitations that inhibit social support networks (Spicker et al., 1987).

Specific options for advanced coursework accessible via the Internet include simulations and WebQuests, virtual field trips, ask-the-expert Web sites, telementoring, and accelerated online courses, such as those offered by Johns Hopkins University's Center for Talented Youth, Northwestern University's Center for Talent Development Learning Links Program, Stanford University's Education Program for Gifted Youth, and some online Advanced Placement courses (VanTassel-Baska & Stambaugh, 2006). Each of these options may provide valuable learning experiences for advanced students in rural school districts; however, educators must be discerning regarding the selection of online options and ensure that the programs are appropriately accelerated for gifted students and have a marked history of research and success in terms of technical assistance, content-mentoring, and student achievement.

Educators cannot assume that technology will solve the academic issues of rural schools. Educators need to monitor student progress and encourage small-group discussions with content experts in addition to online options. Even though some of the specific programs mentioned may be costly, they generally are cheaper than hiring a teacher for a small number of students and could provide advanced coursework alternatives for gifted students. However, one must be cautious when considering learning opportunities via the various technologies. Students need to have a fast Internet connection, motivation to learn a subject area, and moderate independent learning skills—characteristics that not all gifted students possess.

Curriculum

Adelman (1999) explained the importance of student access to rigorous coursework in high school and how that coursework may be a better predictor of college success than grades or test scores. Therefore, advanced curriculum and subsequent management strategies are important catalysts for the talent development of rural gifted students. When working with rural Native American high school students of promise, Montgomery (2001) reported that a challenging curriculum in the core content areas designed to enhance the regular classroom curriculum resulted in an increase in ACT and SAT performance scores, the number of students who applied to college, and authentic growth in a content area based on portfolio assessments.

Scaffolding instruction from lower level to higher level thinking skills through the use of a critical thinking curriculum also has shown promise for rural students in schools of poverty. Slocumb and Payne (2000) suggested that students of poverty need scaffolding in order to bridge gaps from informal to formal speech and to have appropriate behaviors and academic conversations modeled for them. Specifically, the *Jacob's Ladder*

Reading Comprehension Program (available from Prufrock Press) was written to provide background experiences and knowledge of advanced reading skills through scaffolding. This curriculum was piloted in two rural school districts of poverty in the Midwest. The curriculum intervention provides accelerated reading prompts of short stories, nonfiction selections, or poems and then applies an array of lower level to higher level questions that build upon previous learning so that students may increase their understanding of a passage and apply newly created background knowledge and expertise to advanced questions that promote critical reading and thinking. Teachers who use this program are trained to encourage and model student discussion, solicit appropriate responses, and build metacognition in reading through question-asking, modeling of responses, and think-alouds. Results from a quasi-experimental study suggest that when compared to students who used only a basal reading series, the *Jacob's Ladder Reading Comprehension Program* students showed statistically significant and practical gains in reading comprehension and critical thinking (Stambaugh, 2009). This study suggested that when rural students of poverty have exposure to an advanced curriculum and scaffolding, they can achieve at higher levels than expected or provided by the typical on-grade-level curriculum.

Acceleration

Accelerated opportunities may be an economical option for serving gifted students in rural communities, as acceleration does not typically involve an increase in personnel resources. However, accelerated opportunities in rural schools are limited (Jones & Southern, 2004). In a study of 78 urban and rural school districts, Jones and Southern reported statistically significant disparities between accelerated offerings in urban and rural schools. Rural school districts were less likely to provide subject acceleration, Advanced Placement courses, and dual-enrollment options. Instead, these rural districts reported extracurricular options and academic contests as the primary modes of service for gifted students.

In a review of the literature, only one study was found from the past 10 years that specifically examined accelerative practices in a rural school district (see Howley, 2002). In this study, the author suggested that acceleration can be a viable option for serving rural gifted students; however, in many instances teachers were reluctant to incorporate accelerative options, especially at the elementary level. As part of this study, district and building leadership were asked to provide some form of acceleration to students in their respective jurisdiction. Accelerative opportunities included grade skipping, subject acceleration, cross-grade grouping, and in-class advanced curriculum. Regardless of the acceleration strategy employed, Howley found four themes from building teams that successfully implemented accelerative options: (1) curriculum and instruction was based on a student's individual needs and involved multiple stakeholders; (2) instruction matched the student's skill level; (3) student progress was continually monitored by the teacher of the gifted; and (4) pre- and posttesting was documented using a standardized achievement test.

Grouping

Grouping is a highly researched and controversial topic within gifted education in general. However, the research is clear regarding the positive academic results of grouping for gifted students when the groupings are deliberate and include differentiated and advanced instruction (Gentry & Owen, 1999; Kulik & Kulik, 1992; Rogers, 1998; Tieso, 2002). The deliberate placement of like-ability advanced students together in rural schools is essential to the success of these students, possibly even more so than in urban areas due to the paucity of like peers at the same age and geographic isolation. In rural areas where the geographic area is large and there are several small community schools, gifted students may feel more isolated and are more likely to be found in smaller numbers across the entire school district or multiple classrooms, instead of in deliberately grouped cohorts. In some instances, rural gifted students have been deliberately (and wrongfully) separated among several classrooms or schools so that each building or classroom has better opportunities for passing state-mandated tests, further ignoring the needs of gifted students (Stambaugh, 2001).

Jones and Southern (2004) compared the grouping practices of urban and rural school districts by surveying coordinators of gifted programs regarding program offerings and their perceptions toward grouping. Thirteen of the school districts surveyed reported no grouping options for gifted students. Of those 13 districts, 9 were rural. If grouping options were available, rural districts reported fewer grouping options than their urban counterparts, especially at the elementary level. This held true even though the beliefs about grouping were similar across both urban and rural coordinator groups.

Gentry and Owen (1999) examined the effects of cluster grouping (deliberately placing a core group of high-achieving students in one classroom) in a disadvantaged, rural school district of students in grades 3–5. They found that high-achieving students who participated in the cluster groups showed a significant increase in reading achievement and math achievement over their non-cluster-grouped counterparts. Over time the number of high-achieving students increased across the grade levels. In the beginning of the study, many teachers expressed concern about removing the "cream of the crop" from all classrooms and placing them into one. However, by the end of the study, the majority of teachers reported that new leaders emerged within the classroom, and they were better equipped to meet the needs of all of their students by limiting the ability ranges within each classroom and focusing on areas of strengths and remediation for each of the groups. Specific interventions within the cluster-grouped classroom varied and included interest centers, curriculum compacting, and independent study opportunities. The success of cluster grouping is attributed to the administrative leaders, ongoing professional development both within and outside the school district, and strong collaboration and trust among colleagues (Gentry & Owen, 1999).

Similar effects have been noted in smaller scaled studies as well. Stambaugh (2001) compared the effects of cluster grouping on identified gifted students in grades 2–4 in a rural district of poverty. Teachers of all identified gifted students were provided materials and professional development to aid in differentiation, including accelerated mathematics materials, advanced reading books with provided higher level questions, and independent study methods. Students in the cluster group sustained their standardized test scores in reading and math over a 3-year period, whereas those students who were provided similar differentiated activities without the cluster group showed decreased scores over time and were no longer identified as gifted by district and state measures. Moreover, teachers who were assigned the cluster groups were more likely to provide consistent differentiation for gifted students than those who did not have cluster groups, but had at least one or two gifted students in their classroom.

Reform Studies

Data specific to gifted education reform in rural schools are less plentiful than reform studies in the regular education literature. Of those that do exist, the majority suggest that the success of rural schools is linked to the support of school district leadership, ongoing professional development, community relationships, and the adequate provision of resources. In many instances, teachers in rural schools may not have access to learning opportunities specific to gifted education due to geographic barriers, cultural beliefs, and competing resources that seldom include additional monies for gifted students. Therefore, administrative encouragement and ongoing, embedded professional development are especially critical for the continuation of effective practices.

In a study funded by the Jacob K. Javits Grant from the United States Department of Education, five rural and one urban school district participated in professional development activities to educate regular classroom teachers in differentiated instruction for gifted students. Authors of this study found that in order to successfully incorporate differentiated strategies for gifted students into the regular classroom, the following four components were necessary to support change: staff development, strong district leadership, the provision of resources, and ongoing project support (Johnsen, Haensly, Ryser, & Ford, 2002).

In addition, relationships forged between teachers of the gifted, parents, and the community (Montgomery, 2001), as well as parent advocacy initiatives (Kennedy, 2003) produce positive changes in rural school district services for gifted students. Often, parents in rural school districts are more hesitant than their urban counterparts to request different services for their gifted learners (Jones & Southern, 2004). However, when parents and community members become involved in the provision of services, education for gifted students, and advocacy for gifted children's needs, positive results for the continuation or addition of services are enjoyed (Kennedy, 2003).

Conclusion

There are positive aspects to be gained by gifted and promising students who live and attend school in a rural community, including additional opportunities for adult interaction, family-like environments, and smaller class size. However, gifted students in rural communities, especially those of poverty, are less likely to be exposed to accelerated options, homogeneous grouping with like-academic peers, professional mentorships, a variety of course options based on interests and academic precocity, or a challenging curriculum taught by highly qualified teachers in a given content area. When these opportunities are provided, gifted students in rural school districts show positive academic gains.

Teachers and leaders charged with the oversight of gifted programs in rural schools must be cognizant of the belief systems within the community and work to dispel myths regarding gifted education that are antithetical to best practices for these students. In addition, leaders of gifted programs must be prepared to provide ongoing professional development to other staff members; build relationships with community members and parents; provide in-depth career counseling and exposure to a variety of careers not typically found in the community; infuse an advanced curriculum that incorporates higher level thinking into the school day as opposed to disjointed extra-curricular activities; and build solid, alternative identification systems that capitalize on the strengths of gifted students within the local community. Moreover, leaders and teachers of gifted students in rural communities may need to find alternative and creative ways to provide appropriate services for their students that may involve technology or other types of distance learning if community resources are not readily available.

Finally, additional research specific to gifted learners in rural communities is necessary. One cannot assume that the same interventions found effective with urban or suburban students also will be effective with rural gifted students unless empirical data are available to support those assumptions.

References

Adelman, C. (1999). *Answers in the tool box: Academic intensity, attendance patterns, and bachelor's degree attainment.* Jessup, MD: ED Pubs.

Belcastro, F. P. (2004). Rural gifted students who are deaf or hard of hearing: How electronic technology can help. *American Annals of the Deaf, 149,* 309–313.

Belcastro, F. P. (2005). Electronic technology: Hope for rural gifted students who have motor impairment of the hands. *Journal of Developmental and Physical Disabilities, 17,* 237–247.

Clark, G., & Zimmerman, E. (2001). Identifying artistically talented students in four rural communities in the United States. *Gifted Child Quarterly, 45,* 104–114.

Colangelo, N., Assouline, S. G., Baldus, C. M., & New, J. K. (2003). Gifted education in rural schools. In N. Colangelo & G. A. Davis (Eds.) *Handbook of gifted education* (pp. 572–581). Boston: Pearson.

Colangelo, N., Assouline, S. G., & New, J. K. (1999). *Gifted education in rural schools: A national assessment.* Iowa City: The University of Iowa, The Connie Belin & Jacqueline N. Blank International Center for Gifted Education and Talent Development.

Cramond, B. (2005). From the editor. *Journal of Secondary Gifted Education, 16,* 146–147.

Cross, T. L., & Burney, V. H. (2005). High ability, rural, and poor: Lessons from Project Aspire and implications for school counselors. *Journal of Secondary Gifted Education, 16,* 148–156.

Duncan, C. M. (1999). *Worlds apart: Why poverty persists in rural America.* New Haven, CT: Yale University Press.

Gentry, M., & Owen, S. V. (1999). An investigation of the effects of total school flexible cluster grouping on identification, achievement, and classroom practices. *Gifted Child Quarterly, 43,* 224–243.

Gentry, M., Rizza, M. G., & Gable, R. K. (2001). Gifted students' perceptions of their class activities: Differences among rural, urban, and suburban student attitudes. *Gifted Child Quarterly, 45,* 115–129.

Hadaway, N., & Marek-Schroer, M. F. (1992). Multidimensional assessment of the gifted minority student. *Roeper Review, 15,* 73–77.

Han, K. S., & Marvin, C. (2000). A five year follow-up study of the Nebraska Project: Still a long way to go. *Roeper Review, 23,* 25–33.

Hébert, T. P. (2002). Educating gifted children from low socioeconomic backgrounds: Creating visions of a hopeful future. *Exceptionality, 10,* 127–138.

Howley, A. (2002). The progress of gifted students in a rural district that emphasized acceleration strategies. *Roeper Review, 24,* 158–160.

Howley, A., Pendarvis, E., & Gholson, M. (2005). How talented students in a rural school district experience mathematics. *Journal for the Education of the Gifted, 29,* 123–160.

Johnsen, S., Haensly, P., Ryser, G., & Ford, R. (2002). Changing general education classroom practices to adapt for gifted students. *Gifted Child Quarterly, 46,* 45–63.

Jones, E. D., & Southern, W. T. (2004). Programming, grouping, and acceleration in rural school districts: A survey of attitudes and practices. In L. E. Brody (Ed.), *Grouping and acceleration practices in gifted education* (pp. 147–159). Thousand Oaks, CA: Corwin Press.

Kennedy, D. M. (2003). Custer, South Dakota: "Gifted's" last stand. *Gifted Child Quarterly, 47,* 82–93.

Kulik, C., & Kulik, J. (1992). Meta-analytic findings on grouping programs. *Gifted Child Quarterly, 36,* 73–77.

Lohman, D. F. (2005a). Review of Naglieri and Ford (2003): Does the Naglieri Nonverbal Ability Test identify equal proportions of high-scoring White, Black, and Hispanic students? *Gifted Child Quarterly, 49,* 19–28.

Lohman, D. F. (2005b). The role of nonverbal ability tests in identifying academically gifted students: An aptitude perspective. *Gifted Child Quarterly, 49,* 111–138.

Montgomery, D. (2001). Increasing Native American Indian involvement in gifted programs in rural schools. *Psychology in the Schools, 38,* 467–475.

Naglieri, J. A., & Ford, D. Y. (2003). Addressing underrepresentation of gifted minority children using the Naglieri Nonverbal Ability Test (NNAT). *Gifted Child Quarterly, 47,* 155–160.

Naglieri, J. A., & Ford, D. Y. (2005). Increasing minority children's participation in gifted classes using the NNAT: A response to Lohman. *Gifted Child Quarterly, 49,* 29–36.

National Center for Education Statistics. (1994). *Condition of education in rural schools 1994.* Washington, DC: U.S. Department of Education.

National Center for Education Statistics. (2003). *Digest of education statistics 2005.* Washington, DC: U.S. Department of Education.

National Center for Educational Statistics. (2007). *Status of education in rural America.* Retrieved August 28, 2008, from http://nces.ed.gov/pubs2007/ruraled

Office of Management and Budget. (2000). Standards for defining metropolitan and micropolitan statistical areas: Notice. *Federal Register, 65*(249), 1–12.

Olszewski-Kubilius, P. (2007). Working with promising learners from poverty. In J. VanTassel-Baska & T. Stambaugh (Eds.), *Overlooked gems: A national perspective on low-income promising learners* (pp. 43–46). Washington, DC: National Association for Gifted Children.

Payne, R. K. (1996). *A framework for understanding poverty.* Highlands, TX: Aha! Process.

Provasnik, S., KewalRamani, A., Coleman, M. M., Gilbertson, L., Herring, W., & Xie, Q. (2007). *Status of education in rural America* (NCES 2007-040). Washington, DC: National Center for Education Statistics, Institute of Education Sciences, U.S. Department of Education.

Rogers, K. B. (1998). Using current research to make "good" decisions about grouping. *NASSP Bulletin, 82,* 38–46.

Rural School and Community Trust. (2005, May). *Why rural matters: The facts about rural education in the 50 states* (Tech. Rep. No. 3). Arlington, VA: Author.

Shaunessy, E., Karnes, F. A., & Cobb, Y. (2004). Assessing potentially gifted students from lower socioeconomic status with nonverbal measures of intelligence. *Perceptual and Motor Skills, 98,* 1129–1138.

Slocumb, P. D., & Payne, R. K. (2000). *Removing the mask: Giftedness in poverty.* Highlands, TX: Aha! Process.

Spicker, H. H., & Poling, N. (1993). *Identifying rural disadvantaged gifted students. Project SPRING: Special populations resource information network for the gifted.* Washington, DC: Department of Education. (ERIC Document Reproduction Service No. ED404791)

Spicker, H. H., Southern, W. T., & Davis, B. I. (1987). The rural gifted child. *Gifted Child Quarterly, 39,* 88–94.

Stambaugh, T. (2001, Winter). Cluster grouping the gifted: One school's journey. *The OAGC Review,* 4–5.

Stambaugh, T. (2009). *Effects of the* Jacob's Ladder Reading Comprehension Program *on Title I students' reading comprehension and critical thinking ability.* Manuscript submitted for publication.

Stephens, K., Kiger, L., Karnes, F. A., & Whorton, J. E. (1999). Use of nonverbal measures of intelligence in identification of culturally diverse gifted students in rural areas. *Perceptual and Motor Skills, 88,* 793–796.

Tieso, C. L. (2002). *The effects of grouping and curricular practices on intermediate students' math achievement* (Research Monograph 02154). Storrs: University of Connecticut, The National Research Center on the Gifted and Talented.

VanTassel-Baska, J., Johnson, D., & Avery, L. D. (2002). Using performance tasks in the identification of economically disadvantaged and minority gifted learners: Findings from Project STAR. *Gifted Child Quarterly, 46,* 110–123.

VanTassel-Baska, J., & Stambaugh, T. (2006). *Comprehensive curriculum for gifted learners* (3rd ed.). Boston: Allyn & Bacon.

VanTassel-Baska, J., & Stambaugh, T. (Eds.) (2007). *Overlooked gems: A national perspective on low-income promising learners.* Washington, DC: National Association for Gifted Children.

Working With Academically Gifted Students in Urban Settings: Issues and Lessons Learned

Paula Olszewski-Kubilius

The Achievement Gaps

Gaps in the achievement of minority and nonminority students at all ages, socioeconomic levels, and levels of ability continue to be the most central problem in the field of education. Various measures, including grades, standardized test scores, course selections, dropout rates, and college-completion rates, have been used to assess achievement differences, and performance gaps by ethnicity (Caucasians vs. African Americans or Hispanic/Latinos) and socioeconomic status (higher income vs. lower income families) are the largest, most persistent, and most troubling to our nation (*Education Week*, 2007; National Governors Association, 2007). For example, 2003 data from the National Assessment of Educational Progress (NAEP) study showed that 39% of Caucasian students scored at the proficient or advanced level on the fourth-grade NAEP assessments in reading compared to 14% of Hispanic students and 12% of African American students (*Education Week*, 2007). These disparities have been steady over decades and across ages of students. For example, on the NAEP math assessment, differences between Caucasian students and African American students at age 9 were 25 points in 1986 and 23 points in 2004; 24 points in

1986 and 27 points in 2004 for students at age 13; and 29 points in 1986 and 28 points in 2004 for students at age 17. Similar gaps were found for Caucasian versus Hispanic students on the math assessment (age 9, 21 points in 1986 and 18 points in 2004; age 13, 19 points in 1986 and 23 points in 2004; age 17, 24 points in 1986 and 24 points in 2004). Identical discrepancies by ethnicity were found on the NAEP reading assessment as well (see *Education Week*, 2007, for more information).

Racial disparities in academic achievement also are found among the most able students, specifically among high scorers on the SAT-Math and Reading (Miller, 2004). Data from college-bound seniors in 2000 showed that on the SAT-Math, 16% of Asian students and 5.8% of Caucasian students scored 700 or above compared to 0.6% of African Americans, 1.2% of Mexican Americans, and 1.2% of Puerto Ricans. On the SAT-Reading, the percentages of the high school seniors with 700 or above were 6.4% for Asians, 5.3% for Caucasians, 1.2% for Puerto Ricans, 1.1% for Mexican Americans, and 0.8% for African Americans. Differences between minority and nonminority students also were found on Advanced Placement (AP) examinations. In 2002, the racial composition of the students who took AP examinations was 75% Caucasians, 13% Asians, 6.5% Mexican Americans, and 5.6% African Americans. As for the level of performance, Asian (mean = 3.08) and Caucasian (mean = 3.07) students outperformed Mexican American (mean = 2.13, excluding Spanish Language) and African American (mean = 2.14) students on average, and overwhelmingly Asian (39%) and Caucasian (37.2%) students earned high scores (4 or 5 points) compared to percentages of African American (13.3%) and Mexican American (12.9% excluding Spanish Language) students. Miller concluded that "African Americans, Latinos (especially Mexican Americans and Puerto Ricans) and Native Americans are currently severely underrepresented among the nation's highest achieving students, by virtually all traditional academic achievement measures, including GPA, class rank, and standardized test scores" (pp. 1–2).

The achievement gap is not limited to nor defined only by differences in achievement by ethnic/racial group: Poverty plays a huge role. Wyner, Bridgeland, and DiIulio (2007) analyzed data from three national longitudinal studies (Early Childhood Longitudinal Study-Kindergarten Cohort, the National Education Longitudinal Study Data, and Baccalaureate and Beyond Longitudinal Study) to track the performance of high-achieving lower income and high-achieving upper income students. The authors defined high-achieving students as those who placed in the top quartile nationwide on nationally normed examinations, and defined lower income and upper income as the bottom and top halves of the family income distribution. Disparities between high-achieving lower income students and high-achieving upper income students were found at the beginning of elementary school (e.g., 72% of the high achievers came from the upper income families compared to 28% from the lower income families), and these grew larger over time. For instance, compared to high-achieving first to fifth graders from upper income families, a greater number of high-achieving lower income students tended to fall out of the top quartile in reading (31% vs. 44%). In high school, high-achieving lower income students were more likely to fall out of the top quartile in math (16% vs. 25%) and drop out of high school or not graduate on time (4% vs. 8%) than their upper income counterparts. Disparities between upper income and lower income high achievers also were found in higher education in terms of college graduation rates (77% vs. 59%), attendance at prestigious colleges (29% vs. 19%), and attainment of graduate degrees (47% vs. 29%). The fact is, most of our minority students in urban areas also are disproportionately low income and thus doubly handicapped.

Further, there also is evidence of achievement disparities between minority and majority students within every socioeconomic status (SES) level, as determined by family income and parental education levels (what Miller, 2004, calls the within-class problem) and particularly at the higher SES levels (the "within-the-top" achievement problem; Miller, 2004). Data from the 1998 early childhood longitudinal study showed performance gaps in several math areas between minority and majority kindergarteners in the highest SES quintile (Miller, 2004). Particularly, African American and Hispanic children lagged behind Asian and Caucasian children in understanding ordinal sequence (performance rate: Asian, 48%; Caucasian,

41%; Hispanic, 25%; African American, 21%) and performing addition and subtraction (performance rate: Asian 16%, Caucasian 10%, Hispanic 4%, African American 3%). Additionally, likely due to support systems within certain cultures for academic achievement, some low-income groups fare better academically than others. For example, Wyner and colleagues (2007) reported that during high school, lower income, high-achieving Asian students were more likely to stay in the top quartile of performance in math, while lower income African American students were less likely to climb into the high achievement level in math and reading.

Urban Gifted

Achievement differences by racial/ethnic group and SES level are especially pronounced and pervasive within our major urban school districts in the United States, although such disparities are not limited to these settings and are found in large suburban districts located close to major cities as well (see the Minority Student Achievement Network, http://www.msan.wceruw. org). Most of our poor minority children and new immigrants reside in these school districts that are underfunded and struggling to survive. Gifted children within these districts are particularly at risk because they often are overlooked. Indeed, in some instances no gifted programs exist at all, high achievement of students goes unnoticed and unattended to, and the focus of human and other resources is completely on struggling students, preventing dropouts, teen pregnancy, drug use, and the like.

Issues With Schooling

Poor children, minority children, and poor minority children are underrepresented in gifted programs. Literature has documented that most of the students qualified for and placed in gifted programs and advanced classes are predominantly Caucasian or Asian students (Bernal, 2002; Borland & Wright, 1994; Ford, 1996; Ford & Harris, 1999; Ford, Harris, Tyson & Trotman, 2002; Gallagher, 1994; Grantham, 2003; Lee, Matthews, & Olszewski-Kubilius, 2008; Maker, 1996; Morris,

2002; Worrell, 2007; Wyner et al., 2007) and that Black students are underrepresented by as much as 55% nationally in gifted programs (Ford, Grantham, & Whiting, 2008). One of the reasons for this is that gifted programs tend to exist in schools that serve more affluent populations of students. Baker and Friedman–Nimz (2002) analyzed data from the National Educational Longitudinal Study of 1988 on 19,000 students from 802 public schools and found that gifted programs were more likely to be available to students with higher socioeconomic status. Specifically, 18% more students in the third quartile on SES and 28% more students in the fourth quartile on SES attended schools where gifted programs were offered compared to students where family incomes placed them in the first quartile on SES (Baker & Friedman–Nimz, 2002).

Most of our poor minority children find themselves in schools that lack a rigorous curriculum, are less well equipped in terms of educational resources such as libraries, textbooks, and technology, and often employ less experienced or less qualified teachers (Barton, 2003). And, even if students are in schools with gifted programs, poor minority children are far less likely to be referred by teachers for possible participation in the gifted program, regardless of the ethnicity or race of the person doing the referring. Ford and colleagues (Ford, 1996; Ford & Harris, 1999; Ford, Harris, Tyson, & Trotman, 2002) identified this as the "under-referral" problem, which severely limits poor and minority children's access to advanced educational programs and results from low expectations based on racial stereotypes.

Other school-related issues include the confusion about how to identify gifted minority children, because these groups do not score well on typically used measures, such as IQ tests or other standardized achievement tests. Allegations of cultural bias in measures (which is controversial and not agreed upon by all; see Lohman, 2005) has led to considerable time and energy being spent by gifted education researchers on constructing better measures and/or processes to identify the abilities of gifted minority children. Strategies include incorporating more culturally relevant indicators of ability (e.g., oral expressiveness for verbal ability) into identification protocols (Ford, 1996); the use of performance-based assessments (Baldwin, 1994; Sarouphim, 1999; VanTassel-Baska, Feng, & de Brux, 2007; VanTassel-Baska, Johnson, & Avery, 2002); and nonverbal ability tests (Bracken, VanTassel-Baska, Brown, & Feng, 2007; Ford et al., 2002; Naglieri & Ford, 2003; VanTassel-Baska et al., 2007). There is considerable controversy about the validity and reliability of these alternative measures, and current thinking suggests that traditional tests are still the best measures, especially if selected to match the requirements of the learning situation and if students' scores are evaluated in reference to appropriate norming groups consisting of other students who more closely match the characteristics of the students being assessed and their opportunities to learn (Lohman, 2005).

The lack of a truly multicultural classroom is believed to affect the achievement of gifted minority children. Ford, Howard, Harris, and Tyson (2000) called for cultural diversity in gifted classrooms not only in terms of students but also curriculum and instruction so that minority students can experience a sense of belonging and validation as scholars. Others note that many teachers are ill-equipped and poorly trained to create a multicultural classroom (Banks, 1999; Hanushek & Rivkin, 2006; Irvine & York, 1995).

Even if urban schools with high levels of poverty have gifted programs and have appropriate procedures in place to identify students, questions arise as to what to do for students educationally. Often, poor minority children identified with high potential and ability will not succeed in gifted programs filled with high-achieving White students. Despite great potential, they may have gaps in their content backgrounds that need remediation and exposure to advanced content before they can succeed in more accelerated programs. Gifted programs must be designed with the needs and current achievement levels of these students in mind. This often can be done readily at the local school level because school administrators know the students and have the freedom to craft their own programs. In schools systems where there is great diversity with respect to student SES level, race, and achievement, or for programs that pull children from schools across the district, such as full-time gifted schools, the challenge often is one of enabling bright minority or low-SES children to qualify for such programs. Many researchers and educators advocate that minority gifted students participate in preparatory types of educational programs that prepare them to enter advanced and accelerated programs later as well as protect them from potentially negative peer influences and support their goals and aspirations (Grantham, 2002; Robinson, 2003). These preparatory type programs take different forms, and many supplement schooling with afterschool, summer, and weekend courses. There is some evidence of the success of these supplementary or intervention programs.

Olszewski-Kubilius and colleagues (Olszewski-Kubilius, 2006, 2007; Olszewski-Kubilius, Lee, Ngoi, & Ngoi, 2004) provided afterschool, summer, and Saturday enrichment classes in science and math to academically talented minority students beginning in third grade. Minority gifted students were identified via the Naglieri Nonverbal Ability Test and the Iowa Tests of Basic Skills to participate in the program that aimed to have them complete algebra at least before grade 9 and qualify for honors tracks in science and math in high school. Major findings included that the number of minority students who were accelerated in math in middle school and consequently placed into advanced tracks in high school was significantly increased. EXCITE students also improved their performance on state competency examinations and performed better than the average for minority students in the district.

Another preparatory program for minority and economically disadvantaged students was Project Synergy (Borland & Wright, 1994). The program identified low-income, potentially gifted kindergarteners using several measures, including standardized tests, multicultural curriculum-based enrichment activities, classroom observations, portfolios, and teacher nominations, and provided students with a 5-week summer program aimed at preparing them for placement in advanced and challenging educational programs in school. Project Synergy students demonstrated significant improvement in their academic performances following 1 or 2 years of the summer intervention. Examples included higher mean scores and median percentile ranks on the Test of Early Mathematics Ability-2 (TEMA-

2); rankings in the top third nationwide on the Test of Early Reading Ability-2 (TERA-2); and improved general academic aptitude as indicated by higher IQ scores.

The Javits 7+ Gifted and Talented Program (Baldwin, 1994) is another preparatory program that provided intensive school-based activities in order to prepare economically disadvantaged children (from kindergarten to grade 3) and developmentally delayed students to qualify for gifted programs. The children participating in the program were overwhelmingly African American (84%) and Hispanic (8%). Evaluation data using a locally developed teacher rating scale confirmed considerable gains from pre- to postprogram tests on specified behavioral characteristics, such as flexibility, fluency, originality, elaboration, commitment, and performance. Enhanced confidence, communication skills, and knowledge also were reported as evidence of student progress following the program.

Psychological and Social Issues

Even when appropriately designed gifted programs are available to minority students, they may choose not to participate. Why? Scholars have identified psychological and social factors that are operative for gifted minority students, which may not be present for nonminority students. These include associating academic achievement with "acting White," fearing that achievement will be perceived as rejection of one's culture and result in social isolation, and fearing that participation in high-stakes testing and achievement situations will confirm negative stereotypes about minorities' achievement. These beliefs may be at the root of what Ford et al. (2008) and others (Mickelson, 1990) refer to as the attitude-achievement paradox, in which minority students verbally endorse beliefs that education is vital to future success but put little effort into their schoolwork. Black students may agree that in an ideal world, hard work and achievement in school will lead to occupational and financial success, but not for them because of racism and basic inequities in society.

Steele and colleagues (Steele, 1997; Steele & Aronson, 1995) have developed the concept of stereotype threat. For example, African American college students did not perform as well as Caucasian students when they were told to take a test that would assess their reading and verbal reasoning abilities, while they performed comparable to Caucasian students when they were informed that the test was not diagnostic of their intellectual ability.

Ogbu (1992) has studied peer pressure, particularly among involuntary minority groups (e.g., African Americans, early Mexican Americans; also see Ford, 1993, 1996; Fordham, 1988; Fordham & Ogbu, 1986) and has found that minority students tend to shun academic excellence due to the fear of being rejected by their peers who perceive success in school as acting White. Minority students' reluctance to be placed in gifted programs in urban schools, where they often find themselves as one of only a few minority students surrounded by White and Asian students, also has been cited as a mitigating factor of high achievement (Ford, 1996; Ford et al., 2000; Morris, 2002; Tatum, 1997). This is referred to as the concept of "fewness," which represents the condition where only small percentages of students from minority groups (e.g., African Americans, Hispanics, or Native Americans) are in advanced or accelerated classes (Miller, 2004). Miller documented that the conditions of fewness are found early in elementary school and continue through all levels of schooling including the faculties of institutions of higher education. This situation has a comprehensive impact on the academic performance of minority students as indicated by data such as SAT scores or NAEP tests, GPA, enrollment in advanced classes, and attendance at selective colleges. Too many minority gifted students succumb to the perception that success in schooling and placement in gifted or advanced educational programs particularly is a "sell-out" to the mainstream White culture and has social disadvantages including isolation and rejection by other minority peers. Ford and colleagues (2008) studied the attitudes of middle school African American students formally identified as gifted according to state criteria including IQ and achievement test scores. The data indicated that students indeed perceived negative reactions from peers as a result of high achievement; connect acting White with school achievement, intelligence, and positive attitudes toward school; and attribute acting Black to low school achievement, low intelligence, and negative attitudes toward school. On the other hand, Olszewski-Kubilius, Lee, and Peternel (2009) found that high-ability middle school students enrolled in a supplementary program to prepare them for entrance into honors classes in high school did not perceive negative peer reactions as a result of their involvement in the program. However, these authors suggested that supplementary gifted programs may be less stigmatizing than within school programs and less likely to elicit concerns about accusations of acting White from peers.

Family Issues

There is ample research documenting a relationship between SES and achievement outcomes, and disparities between high- and low-income children that appear early in life (e.g., early literacy; Aikens & Barbarin, 2008) and grow larger over time (Wyner et al., 2007). Less well understood is the mechanism by which low family income impacts achievement. Bronfenbrenner (1979) offered an ecological perspective on child development that recognized the role of several dynamic and interacting systems including family, community, and school on developmental outcomes. The role of the family system in talent development, because of its close proximity to the child (as opposed to community, which is more distal) has been the focus of much attention and discussion (Bloom, 1985; Subotnik & Jarvin, 2005). Specific parental practices such as closely monitoring school progress (Robinson, Lanzi, Weinberg, Ramey, & Ramey, 2002), reading to the child and parental involvement in school (Aikens & Barbarin, 2008), and characteristics of the family, such as parental role strain, have been linked to early literacy (Aikens & Barbarin, 2008; Robinson et al., 2002) and offer some insight as to how SES, through parental actions, specifically affects children's achievement.

The talent development literature has suggested that early parental teaching, enriched home environments, a focus on providing cultural enrichment (Gottfried, Gottfried, Bathurst, & Guerin, 1994), support for extra lessons, monitoring of practice, modeling persistence, and encouragement of risk-taking are other ways in which families promote the development of skills and attitudes associated with high achievement (Bloom, 1985; Olszewski-Kubilius, 2008). It is clear from this literature that lack of financial resources and a necessary preoccupation with day-to-day matters would preclude many low-income parents from being able to do the things that more advantaged families can readily do to support their talented children. However, it also is clear that even parents with very limited resources can, by their messages to children and actions in the home, enable their children to succeed. Sampson (2002), via interviews and observations of 12 African American students aged 10 to 14 years and their parents, found that the family and home environment led to differences in students' academic performances as measured by GPAs. Sampson found a difference in values between African American families whose children were achieving at high, average, or below average levels in school and an inconsistency between verbally espoused values and enacted values for low-achieving children. Families of the high and average achieving children stressed the importance of education and structured their family life around schoolwork and school activities. Parents encouraged participation in extracurricular activities, assuming responsibility at home through babysitting and household chores, and provided a quiet, orderly home environment conducive to study. They communicated to students that they alone were in control of their destinies, that nothing could prevent them from meeting their goals except perhaps money and provided a hopeful and positive view of the future to their child. In contrast, families of low-achieving children communicated different beliefs and values and/or verbally endorsed similar values to families of average and high-achieving children, but did not follow through with supportive actions. They may have told their children that getting a good education was important to their futures, but then did not provide a home environment conducive to study nor check on their child's schoolwork or even ask about school at home (Sampson, 2002).

The family typically serves as a filter for children, interpreting events and circumstances from the outside world and in the process creating strong messages about how the world works and what to expect from it, thereby affecting children's attitudes, beliefs, values, and actions. So, for example, the "spin" that parents or other adults put on difficult circumstances such as racism or poverty will have an effect on whether a child will view education and talent development as the key to success or the means of breaking a cycle of poverty, which can impact beliefs about self-efficacy and one's ability to accomplish future goals (see Olszewski-Kubilius, 2008). The research literature on eminent individuals notes that many of them came from poverty and difficult circumstances and used those experiences to develop emotional stamina, independence of thought, risk-taking, and high levels of motivation that were crucial to their success.

Communities

Bronfenbrenner (1979) identified communities as one of the spheres of activity or settings that impacts the developing child. Communities can provide many additional resources to assist in the talent development of gifted children including psychological services, work and apprenticeship opportunities, and cultural institutions that offer lessons, recreation, or other programs. Urban settings typically are resource-rich communities. However, it is not atypical that poor, urban children live in blighted neighborhoods, completely unaware of the opportunities available only blocks away. The parents of advantaged children regularly take their children to museums, libraries, concerts, ballets, restaurants, and events that enlarge their worldview, expose them to adults in various occupations, increase their cultural knowledge, and help them acquire tacit knowledge about education, careers, and different life paths. Urban students often lack opportunities to acquire this knowledge, which puts them at a disadvantage when interacting with and competing with more advantaged peers and makes them feel different and less capable. It is critical that programs for poor minority students specifically work to level the playing field with respect to exposure to culture and cultural institutions. This can be done through field trips and collaborations with cultural institutions, such as museums, to provide gifted programming.

Lessons From Experience

I have been involved in a number of projects that serve low-income, gifted urban students over the last 25 years, but I would like to focus on two current ones: Project Excite, which involves working with underrepresented, low-income youths who are primarily African American and Hispanic, to prepare them to enter advanced science and mathematics tracks in high school (e.g., honors classes and an accelerated chemistry/physics program), and Project LIVE (Launch Into Verbal Excellence), which involves providing enrichment to average and above-average readers in middle school so as to boost their achievement up to levels that qualify them for high school honors classes in English. Both of these programs are "preparatory" types of programs alluded to earlier in that they are designed to prepare talented minority students to enter existing programs for advanced learners within their school districts. Project Excite is in its eighth year of operation; identifies students with talent in mathematics in second grade via parent nomination, using traditional achievement tests as well as a nonverbal ability measure; and involves them in more than 400 hours of science and math enrichment classes after school, on Saturdays, and during the summer for a 6-year period, until students enter high school. Some of the educational classes students take are designed just for Excite students while others integrate Excite students into existing Center for Talent Development (CTD) classes, which draw gifted students nationally. Other components of the project include parent support and education, individual and group tutoring for students, cultural enrichment, systematic exposure to groups of intellectual peers, and psychological services for students who need them.

There are currently 6 cohorts of students involved in Project Excite, each about 15 to 20 students in size. Students are recruited from 7 schools in a school district where 50% of the students are minority but only 5% to 10% of students in the most advanced track in math/science track are minority. On average, 75% of Excite participants complete the program based on several cohorts of students and those who do drop out do so primarily because of family moves. Project Excite is a collaboration between Northwestern University, the local elementary school district, and the local high school district. It is funded by all three partners and by corporate and foundation money.

Project Excite has increased the access of low-income minority students to advanced classes. Achievement results to date include that almost all of Project Excite students currently attending high school are enrolled in or have completed geometry as freshmen. One high school sophomore is taking AP BC Calculus and one high school freshman has been admitted to the Illinois Mathematics and Science Academy. In the first cohort to reach high school, 13 out of 17 Excite students were placed in honors mathematics and science classes as freshmen. In addition, 90% of Black Excite eighth graders "exceeded standards" on the 2006 Illinois State Achievement Test (ISAT) in mathematics compared with 18% of Black eighth graders district wide. Sixty-seven percent of Hispanic eighth-grade students "exceeded standards" on the math portion of the ISAT compared to 27% of Hispanic eighth graders district wide. ISAT data revealed cumulative program effects over time with only 30% of Black Excite and no Hispanic Excite students "exceeding standards" on the 2003 mathematics ISAT 3 years earlier. Interviews with Excite students and their parents revealed that students enjoyed the activities, liked "getting ahead" via the coursework, made attendance at Excite activities a priority, expressed increased confidence for future challenging academic work, and raised parents' expectations, resulting in parents taking a greater interest in their child's schoolwork. It also is true that achievement of Project Excite students has been more variable than expected during the years of the project, often alternating between quarters of A or B grades and quarters of C grades, particularly once students graduate from the program and enter high school (see Olszewski-Kubilius, 2006; Olszewski-Kubilius et al., 2004).

Project LIVE starts with students who have completed grade 6 and provides more than 300 hours of supplemental enrichment in language arts after school, on Saturdays, and in the summer until grade 8. LIVE is modeled after Project Excite. Students are identified via teacher recommendation, a lengthy application that includes student essays and parent statements, and scores on state tests and district curriculum assessments. Students had to be at least average readers with potential to achieve at higher levels. Project LIVE was funded by a grant from the Jack Kent Cooke Foundation. Project LIVE students are a diverse group; the majority of students are minority with an average family income of $38,000 in a community where the average income is $75,000. Program components include parent education, cultural enrichment, test preparation, and exposure to other gifted peers. Beyond the goal of preparing students to enter honors English as freshmen, the LIVE program seeks to raise students' expectations regarding grades and coursework, increase the level and quantity of extracurricular reading, increase students' self-confidence regarding challenging work, and level the playing field in terms of students' knowledge and exposure to cultural institutions. Achievement results indicate that LIVE students' EXPLORE scores at the middle of eighth grade, after the program, were significantly higher than that of eighth graders nationally; were better than that of students districtwide (16.8 composite for district versus 18.4 for LIVE); and increased an average of 3.26 points compared to .2 points for the district over the same 3-year period (see Table 5.1). Regarding high school placements, of the 37 students who completed all 3 years of the program (representing 79% of students who began in year 1), 70% were placed in honors English as freshmen and many others were placed in a mixed honors class. Surveys of parents and students showed that parental expectations about grades along with encouragement of reading and monitoring of homework increased. Although students' voluntary reading and writing did not increase as hoped, likely due to increased homework demands, students did indicate that they planned on taking more honors-level courses during high school.

How Did These Programs Respond to the Needs of Urban Gifted Students?

These programs responded to the needs of urban gifted children in several key ways:
- Both programs were preparatory in nature, built around the needs of the specific populations to be served, and designed to intensely build the skills of students so that

Table 5.1
EXPLORE Test Scores
(Sixth, Seventh, and Eighth Grades)

	Mean			Effect Size (*d*)
	6th grade	7th grade	8th grade	6–8th grade
English	14.25	16.62	18.09	Large
Math	16.29	16.59	17.89	Medium
Reading	13.75	16.68	18.14	Large
Science	16.00	16.97	19.03	Large
Composite	15.14	16.94	18.40	Large

they could enter and be successful in traditional advanced coursework available in their schools. Yet, programs were crafted to not just build up content knowledge and skills but to engender excitement and motivation for learning through activities that were hands-on, discovery-based, problem-oriented, and creativity-generating. They moved from enrichment activities initially to accelerative experiences eventually. Motivation and enthusiasm was created via program activities as students were neither compensated nor offered material incentives for their participation.

- Both programs identified children relatively young and provided multiple program options for a period of 3 to 6 years. Through a long-term commitment, trust was built with teachers, school administrators, and parents who came to rely on program administrators for all kinds of help once they were convinced they were there to stay.

- Both programs were primarily outside-of-school programs, which was less stigmatizing for students and did not create tensions for students with peers within their home schools regarding high achievement, yet gave them additional peer support. Teachers who taught the LIVE or Excite classes often were teachers who worked full time within the school districts of the children's schools. This helped to forge school-to-program linkages that supported the students as well.

- Both programs sought to forge close connections with parents and to assist them in understanding and responding to the needs of their talented child. Both programs involved parents in meetings, seminars with experts, and cultural enrichment activities and field trips. Project staff responded to individual family needs via focused counseling or referrals to other resources and experts.
- Both programs had cultural enrichment as a component and took students to concerts, plays, museums, arboretums, and universities. Both programs emphasized to parents how to provide enrichment to their children through existing cultural institutions.
- Both programs deliberately designed experiences to give children exposure to other gifted students. Both programs initially had students participate in educational classes only with other project participants, but eventually moved students into broader settings (i.e., CTD programs), where they interacted with gifted students from around the nation. This did much to bolster students' confidence that they could compete successfully in classes with more advantaged and nonminority peers, crucial to their choosing challenging coursework in the future.
- Both programs created multiple support structures for students. Both Excite and LIVE had components that sought to enhance peer support for high achievement and ameliorate negative peer influences; build up skills and content knowledge in key subject areas; enable children to acquire tacit knowledge about schooling; provide exposure to cultural institutions; and respond to unique and individual needs of students and families.

Final Thoughts

Successful programs for poor or minority urban gifted children must be multifaceted and flexible. In a field that stresses how individual gifted children are, we tend to construct programs aimed at groups and at the typical low-income, minority child. But, there is no typical child, as the circumstances that lead to poverty are many and varied. There are, at the very least, several different "types" of low-income families. For example, some families are low income because while educated, they are immigrants to the U.S. and cannot work in their professions, but must work at low-level jobs. They will value education, understand what is involved in high achievement, and have high expectations for their child. English will be their and their child's second language. In contrast, some families are poor because parents are not well educated, work at minimum wage jobs because that is all they are prepared for, do not have experience with higher levels of education, and may not have high expectations for their child nor understand what is involved in developing their child's talent. Every family in poverty has strengths and weaknesses, features that support the talent development of their child, and features that work against it. Strengths of even the poorest and most marginalized of families can include the unconditional love and support of a family member for a child or the incredible resilience and psychological strength of a child. Interventions need to recognize, affirm, acknowledge, and take advantage of strengths, and identify, understand, and compensate for weaknesses in schools, families, and communities. I think that a more productive approach to assisting talented children of poverty is one that constructs a support plan for each child based on a profile of the strengths and weaknesses of the child's environment, including not only the family, but the school and community as well (see Olszewski-Kubilius, Grant, & Seibert, 1994). Interventions for individual children and families include tutors, mentors, enrollment in afterschool clubs, weekend programs, psychological services, part-time jobs, and internships. But these interventions will be most successful if they are based on and tailored to identified needs of the specific population of students involved.

Author's Note

Significant portions of this chapter were published previously in Lee et al. (2009), Lee et al. (in press), Olszewski-Kubilius (2007), and Olszewski-Kubilius et al. (2004).

References

Aikens, N. L., & Barbarin, O. (2008). Socioeconomic differences in reading trajectories: The contribution of family, neighborhood, and school contexts. *Journal of Educational Psychology, 100,* 235–251.

Baker, B. D., & Friedman-Nimz, R. (2002). Determinants of the availability of opportunities for gifted children: Evidence from NELS '88. *Leadership and Policy in Schools, 1,* 52–71.

Baldwin, A. Y. (1994). The seven plus story: Developing hidden talent among students in socioeconomically disadvantaged environments. *Gifted Child Quarterly, 38,* 80–84.

Banks, J. A. (1999). *Introduction to multicultural gifted education* (2nd ed.). Boston: Allyn & Bacon.

Barton, P. E. (2003). *Parsing the achievement gap.* Princeton, NJ: Educational Testing Service.

Bernal, E. M. (2002). Three ways to achieve a more equitable representation of culturally and linguistically different students in GT programs. *Roeper Review, 24,* 82–88.

Bloom, B. S. (1985). *Developing talent in young people.* New York: Ballantine Books.

Borland, J. H., & Wright, L. (1994). Identifying young, potentially gifted economically disadvantaged students. *Gifted Child Quarterly, 38,* 164–171.

Bracken, B. A., VanTassel-Baska, J., Brown, E. F., & Feng, A. (2007). Project Athena: A tale of two studies. In J. VanTassel-Baska & T. Stambaugh (Eds.), *Overlooked gems: A national perspective on low-income promising learners* (pp. 63–67). Washington, DC: National Association for Gifted Children.

Bronfenbrenner, U. (1979). *The ecology of human development: Experiments by nature and design.* Cambridge, MA: Harvard University Press.

Education Week. (2007). *Achievement gap.* Retrieved September 5, 2007, from http://www.edweek.org/rc/issues/achievement-gap

Ford, D. Y. (1993). An investigation of the paradox of underachievement among gifted Black students. *Roeper Review, 16,* 78–84.

Ford, D. Y. (1996). *Reversing underachievement among gifted Black students: Promising practices and programs.* New York: Teacher College Press.

Ford, D. Y., Grantham, T. C., & Whiting, G. W. (2008). Another look at the achievement gap: Learning from the experiences of gifted Black students. *Urban Education, 43,* 216–238.

Ford, D. Y., & Harris, J. J., III (1999). *Multicultural gifted education.* New York: Teachers College Press.

Ford, D. Y., Howard, T. C., Harris, J. J., III, & Tyson, C. A. (2000). Creating culturally responsive classrooms for gifted African American students. *Journal for the Education of the Gifted, 23,* 397–427.

Ford, D. Y., Harris, J. J., III, Tyson, C. A., & Trotman, M. F. (2002). Beyond deficit thinking: Providing access for gifted African American students. *Roeper Review, 24,* 52–58.

Fordham, S. (1988). Racelessness as a factor in Black students' school success: Pragmatic strategy or Pyrrhic victory? *Harvard Educational Review, 58,* 54–84.

Fordham, S., & Ogbu, J. U. (1986). Black students' school success: Coping with the "burden of acting White." *The Urban Review, 18,* 176–206.

Gallagher, J. J. (1994). Current and historical thinking on education for gifted and talented students. In P. O. Ross (Ed.), *National excellence: A case for developing America's talent: An anthology of readings.* Washington, DC: U.S. Department of Education.

Gottfried, A. W., Gottfried, A. E., Bathurst, K., & Guerin, D. W. (1994). *Gifted IQ: Early developmental aspects: The Fullerton Longitudinal Study.* New York: Plenum Press.

Grantham, T. C. (2002). Straight talk on the issue of underrepresentation: An interview with Dr. Mary M. Frasier. *Roeper Review, 24,* 50–51.

Grantham, T. C. (2003). Increasing Black student enrollment in gifted programs: An exploration of the Pulaski county special school district's advocacy efforts. *Gifted Child Quarterly, 47,* 46–65.

Hanushek, E. R., & Rivkin, S. G. (2006). *School quality and the Black-White achievement gap* (Working paper 12651). Cambridge, MA: National Bureau of Economic Research.

Irvine, J. J., & York, E. D. (1995). Learning styles in culturally diverse students: A literature review. In J. A. Banks & C. A. M. Banks (Eds.), *Handbook of research on multicultural education* (pp. 484–497). New York: Macmillan.

Lee, S.-Y., Matthews, M. S., & Olszewski-Kubilius, P. (2008). A national picture of talent search and talent search educational programs. *Gifted Child Quarterly, 52,* 55–69.

Lee, S.-Y., Olszewski-Kubilius, P., & Peternel, G. (2009). Follow-up with students after six years of their participation in Project EXCITE. *Gifted Child Quarterly, 53,* 137–156.

Lohman, D. F. (2005). The role of nonverbal ability tests in identifying academically gifted students: An aptitude perspective. *Gifted Child Quarterly, 49,* 111–138.

Maker, C. J. (1996). Identification of gifted minority students: A national problem, needed changes and a promising solution. *Gifted Child Quarterly, 40,* 41–50.

Mickelson, R. A. (1990). The attitude–achievement paradox among Black adolescents. *Sociology of Education, 63,* 44–61.

Miller, L. S. (2004). *Promoting sustained growth in the representation of African Americans, Latinos, and Native Americans among top students in the United States at all levels of the education system.* Storrs: University of Connecticut, The National Research Center on the Gifted and Talented.

Morris, J. E. (2002). African American students and gifted education: The politics of race and culture. *Roeper Review, 24,* 59–62.

Naglieri, J. A., & Ford, D. Y. (2003). Addressing underrepresentation of gifted minority children using the Naglieri Nonverbal Ability Test (NNAT). *Gifted Child Quarterly, 47,* 161–169.

National Governors Association. (2005). *Closing the achievement gap.* Retrieved October 5, 2007, from http://www.subnet.nga.org/educlear/achievement/index.html

Ogbu, J. U. (1992). Understanding cultural diversity and learning. *Educational Researcher, 21*(8), 5–14.

Olszewski-Kubilius, P. (2006). Addressing the achievement gap between minority and nonminority children: Increasing access and achievement through Project EXCITE. *Gifted Child Today, 29,* 28–37.

Olszewski-Kubilius, P. (2007). Working with promising learners from poverty: Lessons learned. In J. VanTassel-Baska & T. Stambaugh (Eds.), *Overlooked gems: A national perspective on low-income promising learners* (pp. 43–46). Washington, DC: National Association for Gifted Children.

Olszewski-Kubilius, P. (2008). The role of the family in talent development. In S. I. Pfeiffer (Ed.), *Handbook of giftedness in children: Psycho-educational theory, research, and best practices* (pp. 53–71). New York: Springer.

Olszewski-Kubilius, P., Grant, B., & Seibert, C. (1994). Social support systems and the disadvantaged gifted: A framework for developing programs and services. *Roeper Review, 17,* 20–25.

Olszewski-Kubilius, P., Lee, S.-Y., Ngoi, M., & Ngoi, D. (2004). Addressing the achievement gap between minority and nonminority children by increasing access to gifted programs. *Journal for the Education of the Gifted, 28,* 127–158.

Robinson, N. M. (2003). Two wrongs do not make a right: Sacrificing the needs of gifted students does not solve society's unsolved problems. *Journal for the Education of the Gifted, 26,* 251–273.

Robinson, N. M., Lanzi, R. G., Weinberg, R. A., Ramey, S. L., & Ramey, C. T. (2002). Family factors associated with high academic competence in former Head Start children at third grade. *Gifted Child Quarterly, 46,* 278–290.

Sampson, W. A. (2002). *Black student achievement: How much do family and school really matter?* Lanham, MD: The Scarecrow Press.

Sarouphim, K. M. (1999). DISCOVER: A promising alternative assessment for the identification of gifted minorities. *Gifted Child Quarterly, 43,* 244–251.

Steele, C. M. (1997). A threat in the air: How stereotypes shape intellectual identity and performance. *American Psychologist, 52,* 613–629.

Steele, C. M., & Aronson, J. (1995). Stereotype threat and the intellectual test performance of African Americans. *Journal of Personality and Social Psychology, 69,* 797–811.

Subotnik, R. F., & Jarvin, L. (2005). Beyond expertise: Conceptions of giftedness as great performance. In R. J. Sternberg & J. E. Davidson (Eds.), *Conceptions of giftedness* (2nd ed., pp. 343–357). New York: Cambridge University Press.

Tatum, B. D. (1997). *"Why are all the Black kids sitting together in the cafeteria?" and other conversations about race.* New York: Basic Books.

VanTassel-Baska, J., Feng, A. X., & de Brux, E. (2007). A study of identification and achievement profiles of performance task–identified gifted students over 6 years. *Journal for the Education of the Gifted, 31,* 7–34.

VanTassel-Baska, J., Johnson, D., & Avery, L. D. (2002). Using performance tasks in the identification of economically disadvantaged and minority gifted learners: Findings from Project STAR. *Gifted Child Quarterly, 46,* 110–123.

Worrell, F. C. (2007). Identifying and including low-income learners in programs for gifted and talented: Multiple complexities. In J. VanTassel-Baska & T. Stambaugh (Eds.), *Overlooked gems: A national perspective on low-income promising learners* (pp. 47–51). Washington, DC: National Association for Gifted Children.

Wyner, J. S., Bridgeland, J. M., & DiIulio, J. J., Jr. (2007). *Achievementrap: How America is failing millions of high-achieving students from low-income families.* Lansdowne, VA: Jack Kent Cooke Foundation.

The Patterns and Profiles of Gifted African American Children: Lessons Learned

Bronwyn MacFarlane & Annie Xuemei Feng

What does research tell us about this group of gifted children? A survey of existing literature reveals that while there is a growing body of research on gifted African American students, there is a paucity of studies informing educators about specific and effective interventions. In many studies, gifted African American students and other gifted minority students are not analyzed by ethnicity nor by poverty factors. Consequently it becomes difficult to be specific about what would help particular at-risk learner groups. Moreover, we know little about the impact of gifted programs on these groups at either cognitive or affective levels.

Literature Review

Much has been written about the achievement gap and differential identification patterns between different groups of students. In analyzing inadequate school performance and outcomes among African American students, 14 factors have been strongly associated with the differences in achievement levels between White and Black students. Barton (2003) categorized these factors as school influences and before- and afterschool influences. School influences related to the degree of rigor to which African American students were exposed, less access to technology-assisted instruction, less access to qualified teachers, less experienced teachers, and lower levels of feeling safe at school. Before- and afterschool influences included less family participation, lower levels of parental availability to their children, lower rates of parents who read to children, and more hours of television watching. Also included were health-related variables such as higher rates of low birth weight, lead poisoning, and poorer nutrition and overall health.

A disproportionate amount of the literature on this population focuses on identification and recruitment of African American students (Ford, 1994, 2004). Low standardized test performance and low teacher expectations of these students are cited as the most salient reasons explaining the underrepresentation of African American students in gifted programs (Baldwin, 2005; Castellano & Diaz, 2001; Ford, 2004; Ford & Grantham, 2003; Frasier, Garcia, & Passow, 1995; Whiting & Ford, 2006). To address the issues of under- and low representation of African American students in gifted programs, Ford (1994, 1996, 2004) has suggested a greater emphasis on recruitment and retention of students in special programs.

Ford, Grantham, and Whiting (2008a) have recommended that more research is needed in gifted education to increase understanding of underrepresentation and underachievement among these students. In studying academic achievement, they found that more than one fourth of students responded "no" when asked whether they put forth their best effort in school; 69% responded that they do not study or do homework on weekends; and 42% reported that they have been teased for doing well in school. Students reported that they spend their out-of-school time being with family, watching TV, being with friends, and listening to music. When asked about the term "acting White," students characterized the idea behind the phrase in terms of language, behavior, intelligence, and attitude. When asked why smart students do not do well in school, the majority of students indicated that peer pressures contribute to students' underperforming in school.

Test scores play a significant role in identification and placement decisions in gifted programs (Davidson Institute, 2006; Davis & Rimm, 2003; Ford, Grantham, & Whiting, 2008b).

It is a belief of many in the field of gifted education that new conceptions of giftedness and a new paradigm for identifying and selecting students will help low socioeconomic status (SES) and minority students become more represented in gifted programs (Ford, 1996; Patton, Prillaman, & VanTassel-Baska, 1991). Instead of basing identification solely on intelligence and achievement test scores, multiple criteria would be employed, including more nontraditional measures, such as observing students interacting with a variety of learning opportunities (Passow & Frasier, 1996), dynamic assessment (Feuerstein, 1986; Kirschenbaum, 1998), and nonverbal tests (Bracken & McCallum, 1998; Naglieri & Ford, 2003; Naglieri & Kaufman, 2001).

Based on current understanding of the problem of underrepresentation of low-income and minority students in gifted programs and preliminary studies, the use of performance-based assessment as a nontraditional tool for enhancing the possibility of greater representation of such students in these programs appears to be a promising development (VanTassel-Baska, Johnson, & Avery, 2002). Studies have not really focused, however, on the comparative efficacy of this approach in relation to more traditional models of identification.

To recruit and retain students in gifted programming, an optimal match between students and programming design is necessary. To design a program that is an optimal match to underrepresented groups of students, it is necessary to identify specific characteristics and traits and patterns and profiles of these groups of students to better serve them in gifted programming formats.

A Vignette Study of Gifted African American Low-Income Learners

Underrepresentation of African American students in gifted education school-based programs has been a topic of discussion in the field of gifted education for more than 30 years. In tackling this area of concern head-on, researchers at the Center for Gifted Education at the College of William and Mary in collaboration with The South Carolina Department of Education designed alternative assessment performance tasks to identify more gifted African American students who were not found through traditional identification tools. The research project, known as Project STAR, evolved in two stages following the development of the Project STAR performance tasks protocol in 1996. The first quantitative study with Project STAR performance task-identified students was conducted in 2002, and the follow-up interview study involved teachers, parents, and students across a 2-year research period.

Based on pilot, field test, and statewide implementation data from the project's first study, the performance tasks were found to be useful tools in identifying more low-SES and African American students, finding 12% to 18% more underrepresented students annually. A second study was undertaken to examine prototypical characteristics of five groups of gifted low-income learners (i.e., low-income African American students; low-income other minority students; low-income White students; high nonverbal, low verbal students; and twice-exceptional students) through in-depth interviews with the students, their parents, and two teachers who had worked with them.

Demographic Profiles of the Students

The vignette study focused on nine low-income African American students, five of whom were identified for gifted programs through Project STAR performance tasks (three male and two female), and four of whom were identified through traditional ability and achievement tests. There were five female and four male students in the sample. No distinctive differences were found between the students based on method of identification, suggesting that differences were negligible in their profiles.

Across the sample, the majority of the students had been enrolled in both math and language arts strands of the gifted program in their middle schools (n = 7) and maintained outstanding academic performance in one or more subject domains. There appeared to be few differences between the gifted male and female low-income African American students in terms of their identification profile, grades, cognitive characteristics, learning motivation, and social-emotional features within the study sample. The two students whose teachers explicitly noted that their outstanding performance was due to extra efforts happened to be female students; however, it was hard to draw any lines between gender and such perceptions of teachers from the data.

African American Student and Parent Reactions to the Gifted Program

Both students ($n = 8$) and a few parents ($n = 3$) noted the positive impact of gifted program participation. Students expressed their appreciation of the benefits they received from their past and current gifted classes, citing the challenges of the curriculum, acquisition of basic skills and high-level thinking skills, more extracurricular activities, and an environment focused on learning as typical examples. Parents ($n = 7$) noted particularly that their children became more motivated to learn in the gifted class. Some parents attributed the increased achievement of their children to gifted program experiences.

One student, Barrett, felt positively about his gifted program experiences, noting that it "increased my learning a lot and made me want to learn more." He hoped to become an electrical engineer in the future. He liked language arts better than other subject areas, and he said he loved poetry. Yet, he was not very comfortable with writing.

Another student, Kassidy, liked being in gifted classes: "It's a good thing." When asked to specify what is good, she said, "[You are] able to be more open" because "you are surrounded by other children who basically think like you." For her, the gifted program created a more positive attitude toward school. For example, she did her homework and completed projects and papers on time. She stated, "I always think of myself as a normal person. I'm just a level ahead of other students 'cause everybody learns at their own pace." She felt more of a sense of belonging in her gifted classes, but also commented that due to her personality, she found it easy to make friends. In her gifted classes, she said, "We think on the same level. The books we read are all the same books, and our writing is almost equal."

Family members cited that gifted program participation increased their child's academic motivation. One student noted that the program "made her want to do more and get into deep level things and it had a lot of interesting activities."

William fit the profile of a low-income African American student who was identified through traditional methods. When asked how placement in the gifted program made him feel, William responded, "I felt like I had achieved something. I felt special that I had done something really great." It was obvious that William considered placement in the gifted program to be a great achievement. Similarly, his mother believed that placement in the gifted program had a positive impact on him. She remarked, "He started excelling in school. His grades went up. His math teachers used to say that math was not challenging enough for him before that [placement in the gifted program]." She also believes that the gifted program influenced William's self-esteem in a positive way: "When he joined the gifted program, he started to talk about what he wanted to be—an engineer, a computer technician, and he wanted to grow up quickly so that he can be all these. He has also started talking about going to good colleges."

William also cited many things that he liked about being in the gifted program, such as being mixed in with older students in classes and getting high school credit (for algebra) in middle school. Yet, he disliked the amount of math homework. He said: "In algebra there is more and more homework. Every weekend there is homework and it takes time from playing." He also disliked that algebra was getting harder and harder for him. One of his suggestions for improvement of the gifted program was the reduction of the use of the program's "Word Within the Word" activities. He reported that the activities were useful, so they shouldn't be eliminated, but students should not have to do so many of the exercises. He also reported that he would like to see more time for independent reading of student-chosen selections, such as the nonfiction murder mysteries he enjoys. William believed that the honors science class should have an emphasis on biology and chemistry, with some opportunities for dissection included.

In keeping with the gifted class's emphasis on group work, one female student, Barbara, indicated a wish that the class would "slow down more if the teacher sees more kids having problems" and also would like it if the class would "do more hands-on activities in groups and with other people."

The Role of Effort in Learning

A common theme found among most of these African American student vignettes was the increasing amount of effort they were willing to spend in learning. They did not sit idle and daydream in a regular class anymore; instead, they had to spend more time on their work and be more focused on learning in order to keep up with other peers in the gifted class. Some of these students (n = 3) appreciated the fact that the gifted class provided them with a healthy and constructive learning environment that they wouldn't have had in a regular classroom setting where behavioral disruptions often mingled with slow-paced instruction.

One student, Jessica, noted that learning and study skills were included in her gifted classes. "I have learned better organization and time management. I feel that I am more organized and more in control of my work, teaching myself and my mom that I am the learner, the person responsible for my learning." She credited the program with challenging her, helping her see connections in her learning, and providing her with strategies to compensate for weaknesses. "Before the gifted program, [I was] not much of a note taker. Now I try to do very detailed notes. [I have] learned not to procrastinate, especially in the gifted program." She disliked the number of assignments and the fact that she procrastinates, causing the work to "pile up." Practicing with a timer helped her to focus. She liked "how I am actually challenged. I can learn something else other than what I know. It is really great to see connections with the real world."

Bonnie also characterized her enjoyment with her gifted program experiences and credited the program with providing her an opportunity to learn more knowledge and grasp higher level thinking skills. She elaborated that her elementary gifted program participation helped her to comprehend literature better and teach her to think logically and analytically. These thinking skills facilitated her learning in math and science at the middle school. Despite positive program experiences, Bonnie also felt greater pressure being a student in a gifted class, preparing for higher expectations from teachers and parents, and remaining friends with peers in her regular classes. She noted that she would like to see more field trips and outside of school learning in her gifted program. Stating that she would like the program to continue, she felt that the curriculum in the gifted class could have been more challenging. She said that "the curriculum in gifted class is almost the same as the regular class, but just had more work to do," suggesting quantitative instead of qualitative curricular differences between gifted and regular classes. Among her learning strengths, Bonnie cited good memory and hands-on learning as her two most important strengths: "I like to be hands-on [in learning], I can sit and learn by listening and taking notes, but I like to learn by using my hands, not just sit there and listen."

Social Relationships

Although the learning environment of the gifted class was intellectually gratifying for many students, many of them also felt socially divided due to the fact that most of their friends (often African American) were not identified and placed in the same program as they were, remaining instead in regular classes. This finding is in keeping with the literature base regarding the effects of achievement and peer pressure among African American students (Ford, 1994, 1996; Ford et al., 2008a).

One student, William, noted that he felt a greater sense of belonging in his regular classes. He was in mixed classes until the sixth grade, when he was placed in honors classes. He talked about the fact that in the honors classes he was with the same people all day. In the seventh grade he had both honors and regular classes. He described the social aspects of those classes: "I just felt more at home in those regular classes. It is easier to make friends in regular classes. There is more time to communicate (in regular classes). In honors classes, there is so much work to do, you do not have time to communicate."

In the sample of nine African American students, four of them had once been or were still the only African American student in their gifted classes. That sense of difference, loneliness, and isolation were articulated by both the students and their parents and perceived by some of the teachers. These students ($n = 7$) chose to retain close friendships more often with those in their regular class or from their community than from the gifted class.

Wanda's grandmother also voiced her concerns about Wanda's feeling of isolation in the gifted class. Wanda was the only identified gifted kid from her neighborhood. The grandmother said that, "Wanda was initially discouraged, and it took a while for her to adjust to the program and to socialize with other kids." Although she got along well with her classmates in the gifted class, Wanda typically hung out with her friends from her neighborhood.

Code-Switching

Many of these gifted students were faced with a dilemma, that of wanting to learn more in a class environment where their minds could be challenged and yet longing for friendship in another class setting. To cope with this dual desire, some of them ($n = 5$) articulated that they became more sensitive to the language or behaviors they would present in front of their old friends, striving not to impress upon their friends that they were smarter and avoiding any boasting or showoff behavior. The issue of "code-switching" has been highlighted in recent literature on African American student behavior (Ford et al., 2008a, 2008b). Teachers negatively viewed their students' choice to hang out with friends of a group that had lower grades, worrying that such friendship patterns might affect their grades and attitude to learn in the long run.

There was a gap between attitude and achievement displayed by some of the students. The same students who professed a belief that getting an education is important and valuable for success in life also reported that they do not put forth much effort in school. This attitude-behavior-achievement discrepancy often has been noted among African American students (Ford, 1996; Ford et al., 2008a, 2008b; Ford & Harris, 1996).

With respect to her sense of belonging, Bonnie felt that she belonged to the gifted class in terms of learning yet preferred the regular class with regard to friendship. When Barrett was asked to comment on friendships, he said he liked his friends in the regular class. He felt the academic pressure in the gifted class engaged students in the academic work rather than talking and thinking about friends. He noted that "you wouldn't have to get another race in the regular class" as one did in the gifted class. Barrett voiced his anger with some students in the gifted class who were arrogant and liked to tease other people, saying that it was a challenge not to hit such students.

Conversely, Jessica said that she fit in well in both her gifted and regular classes. "In gifted classes, [I] can talk with people about books in great depth and detail. In regular classes, [I] can teach others. [I] fit with both." Jessica preferred what she called "more of an order in gifted classes than regular classes." She expressed an interest in receiving more information about college, scholarships, and specific coursework necessary for certain professions.

Family Issues and Involvement/Support

All of the nine African American students in the vignette sample came from a low-income family, and several of them (n = 3) lived with a single parent. Financial and educational resources in these families obviously were limited. Many of the parents reported never having an opportunity to go to college. These parents had to spend more hours in working nightshifts or several different jobs for the survival of the family. The quality time that these parents were able to provide to their children was scarce. Yet, despite poverty, health problems, single-parent homes, and other family issues, a majority of these parents had high expectations for their children, hoping that they would go to college, and they provided for their children the best they could. As one parent confessed, "I want and wish my kid to get what I did not get." To many of these students, living in a poor family also has become a stimulant for them to work harder.

Keith has a strong and close relationship with his mother. He was willing to look after his sick mother at home, instead of playing outside like his big brother did, noting that he would hang out with his friends after his mother's surgery. Keith conveyed his aspiration of becoming a pediatrician, noting that he liked to work with kids, plus being a pediatrician would make him a good contact in the hospital if family members got sick, particularly his mother.

During a second interview with one of the student's grandmothers, she noted: "Barrett wanted you to know that he learned everything from me." Bonnie added positive comments on her parents' help and her brother's influence on her, noting that "If I have a question, they won't say 'I don't know,' they will try their best to have me an answer."

Learning Styles and Subject Preferences

In regards to learning style and subject preferences expressed, both students and their parents noted that they had a tendency to prefer hands-on activities and project-based learning. Among students ($n = 5$) who personally noted or were noted by their parents to have a preference, three were female students. However, it is unclear whether gender has anything to do with learning style preferences, based on the interview data. The gifted class emphasis on group work and hands-on learning also might have contributed to preferring such a "learning style."

According to her mother, Bonnie was good at both math and English all through her elementary years except for the year when she was a sixth grader, when there was no gifted program service at her school and she had a slippage in her math grades. Among her strengths, the mother cited reading comprehension, good learning motivation, visual learning, and group work.

There seemed to be a pattern of strong subject preferences among these students. Except for two of them who seemed to be well-rounded in all domains of learning, a majority of these students ($n = 7$) tended to prefer one subject over others. Five of them noted math as their favorite subject, consistent with their identification profiles with strength in quantitative or nonverbal tasks ($n = 3$) or in alignment with both of their identification profiles and current grades in math ($n = 2$). Writing appeared to be a less preferable subject among four of these students.

Other Areas of Talent

Parents provided a unique perspective on their children's strengths and talents in domains other than in academics. Several of them ($n = 5$) reported that their children loved and practiced music, dance, or sports.

Jessica's mother shared an extensive list of hobbies and activities Jessica is involved in outside of school. Those activities include music, singing, piano, jewelry making, making things out of cloth, working with clay, painting, cooking, designing (clothes, rooms), inventing, and writing books and stories at home. Her mother stated that Jessica "has written several little books in her notebooks. This [at-home] writing was interfering with her homework. She was writing stories instead of doing her homework."

Two students appeared to be strong leaders in both their circle of friends and their school life, one acting as president of the student council at school. These students appeared not only to perform well in academics but also remained active in other outlets of talent, consistent with the literature on characteristics of giftedness (Robinson, Shore, & Enersen, 2007). Barbara's father cited leadership among her peers as evidenced by her election to the student council while William's teacher mentioned his role as student body president and his performance as a leader and not as a follower: "He is good around all kids."

On the social front, Bonnie's mother noted that she has demonstrated a leadership mentality at an early age. Despite being the only African American in her class, Bonnie has always played the role of leader instead of a follower. "Bonnie was able to draw people toward her, liked by her friends both in gifted class and regular class . . . and she treated peers equally." The mother felt that Bonnie was a person with both good book sense and common sense.

Barrett, for example, demonstrated maturity in the way that he got along well with his classmates including those who were problems in the class. One of the science teachers noted, "He has been sitting beside the worst kid, and was able to maintain his cool, and he was able to have a positive influence on that student."

Developmental Milestones

Many of these students did not demonstrate their talents and giftedness until kindergarten age, when neat schoolwork and ease of learning served as a wake-up call to their parents. The early years of growth of these gifted students appeared to be as normal as many other children of the same age. The early signs of giftedness identified by parents included early reading ($n = 4$), quickness in learning, and the inquisitive nature of their mind. Interestingly, many parents tended to correlate effortless learning of their children in elementary school ($n = 5$) to signs of giftedness; and they were proud of their children and believed in their smartness. Teachers, on the other hand, tended to be milder in their views of these students' intelligence, admitting their capability, but not being as enthusiastic as parents in embracing the behavior as gifted. From teachers' perspectives ($n = 4$), these students "are capable but not outstanding or spectacular"; their outstanding performance more often was viewed as extra effort expended.

This juxtaposition of family and teacher views of the students' performance was illustrated with the case of Keith. According to his mother, Keith was more advanced intellectually than many other children of his age. She was well aware of her son's giftedness when Keith was in kindergarten when she brought him to a math and science fair, where he was able to figure out the formula of a math problem that was several grades above him. The mother also noted that Keith often came up with ideas that were not typical of his age peers, giving as an example a conversation she had with him about the blue sky while he was little, and he was relating it to the ozone of the atmosphere. In his mother's words, "He thinks at a deeper level." However, his mother also was worried about her son's nonconforming way of thinking and responding to questions, fearing that it both might affect his grades and the impression he left on his teachers. Conversely, Keith's teachers reported a different perspective. Both teachers who were interviewed saw Keith as "not a strong student" neither in terms of his grades nor his performance in class. Both categorized him as a "B" student. The elementary teacher noted that Keith liked to build things, using manipulatives. However, he "orally lost track." Acknowledging that he enjoyed being in the gifted class and contributing to class discussions, the same teacher did not find him to be a highly motivated learner and commented that Keith seemed to have trouble with the high-level thinking activities that were central to most of the gifted program routines.

Barbara's parents noted that she was bright at a very young age, prior to her beginning school. By the age of 5, she was answering the phone and taking down detailed information. Her father noted,

> We had no day care with her; my wife stayed at home with her. I remember certain things; she would catch on quickly. She missed the cut-off for first grade by one day, so she had to wait out for one year. The teachers noticed how smart she was and asked, "What did you do with her?"

Her parents indicated that she was a "quick study" who caught on easily. She was strong in number sense and comprehension. Her parents were concerned when she became bored in school and advocated for her to grade skip. The district told them that they did not practice acceleration. Her father observed that Barbara was mature beyond her age in some ways. She helped with family responsibilities like cooking and caring for her brother, because her mom had been ill with multiple sclerosis for several years. According to her father, that illness caused Barbara to grow up faster than normal. She took responsibilities such as getting her brother off to school when her dad had to go to work.

Teacher Perceptions

Although Barbara was seen as highly motivated, focused, and hard working by her language arts and science teachers, her math teacher could not think of any evidence of giftedness nor any strengths in Barbara. In terms of her weaknesses, Barbara's math teacher saw a lack of motivation and persistence and weak mathematical reasoning and problem solving. All of Barbara's teachers commented on her social nature and popularity. Her math teacher saw this as a negative. She noted that Barbara is "more interested in socializing than in hard work." She suspected that Barbara's less than stellar performance in math could be attributed to negative peer influence on Barbara's attitude toward math class.

Further, she believed Barbara may be having self-esteem issues because she is struggling so much with math. She said,

> Barbara is not motivated, but she is expecting to make an A without the work. She is more interested in socialization, friends. I can see the look on her face. Everyone around her is doing well and achieving. She is the lowest grade in the class. I'm pretty sure that it is bringing her self-esteem down a lot.

The math teacher also wondered about all that Barbara is involved in beyond school:

> Maybe having to play a role at home that a seventh grader may not normally have to play [in caring for her ill mother] is part of the problem. She is a cheerleader after school, too. The workload of math is pretty extensive. All combined, it is a heavy load for a seventh grader.

Barbara's science teacher noted her strong verbal and written expression with extensive vocabulary. Her language arts teacher shared her perspective on weaknesses: "The one weakness would be in oral expression; she is not very vocal in class. She will answer when called upon but does not volunteer. She is also a little bit timid in a presentation setting."

Special learning characteristics her teachers have noticed are that Barbara desires and seeks to work with other students. Her language arts teacher noted that Barbara is different from other gifted students in that "She is a little more social. Her focus is more on the social aspects of middle school. A lot of gifted students don't get into all of the 'socialness.'" When asked about special characteristics, her math teacher said, "I would think she is more kinesthetic at this point." Her science teacher stated, "[Barbara] wants to do well. [She is] very creative on projects.

She uses drawings and is very neat. She goes to the next higher level of thinking."

Ricky's gifted teacher knew that he had been identified through nontraditional means and stated, "I believed all along [he was] gifted even though [he] did not fit the mold as some others did."

Wanda's gifted teacher viewed her as "a capable but socially divided child," noting that Wanda was not a very strong student in her class and her performance in class had been uneven. Interestingly, Wanda's science teacher also was concerned that she spent too little effort on her schoolwork, noting that "she is at an age where friends are more important than academics. If she could put more effort in her studies, she could be a straight A student." Addressing the social development aspect of Wanda, the science teacher, who herself is African American, gave her insights about the dilemma an identified African American student like Wanda typically faces:

> Social development is a matter of whom she chooses to be friends with. Her friends are not likely to be the girls that will put more effort in to make an A, or put forward more effort to make a B. Nobody in her group that she hangs with will push themselves, and she will soon pick that up, too. She will try to accommodate them . . . I've noticed that with Black kids, they don't want to embarrass their friends, and they don't want to be different and feel so smart. So that is the issue, academically they don't want to push themselves because they are so worried about the image of people thinking you are smart.

She hoped Wanda could understand that people that she was friends with now are not likely people she will be friends with years later and that she needs to apply herself more because she is capable. The science teacher noted that the peer pressure was such an overwhelming force that she felt inadequate to convince Wanda to change her mind. As her science teacher put it, "I think if she knew what she could become, what kind of future she would like to have, what kind of career she wants, and what kind of economic and life style she would want, she would study more and apply herself."

Internal Factors

Despite perceptual differences about these African American students' growth pattern, parents, students, and teachers were unified in recognizing the enhanced motivation to learn and to achieve as one of the changes the gifted program participation brought upon these students. These students enjoyed their program experiences, noting that the program made them "feel good" about themselves, and "feel smarter." The program experiences appeared to be a confidence booster, helping them to have better self-esteem.

Changes that Ricky's father had noticed since his son began the gifted program are that his

> conversation has increased [and is] more in depth. [His] subject areas are more in depth, and he is always motivated. [He is] very social and gets along with everyone. [His] self-esteem is great; he feels good about himself and what he is doing. He is very determined; if he thinks something is right, he sticks to it.

Poor time-management appeared to be another theme that surfaced from both parents' and teachers' perspectives. Two students admitted that the gifted program has helped them to be better organized. Weaknesses noted by one father were time management and procrastination: "She waits until the last minute to do work and assignments. She wants to make good grades." Sticking to difficult, challenging situations also was hard for Barbara as evidenced through her desire to drop her gifted math class if it did not go well.

Summary of African American Low-Income Vignettes

This in-depth analysis of nine low-income African American students' performance and developmental profiles suggested both common and unique characteristics of this group of gifted students. They enjoyed the gifted program experience, and became more eager to learn and to work hard willingly. They particularly appreciated the gifted class environment for learning. Participation in the program itself played an important role in enhancing their self-esteem and increasing their confidence in themselves. In addition to their continuing academic excellence, many of them possessed other creative outlets in music, dance, arts, or sports.

What was unique to African American gifted students was their friendship choices outside of the gifted class and the tendency to be perceived as loners by gifted class teachers. They seemed to be facing some pressure from their peer culture against "acting White" on the one hand, and an increasing hunger for social life as a middle schooler, on the other. Many of them, however, presented a high level of maturity in handling peer relationships.

Another emergent theme unique to this group of gifted students was the moral support they received from their families to achieve and the opportunities the gifted program provided. These students, like others across the low-income sample, found that identification and participation in gifted programs strengthened their self-esteem, confidence, and view of a better future. These students also, more than their parents and teachers, tended to be sensitive to affective and social issues in their school lives. Yet, the group also experienced personal issues such as lack of persistence and task commitment, and frustration with tasks that seemed overwhelming.

Key Points to Guide Practice

Implications from these findings can be applied to work with gifted African American low-income students. Based on the understandings from the vignette analysis, educators should apply the following key points to guide their practice.

1. Educators should use diagnostic-prescriptive techniques to target students' needs. As evidenced by the vignettes, gifted students from special populations have special needs that must be met in order to provide an environment conducive to the development of their

talents. With a diagnostic-prescriptive technique, educators can first assess students' skills and understandings and then adapt their instruction prescriptively to assist the gifted student in progressing as his or her profile indicates. These diagnostic-prescriptive methods should be well-documented and shared across grades as these students progress through the K–12 scope and sequence.

2. Providing a professional development model, focused on nontraditional gifted learners, is necessary for educators to enhance their awareness and reduce bias that may impede the opportunities presented to their poor and minority students. By enhancing the cultural competency of educators through targeted professional development, greater emphasis/awareness on identifying and serving gifts and talents among nontraditionally identified gifted students may accrue. Consulting the new teacher education standards approved by the Council for Exceptional Children and the National Association for Gifted Children (Kitano, Montgomery, VanTassel-Baska, & Johnsen, 2008) would provide a strong program for in-service education, including confronting stereotypes, acknowledging the role of culture and race in education, and constructive approaches to working with students from both different cultural backgrounds and students of poverty.

3. Another key point to guide educational practice is that of providing value-added classes and targeted options for these students in domains of strength. This targeting of classes for specific academic talents may provide the necessary acceleration with the appropriate challenge at the appropriate time for these students. This approach aligns and expands the earlier recommendation regarding diagnostic-prescriptive techniques in which students are assessed on their existing level of functioning and then placed in classes where their talents can be developed further. Moreover, value-added options outside the academic core also would be useful to sustain interest and motivation for learning as well as

enhance affective development. Providing opportunities for the arts, for leadership, and for social skill development all would promote important talent development in these learners.

4. Working effectively with parents from other cultural backgrounds and poverty will need to include opportunities for parents to meet teachers and discuss their child in community settings outside of school where they will feel safer and can bring younger children, have support for transportation, and receive practical ideas for easy implementation at home such as games and specialized materials for home use.

Tailoring instructional opportunities based on diagnostic information, offering professional development for serving diverse gifted learners, enhancing targeted academic and non-academic options to fit strengths and develop talents, and working with parents will contribute significantly to providing gifted education services that optimally fit gifted African American students from poverty. Yet barriers to the implementation of such practices abound. Schools are not set up to address the needs of small groups of learners nor to provide individualized approaches so needed by this group of learners. Moreover, professional development time is at a premium, often not amounting to more than 2 days per year on any topic. Parent education as a systematic intervention also often is lacking, rendering the implementation of ongoing parent workshops less likely.

Implications for Future Research

More research clearly is needed to disentangle the effects of poverty from cultural group membership if we are to do a credible job in tailoring interventions to both groups. Although many African American children live in poverty, it would be presumptuous to assume that both the poor and middle class require the same value-added options. Moreover, we still lack data on the positive impacts of value-added programs on a longitudinal basis for these students. The vignette study looked back on 3 years of gifted programming in a part-time model.

What would the effects have been if the students had been in full-time programs? What would be the effects after 10 years of schooling? Longitudinal studies that track outcomes across the years in school would provide better guidance on crafting meaningful interventions.

References

Baldwin, A. (2005). Identification concerns and promises for gifted students of diverse populations. *Theory Into Practice, 44,* 105–114.

Barton, P. E. (2003). *Parsing the achievement gap.* Princeton, NJ: Educational Testing Service.

Bracken, B., & McCallum, R. (1998). *Universal Nonverbal Intelligence Test (UNIT).* Chicago: Riverside.

Castellano, J., & Diaz, E. (2001). *Reaching new horizons: Gifted and talented education for culturally and linguistically diverse students.* Boston: Allyn & Bacon.

Davidson Institute. (2006). *State mandates for gifted programs as of 2006.* Retrieved from http://www.davidsongifted.org/db/state_policies.aspx

Davis, G., & Rimm, S. (2003). *Education of the gifted and talented.* Boston: Allyn & Bacon.

Feuerstein, R. (1986). Learning to learn: Mediated learning experiences and instrumental enrichment. *Special Services in the Schools, 3,* 49–82.

Ford, D. (1994). Nurturing resilience in gifted Black youth. *Roeper Review, 17,* 80–85.

Ford, D. (1996). *Reversing underachievement among gifted Black students: Promising practices and programs.* New York: Teachers College Press.

Ford, D. (2004). Recruiting and retaining culturally diverse gifted students from diverse ethnic, cultural, and language groups. In J. Banks & C. Banks (Eds.), *Multicultural education: Issues and perspectives* (5th ed., pp. 379–397). Hoboken, NJ: Wiley.

Ford, D., & Grantham, T. (2003). Providing access for culturally diverse gifted students: From deficit to dynamic thinking. *Theory Into Practice, 42,* 217–225.

Ford, D., Grantham, T., & Whiting, G. (2008a). Another look at the achievement gap: Learning from the experiences of gifted Black students. *Urban Education, 43,* 216–239.

Ford, D., Grantham, T., & Whiting, G. (2008b). Culturally and linguistically diverse students in gifted education: Recruitment and retention issues. *Exceptional Children, 74,* 289–306.

Ford, D., & Harris, J. J., III. (1996). Perceptions and attitudes of Black students toward school, achievement, and other educational variables. *Child Development, 67,* 1141–1152.

Frasier, M., Garcia, J., & Passow, A. H. (1995). *A review of assessment issues in gifted education and their implications for identifying gifted minority students.* Storrs: University of Connecticut, The National Research Center on the Gifted and Talented.

Kirschenbaum, R. J. (1998). Dynamic assessment and its use with underserved gifted and talented populations. *Gifted Child Quarterly, 42,* 140–147.

Kitano, M., Montgomery, D., VanTassel-Baska, J., & Johnsen, S. K. (2008). *Using the national gifted education standards for pre K–12 professional development.* Thousand Oaks, CA: Corwin Press.

Naglieri, J., & Ford, D. (2003). Addressing underrepresentation of gifted minority children using the Naglieri Nonverbal Ability Test (NNAT). *Gifted Child Quarterly, 47,* 155–160.

Naglieri, J. A., & Kaufman, J. C. (2001). Understanding intelligence, giftedness, and creativity using PASS theory. *Roeper Review, 23,* 151–156.

Passow, A. H., & Frasier, M. M. (1996). Toward improving identification of talent potential among minority and disadvantaged students. *Roeper Review, 18,* 198–202.

Patton, J., Prillaman, D., & VanTassel-Baska, J. (1991). A state study on programs and services to the disadvantaged gifted. *Gifted Child Quarterly, 34,* 94–96.

Robinson, A., Shore, B. M., & Enersen, D. L. (2007). *Best practices in gifted education: An evidence-based guide.* Waco, TX: Prufrock Press.

VanTassel-Baska, J., Johnson, D., & Avery, L. D. (2002). Using performance tasks in the identification of economically disadvantaged and minority gifted learners: Findings from Project STAR. *Gifted Child Quarterly, 46,* 110–123.

Whiting, G., & Ford, D. (2006). Under-representation of diverse students in gifted education: Recommendations for nondiscriminatory assessment (Part 2). *Gifted Education Press Quarterly, 20*(3), 6–10.

The Patterns and Profiles of Gifted Low-Income Caucasian Children

Julie Dingle Swanson

This chapter begins with a literature review exploring aspects relevant to this special population. The second part of this chapter draws upon case study findings of special needs gifted learners (VanTassel-Baska, Feng, Swanson, Quek, & Chandler, 2009) to discuss and illustrate unique character- istics and resulting educational needs, as well as the learning opportunities these students experience. The chapter con- cludes with an integration of literature and case study find- ings, with key points to guide school-based practitioners and gifted coordinators in development of gifted, low-income, Caucasian children.

What Research Tells Us

Currently, one in five children in our country lives in pov- erty (Robinson, Shore, & Enersen, 2007). Harold Hodgkinson (2007), President of the Center for Demographic Policy, stated that "poverty is a universal handicap" and "the most pervasive, inhibiting force" to a child's success in school (p. 7). Children lose ground when they grow up in poverty. As reported by Hodgkinson, relevant demographic data from the 2000 United

States Census provides a context for understanding the prevalence of the phenomenon:

- 3.9 million women give birth yearly in the United States.
- White females birth 60.8 children per 1,000 women of childbearing age, as compared to 62.9 for Black and 84 for Hispanic.
- The lowest income families (i.e., under $10,000/year) have 73 babies per 1,000 women, as compared to those families of $75,000/year and up, who have 50 babies per 1,000 women.
- Children raised by single mothers are two to three times more likely to be poor.
- Ten percent of White female births are by teenaged mothers, which almost guarantees the children will be raised in poverty.
- The majority of poor children in America are White. Of 14 million poor children from birth to 18 years old, 9 million of them are White.
- Low-income children start kindergarten with the lowest level of math and reading achievement compared to children of other income levels. (p. 15)

We know that poverty negatively impacts children and how they develop physically, socially, intellectually, and emotionally. We know that developmental issues and lack of educational opportunity mean that potential is lost. We know that finding gifted students from poverty has been difficult, but we are strongly aware that the search for these youngsters demands our continued efforts. "Poverty and the parental characteristics and practices associated with it play a greater role than race or ethnicity in determining students' school achievement" (Robinson, 2003, p. 252).

What does research tell us about the gifted low-income Caucasian students subgroup within children of poverty? A survey of existing research reveals a growing body of knowledge on gifted students from poverty, but studies where low-income Caucasian gifted students are the primary research focus are rare. In many studies, low-income gifted students are not separated into groups by ethnicity. It is not clear why few studies focus on gifted low-income Caucasian youngsters, but one hypothesis is that researchers choose to concentrate on minority status as it relates to poverty and school achievement. In a review of the literature on poverty's impact on high achievement, Burney and Beilke (2008) argued that

> Neither locale nor race is helpful as a grouping factor. David Cotter (2002) pointed out that "since at least the early 1960s poverty has been treated in scholarly research, public policy, and popular culture as a largely urban, mostly black problem" (p. 534). This may be part of the reason that race and poverty are frequently linked. (p. 298)

Further, Burney and Beilke noted that categorizing by race and ethnicity is becoming more difficult. Additional research is needed to deepen our understanding of the unique challenges gifted low-income Caucasian children face as well as how their patterns and profiles are similar to and different from those of other gifted low-income youngsters.

Effects of Poverty

Families in poverty face "underemployment, undereducation, single parenting, inadequate medical care; reduced access to first-rate child care; drug and alcohol addictions; [and] unsafe neighborhoods" (Robinson, 2003, p. 253). Families struggle to survive daily because of these constant battles. "Poverty and near poverty can grind down the best efforts of well-meaning parents . . . Poverty is a vicious killer of potentially fine minds" (Robinson, 2003, p. 262). Jimerson, Egeland, and Sroufe (2000) found poverty is a strong predictor of students most likely to drop out of school. In this study, poverty's influences on the students who dropped out of school were their home environment, their care as young children, and lack of parental involvement in school.

One way to head off such results of poverty on achievement is early intervention, a promising solution for bright youngsters from poverty. Hodgkinson (2007) contended that by the time children enter kindergarten at age 5, some have already been left behind in achievement status. The main reason for this is poverty. He argued that because birth to age 5 is the most vulnerable period for social, psychological, and intellectual development for children, a formal preschool structure to enable the success of children from poor families must be provided.

Robinson, Lanzi, Weinberg, Ramey, and Ramey (2002) reported evidence from the National Head Start/Public School Early Transition Demonstration Project study that early intervention positively impacts the social and academic achievement of bright students. Burney and Beilke (2008) cited early intervention in preschool and kindergarten as a strategy for success. Not only is early intervention a critical factor in the social and intellectual development of all youngsters, but accessible healthcare and affordable, safe housing also are parts of the solution.

Identification Route Influences

Finding low-income Caucasian gifted students has not been easy. Low-income gifted learners can be found through traditional means of identification, but they continue to be underrepresented. An investigation of potential causes of underrepresentation of low-income White gifted students (Borland, 2004) revealed several obstacles in their identification, including misconceptions about what giftedness is and how it is manifested, and the instruments, tools, and procedures commonly used in identifying gifted learners.

In many schools, teachers act as gatekeepers of gifted programs, and their assumptions about gifted learners may block identification of low-income gifted learners (Swanson, 2006). Teachers with less experience and knowledge about gifted students believe that motivation and high performance are the primary indicators of giftedness. Because some low-income gifted students may have poorly developed skills and need to learn how to learn, teachers may not see these students as truly gifted (VanTassel-Baska, Feng, Quek, & Struck, 2004). These assumptions contribute to underidentification of this special population.

States report varied approaches in identification procedures for the gifted (Brown, Avery, & VanTassel-Baska, 2003). From a policy perspective, use of unbiased identification instruments and procedures that reflect understanding of how giftedness is manifested in a wide range of groups is essential (Frasier et al., 1995). VanTassel-Baska, Johnson, and Avery (2002) described a promising identification protocol in one state incorporating performance tasks as an effort to find low-income and minority gifted students. The identification protocol combines traditional and nontraditional measures in a multistep process, and has increased the percentage of low-income gifted students identified for services (VanTassel-Baska, Feng, & Evans, 2007).

Piirto (2007) pointed out the need for identification protocols with multiple methods and measures to find students from underrepresented groups: "Researchers and thinkers are now beginning to realize that test scores and checklists themselves can even be harmful to students, because they are scored in the aggregate, the total, the accumulation" (p. 617). This type of approach to identifying talent may miss students who show evidence on only one measure. More inclusive approaches that Piirto advocated are a revolving door method, a modified quota system, a case study approach, portfolio assessment, performance assessment, and dynamic assessment.

Burney and Beilke (2008) advocated for "holistic identification of high-ability students in poverty" (p. 309). Seeking talent and providing opportunities to develop talent, identifying students with potential early, and offering a continuum of services are more holistic approaches they described. In an interesting example reported through an action research study, Jatko (1995) used a whole-class tryout for the Future Problem Solving Program, a component of the gifted program. She found the tryout for this particular part of the gifted program effective in identifying economically disadvantaged gifted students. VanTassel-Baska and colleagues (2009) described one state's use of a combination of traditional (aptitude and achievement measures) and nontraditional measures (performance tasks) as promising in finding low-income and other underrepresented gifted students.

Feeling a sense of belonging is a basic need all humans possess. A sense of belonging may come from family, peers, or other group affiliations. Because gifted students often feel different from the norm, some struggle to find that group where they feel comfortable and accepted. Low-income gifted students may experience double jeopardy because they likely are "different economically and experientially from their intellectual [peer] group" and at the same time feel "different intellectually from their economic peer group" (Slocumb & Payne, 2000, p. 223). Because many adults in poverty are undereducated, parents may not understand their gifted children. Low-income gifted children may have only one parent in the home; this parent may be working two or three jobs to make ends meet (Begoray & Slovinsky, 1997). For these reasons, the social support for academic achievement provided at home for many children may not be present in some low-income households. One study of middle school youngsters found that gifted students from low-socioeconomic backgrounds had significantly lower perceived social self-competence than students from more economically advantaged backgrounds (VanTassel-Baska, Olszewski-Kubilius, & Kulieke, 1994).

Clearly, low-income gifted students need opportunities and assistance in developing necessary social support systems. Olszewski-Kubilius, Grant, and Seibert (1994) advocated for planned opportunities for exposure and enrichment, leadership development, and academic support to build those necessary social networks. They found that extracurricular opportunities (i.e., school clubs, summer enrichment programs, cultural opportunities, and mentors) helped low-income gifted learners develop talent and aspirations for the future. Their findings indicate that guidance support relative to careers, scholarships, and motivation is a key element to the success of these young people.

Family Issues

As with all students, parents' support and participation in their children's lives is important in their success. From their national study, VanTassel-Baska, Patton, and Prillaman (1991) noted, "Students who come from low-income families in which the parents' educational level and occupational status are also commensurately low creates a special constraint" (p. 614) in their talent development. Just because parent participation in schooling may be lower than participation of parents from more economically advantaged backgrounds, lack of interest, low expectations, and lack of aspirations for their children should not be assumed (Robinson et al., 2007). Parents of gifted low-income students may have misperceptions about their children's abilities; they may not understand the purpose of the gifted program. VanTassel-Baska et al. (2004) observed that some parents from low-income backgrounds may believe participation in the gifted program requires that they pay a fee or parents may fear that gifted program participation could create negative changes in their child. For example, encouraging college as a goal may be negatively perceived by these parents because they know they cannot pay for college for their child (VanTassel-Baska et al., 1994).

Although one study showed low-socioeconomic status as a negative factor in parent participation in schools (Griffith, 1998), other research has focused on the need to increase participation by providing additional educational resources and support for low-income parents of gifted students (Newberg, 2006; Shumow, 1997). Hunsaker's (1995) review of the literature found that school and community support for low-income families and the culture they bring was important, especially in recognizing gifted learners from poverty.

Learning Needs and Supports, Styles, and Preferences

Several studies have provided examples of learning opportunities and support systems that nurture and grow potential in gifted low-income learners (Barone & Schneider, 2003; Burney & Cross, 2006; Hébert, 2002; Swanson, 2006). These and other studies have provided insight into the learning needs, styles, and preferences of this special population of gifted students. Enriched and challenging curricula, mentors and role models who give students a picture of future possibilities and offer a caring relationship outside of the family, and targeted counseling that deals with the unique social and emotional issues of low-income gifted youngsters are critical elements in developing student potential.

Enrichment, exposure, and challenge *do* matter. In a case study of three low-income students, Hébert (2002) found an enriched teaching/learning environment, extracurricular activities, and mentors significant for these youngsters. Mentors afforded a different perspective and exposed students to different views and ways of solving problems. Results from Project Breakthrough, a Javits demonstration project in three Title One elementary schools, suggested that minimal interventions with challenging and advanced curricula significantly impact low-income student achievement (Swanson, 2006). VanTassel-Baska et al. (1994) advocated for mentors and role models to assist gifted students from poverty as they seek to understand future possibilities. Counseling, particularly career counseling, is a key aspect in enabling the aspirations of these students. Moon and Callahan's (2001) longitudinal study of interventions to improve achievement of low-income students found that mentoring, parent involvement and specialized curriculum helped improve student performance the most. In a talent search study, where low-income students were provided specific supports such as exploration of careers and counseling, Brewer (2005) found it was more likely for those students receiving support to go on to postsecondary education.

Careful consideration of altering the instructional diet with gifted low-income students is important. For example, Barone and Schneider's (2003) case study of a low-income gifted student in a high-poverty school using a literacy model described the approaches that this particular gifted student responded to as the teacher differentiated his literacy instruction. The school's literacy model with a phonics and skills emphasis designed for low-achieving students was one aspect about which the researchers were curious. What was the impact of this instructional model on a low-income gifted student already advanced in reading, writing, and speaking? Instead of relying on the literacy model for this advanced student's instruction, the teacher in the case utilized open-ended activities, choice, multigrade level materials, flexible learning and teaching, and an individualized, project-based approach. The modified teaching and learning allowed the student to further develop his potential talent in reading, writing, and speaking. The experiences provided him with opportunities to take risks and develop his creativity. "This support allowed him to take great risks with his writing and . . . to move on to more complex understandings than those usually explored" by older students (Barone & Schneider, 2003, p. 265).

Enrichment, choice, relevance, and encouragement positively impacts students' learning attitude and motivation. Commenting on the enrichment opportunities the students in his study received, Hébert (2002) stated, "Learning is more effective when youngsters enjoy what they are doing . . . Learning is more meaningful in the context of a real problem" (p. 136). The study's focus on providing students opportunities to study what they enjoy and "personalizing" learning with choice were important in keeping these youngsters engaged. Students must be engaged in learning if we hope to develop their talent. Hébert also found that extracurricular activities served as talent development experiences. Extracurricular activities made available "tangible products, caring adult relationships, a sense of accomplishment and impact on self-confidence, and opportunities for success" (Hébert, 2002, p. 136).

Internal Factors

Children who live in poverty find themselves and their families in a daily struggle for survival. They often are surrounded by pessimism and hopelessness. Life circumstances have impacted how these children view themselves and their capabilities in relation to others. Self-concept has a critical role in academic achievement. VanTassel-Baska et al. (1994) found that low socioeconomic status gifted students showed significantly lower academic self-confidence than those who came from middle and high socioeconomic status. In another study, participation in a gifted program had a positive influence on self-confidence and self-esteem (VanTassel-Baska et al., 2004). Hébert (2002) noted that teachers with high expectations for students, no matter what the student's life circumstances, have a positive impact on low-income gifted student performance. In a literature review of resilience and gifted students, Kitano and Lewis (2005) suggested strategies to assist in developing the ability to overcome obstacles, a disposition that would clearly strengthen confidence and success for students in difficult life circumstances.

Perceptions of Giftedness

Sennett and Cobb (1972) argued that cultural and social constructions of class influence definitions of intelligence. They linked class and individual perception of ability as evidence that those raised in lower classes fail to achieve success because they do not believe in themselves or their abilities as much as those raised in the upper classes. In school, teachers treat lower income children differently from upper income children, and give lower class children the message that, compared to those of higher social standing, they will not succeed in life. Sennett and Cobb suggested that this perception lingers with the individual and may become a self-fulfilling prophesy.

A deficit view of youngsters, where teachers focus on weaknesses and ignore student strengths, blocks many teachers from recognizing the ability of low-income gifted learners. Teacher development in recognizing and nurturing potential is critical—both in terms of the low-income gifted student and his or her family. Teachers need to understand their own biases and assumptions as they work to develop potential and provide the additional supports needed for these youngsters. For example, building a strong family-school connection relies upon a teacher skilled in understanding parents who may lack trust and confidence in schools and authority figures based on their life experiences. VanTassel-Baska and colleagues (2004) noted that teachers in focus groups stated they had to lower expectations and slow the instructional pace for low-income and minority gifted students. Teachers perceived these students as having more gaps in their knowledge and needing more individual instruction than other gifted students.

To counter teacher perceptions of low-income gifted students is carefully designed teacher development. "Teachers often refer students to gifted programs who are well-behaved, well-dressed, and who obtain good grades" (Clark, 1992, cited in Frasier et al., 1995, p. viii). Teacher expectations about students and their potential for achievement have been linked to "student attractiveness, conduct, cumulative folder information, race/ethnicity, and social class" (Dusek & Joseph, 1983, p. 327).

The similarities of low-income gifted students of various ethnicities (e.g., Caucasian, Hispanic, African American) are implicit in the research reviewed in this chapter, but it is unclear whether these implied similarities hold true because few studies make distinctions among the subgroups within the larger group of low-income gifted students. However, the examples discussed illustrate promising practices that assist in identification and academic/affective development of low-income Caucasian gifted students. The next section examines case study findings focused on this particular subpopulation.

Case Study Findings:
Characteristics, Needs, and Perceptions

In a study of one state's efforts to shape a more inclusive identification policy (VanTassel-Baska & Feng, 2006; VanTassel-Baska, Feng, & deBrux, 2007; VanTassel-Baska et al., 2002), case studies of 37 special needs gifted youngsters from distinct special needs populations were developed. Those gifted populations included low-income African American students (n = 9), low-income Caucasian students (n = 13), twice-exceptional students (n = 5), and high nonverbal, low verbal students (n = 9). This discussion will focus on excerpts from vignettes written on the low-income Caucasian students and what the vignettes reveal about these children.

Interviews of the students, their parents, their gifted teacher, and their science teacher comprised a major portion of the data collected, and short descriptive stories or vignettes were written up from the data. The cases illustrate important understandings about low-income Caucasian gifted students, and although not generalizable to the larger population, these students' stories exemplify important facets of these learners. Table 7.1 gives an overview of the sample (n = 13) by providing the students' pseudonyms, gender, identification route, school performance, and talent area (where applicable). In this subsample of the larger study, most of the students were female and identified through a nontraditional pathway that included performance tasks. At the time of the study, the students were in middle school, either the seventh or eighth grade, and most

Table 7.1
Low-Income Caucasian Gifted Students: Gender, Identification Route, Performance, and Talent Areas

Students (n = 13)	Gender	Traditional Identification (n = 4)	Nontraditional Identification (n = 9)	School Performance	Talent Area(s)
Alicia	Female	Yes		GPA = 3.7	N/A
Andrea	Female		Yes	GPA = 3.8	Writing, visual arts
Betty	Female		Yes	Math =A ELA = B	Writing
Blair	Female		Yes	GPA = 2.75	N/A
Blythe	Female		Yes		Artistic talent
Bronwyn	Female		Yes	Math = A ELA = A	Artistic talent
Cutler	Male	Yes		Math = A ELA = B	Writing
Derek	Male		Yes	GPA = 3.7	N/A
Kassandra	Female		Yes	GPA = 3.6	N/A
Kelly	Female		Yes	Making B's and C's	N/A
Terry	Male	Yes		Making D's	Leadership
Tom	Male		Yes	GPA = 3.8	Artistic talent
Travis	Female	Yes		Making A's	Extracurricular activities (e.g., cheerleading, gymnastics)

Note. ELA = English/language arts, GPA = grade point average, N/A = not explicitly stated.

of them had been in the gifted program for 3 or more years. Almost all were performing well in school; many were seen as having strong talent in one or more areas.

Program Participation

As a group, these students saw the gifted program as a positive force in their lives. They understood the benefits of their participation on their schoolwork, achievement, and self-confidence. Excerpts from the vignettes of Travis, an eighth-grade girl; Tom, an eighth-grade boy; and Blythe, a seventh-grade girl, illustrate how students felt about their participation in the gifted program.

> When first identified, Travis felt special and smart. She said, "I was chosen to do this. I felt smarter than other people. I might have a better chance at learning new things. We might have a little more work, but in the end, it will be worth that little bit of extra work. So I don't complain about it." She thinks about her future and how the gifted classes will help her, stating, "When I am taking the SAT test and I get a good score and get into a good college and get a good job and make good money [that will be a benefit of my gifted classes]." (VanTassel-Baska & Feng, 2006, p. 101)

Travis saw that her aspirations for college were potentially affected by her participation in the gifted program. Building the likelihood of financial possibilities for college can provide hope and motivation for the low-income student. Tom, described below, experienced the impact on his learning as well as an impact on his confidence and self-esteem.

> Tom acknowledged that gifted program participation provided him an opportunity to learn at an advanced level in a healthy environment with other students of similar minds. The placement made him feel good about himself and become more confident. There seemed to him a carryover effect of gifted program participation, whereas what he learned in the gifted classes in language arts and mathematics has helped him a great deal in science and social studies and helped with his [achievement test scores given at the end of the year]. (VanTassel-Baska & Feng, 2006, p. 98)

Tom, too, saw an impact from gifted program participation on his current achievement level. Blythe liked the challenge of her gifted class and felt empowered. Conversely, she felt the pressure of high expectations that came along with the gifted label.

> Positive aspects of the gifted classes from Blythe's perspective are the level of challenge and learning more than the regular students. She stated, "I like it (GT) because it's more challenging, 'cause whenever something is easy, I just breeze right through it. But whenever something's challenging, you have to stop and think about the problem. I like it because I'm learning more stuff than regular classes. It makes me feel powerful, makes me feel smarter than other people. But really, I'm not." The pressure of those classes is a negative for Blythe. "One thing I don't like about the honors classes is the pressure is too much. You're the cream of the crop and you have to set an example for all of the kids." (VanTassel-Baska & Feng, 2006, p. 78)

These examples illuminate the importance of finding and placing low-income Caucasian gifted students.

School Performance, Strengths, and Talents

Most of the low-income Caucasian gifted students in the study performed well in school, and reading and writing were the academic strength areas of most. Parents and teachers commented on the creativity and varied talents of these students. As a group, the student performance is high (see Table 7.1), so low-income status does not appear to negatively impact most of these youngsters' school performance. Two students' (Bronwyn and Kelly) contrasting performance in school are described below. An excerpt from Bronwyn's vignette shows how her performance in mathematics improved. Kelly performed as an average student but had low motivation.

> [Bronwyn's] mother described her daughter's problems in mathematics when she was at the elementary school, but added that she has grown out of the problem and gets A's in her algebra class, and is able to "think out

of the box." Ms. Henly (her mother) noted that the gifted program greatly influenced Bronwyn on both her achievement in math and her self-confidence in a favorable direction, noting that "before the gifted program, she was panicked a little and slow in math, but now she thinks things through a lot better . . . the program makes her confident and she is more motivated to learn even more, even though she is quite competent already." (VanTassel-Baska & Feng, 2006, p. 82)

Bronwyn's mother attributed her daughter's improved performance to enhanced confidence and motivation that came from her growth in the gifted program.

Kelly, a student with deep emotional problems related to a difficult childhood living with a drug-addicted mother, had been seeing a counselor for a few years. It was apparent that the emotional issues Kelly was experiencing were connected to her school performance. An excerpt from Kelly's story follows.

The gifted class teacher thought Kelly was a "good 'C' student, who could be a 'B'." She found her academic performance "average," and said she had not seen evidence of her giftedness. [The gifted class teacher] felt Kelly's work on stem cards was not as well done as the others, and [the teacher noted Kelly] does not maintain her reading logs. [The teacher] observed that Kelly does not talk much in class, and appears to be a loner. She felt that Kelly lacks motivation, although she does get her work done, and her assignments are always done in class . . . The teacher said that she "overreacts in class sometimes," and remarked twice that Kelly "will snap back at you" and "jump down teachers' throats." (VanTassel-Baska & Feng, 2006, p. 94)

Bronwyn learned how to handle challenge better through her experiences in the gifted classes. Kelly's behaviors indicated some deep emotional issues that were affecting her learning and performance in school and illustrated the need for supports such as counseling.

Family and Peer Relationships

A few of the students reported family problems, but there was evidence that most parents were interested and involved in their children's schooling. Kelly, the student mentioned above, moved in with her dad and stepmother 3 years before the study occurred. Prior to that, she was living with her birth mother who suffered from substance abuse problems.

> According to [her stepmother], Kelly had a traumatic childhood, and "has a lot of rage in her." She was living with her birth mother who was a drug addict, and as such, Kelly had to play mom to her two younger stepbrothers, children of her mother's second husband. (VanTassel-Baska & Feng, 2006, p. 93)

Although Kelly now has family support that is consistent and caring, she also has unresolved issues related to her family background.

Outside of the family, social relationships patterns included: (1) conscious choices of friends with similar values (e.g., good grades, not "running wild"); (2) a preference for friends from outside of gifted classes (about a third of the students); and (3) friends both in their gifted classes and in other classes (about half of the students). An excerpt from Betty's story illustrates the first pattern. Cutler exemplifies the last pattern. Andrea provides an example of a student shifting her priorities from academics to peer relationships, a pattern often seen during the transition to middle school. "[Betty's mother] discussed [her daughter's] peers by saying: 'A lot of her friends run wild. I don't allow her to run around; she can only go to houses where I know the parents'" (VanTassel-Baska & Feng, 2006, p. 73).

Although Cutler indicated no preference for friends from inside or outside of the gifted classes, he commented on the value for time with those on his mental wavelength: "Cutler was comfortable making friends in both the regular and gifted classes, although he felt he loved being in the gifted class with intellectually similar kids, since he could learn more" (VanTassel-Baska & Feng, 2006, p. 85).

Andrea, a popular student with lots of friends, appeared to have shifted her focus from academics to her peers.

> Andrea appears to be a girl lacking no friends, pro-claiming that she can make friends with everybody, but further explaining that most of her friends are in her gifted class . . . Her enthusiasm and yearning for friend-ships has become intensified in middle school, and has resulted in her placing a high premium on social relationships and being popular . . . A socially popu-lar student, Andrea appeared not to be very smooth emotionally. The science teacher shared that, "She did not have any problems with other kids, but I know she wasn't happy all the time. Middle school was really hard and she had some family problems." (VanTassel-Baska & Feng, 2006, pp. 70–71)

Andrea's mother had become worried about her daughter's boredom and lack of attention to her school subjects. Her teachers noted that she rushed through her work and did not pay attention to details. Andrea's current situation exempli-fies the struggle with priorities that many young adolescents experience. The potential repercussions of making the wrong choices can be life-altering for low-income students who may not have second chances.

Perceptions of Giftedness

Most parents recognized early that their children were bright. Two of the parents interviewed felt their children were smart but not necessarily gifted. Blythe's mother discussed her daughter's giftedness:

> Natalie Land, Blythe's mother, said that even as a young child her daughter caught on to things quickly. Mrs. Land stated, "[When she was] little, before she started school, she was smart. She caught on fast. She was sneaky, you know what I mean—playing dumb when she knew what was going on." (VanTassel-Baska & Feng, 2006, p. 79)

Alicia's mother and her science teacher both recognized her giftedness and commented on the traits she displays relative to her strengths.

> Alicia's mother . . . indicated that she knew her daughter was gifted early on during her development, around the age of 4 or 5. She said that [Alicia] did everything early. At age 5, she could read fluently and had a good memory. By the age of 10, her love of reading was apparent, as well as an aptitude in math; all of her elementary grades were good . . . [Her science teacher] observed that Alicia is an avid reader who excels in reading and understanding technical material. Alicia is what she would consider "more traditionally gifted" because she is "super smart" and above average in just about everything. (VanTassel-Baska & Feng, 2006, p. 68)

Betty remarked on her self-perception when she was identified as gifted. "When they told me I was going to an honors class, it was kind of shocking because I did not think I was cut out to be an honors student. I thought it was a stretch for me" (VanTassel-Baska & Feng, 2006, p. 72).

Internal Factors

Most of the students appeared to be well-adjusted, but about half of the 13 were perceived to have problems in motivation, time management, organization, procrastination, distractibility, and a tendency to rush through work. A few were seen as perfectionistic. Derek, perceived as an underachiever; Blair, who demonstrated time management issues and distractibility; and Terry, who lacked motivation but is confident and happy-go-lucky, are described below.

> [Derek's] middle school [gifted] language arts teacher believed Derek was definitely gifted, but was an underachiever. She noted that he enjoyed learning, but was frustrated with anything (such as logic problems) that required a great deal of mental processing. Initially, he

struggled in the [gifted] classes because they required different types of thinking; once he adjusted to the thinking, he was successful. The teacher said that Derek complained quite a bit about the work required by the teacher, although he was capable of doing the work. Academically, he was the top student; he was an underachiever because he had the capability but was not motivated and struggled to get his work done. (VanTassel-Baska & Feng, 2006, pp. 88–89)

Was Derek's level of challenge appropriate for him? What social supports would build his self-efficacy? These questions and others that allow for deep analysis of struggling students' profiles need careful consideration if planned interventions are to be effective.

Blair's mother and her science teacher commented on weaknesses they saw in Blair:

[Blair's mother] stated that Blair has good self-esteem and a good attitude towards learning, but observed that her daughter has become a procrastinator. "She puts it (schoolwork) off, does it at the last minute, and still pulls off a good grade . . . [Her science teacher] commented on Blair's distractibility: "She may get halfway through work and go to another task or play with something. She is easily distracted and likes to play sometimes." (VanTassel-Baska & Feng, 2006, p. 76)

Terry's mother recognized his weaknesses, but it was his teachers who were worried about him.

Mrs. Teasdale (Terry's mom) did not seem too perturbed about Terry's problems in school, commenting that her own brother was also troublesome when he was in school, but because he was smart, he still made it to college . . . When asked about Terry's learning weaknesses, she said he was "too smart," and "catches on to stuff quickly," was bored and lazy. He did not like to write, writes "so slow," but reads all the time

. . . Both of his teachers said Terry was very verbal . . . but he "talks more than he writes," and "will tell you things, but refuses to put them on paper." [His science teacher observed] that Terry appeared to like science, but lacked the task commitment and motivation, which had contributed to his poor academic performance . . . She felt that [Terry] lacked time management and organizational skills, and was a perennial procrastinator. In fact, his gifted teacher expressed surprise that he was even in the honors class as he lacked the motivation most honors students had. She found him lazy, and remarked that his work ethic needed improvement. (VanTassel-Baska & Feng, 2006, p. 96)

These excerpts provide commentary on perceived weaknesses in Derek, Blair, and Terry, three Caucasian low-income students experiencing some problems academically that could mushroom in high school if motivation is not improved and better work habits employed.

The Role of Identification

Finally, most of these students would not be in the gifted program if the identification process relied solely on traditional measures (i.e., aptitude, achievement). In this group, 70% were identified as gifted using a nontraditional performance task as one of the indicators of potentiality. This evidence underlines the need for a combination of approaches when attempting to include gifted low-income Caucasian students in gifted programs.

Guidelines for Practice

As teachers, counselors, and other educators, what are the key points we need to keep in mind to shape powerful growth opportunities for low-income Caucasian gifted students? Guidelines for school-based practitioners and gifted coordinators have been synthesized through an integration of literature and case study findings. Table 7.2 summarizes the guidelines and offers concrete, expanded examples for practice.

Table 7.2
Guidelines for Practice: Gifted Low-Income Caucasian Children

Guideline	What Can be Done in Schools and Districts	Examples of How Each Guideline Can be Addressed
Community Supports	• Know the community support systems for low-income families that exist locally. • Connect low-income parents and students with these supports. • Help them learn to navigate these systems.	• Create a listing of free and low-cost healthcare (e.g., Medicaid, resources through the local United Way agency). • Communicate with parents what they need to know and how to gain access to early childhood education and quality childcare (e.g., Head Start, 3- and 4-year-old programs in public schools). • Have contact information for the local housing authority to ensure access to safe, affordable housing. • Connect parents with job training agencies and opportunities. • Track and publicize educational opportunities (e.g., adult education and GED classes, before- and afterschool programs for youngsters, scholarships for college and summer programs).
Identification Routes	• Ensure that teachers provide identification pathways that reveal these hard-to-identify gifted youngsters. • Use traditional *and* nontraditional measures in identification procedures.	• Screen students in many ways (i.e., use of multiple measures) and over time (at several key points in schooling). • Use varied assessments (e.g., portfolio, performance, and/or dynamic assessments). • Utilize try-outs, where students demonstrate their abilities (e.g., critical and creative thinking and problem solving). • Employ trial placement, with potentially gifted students placed in the gifted class for a period of time. Establishing specific criteria for trial placement is important.
Curriculum	• Know low-income gifted learners' traits and how to match effective curricular and instructional practices with their unique traits. • Be aware of the unique affective needs of these youngsters and plan for curricular approaches that address these needs.	• Traits include openness to experience, nonconformity and independence, creativity and fluency in thinking, preference for oral expression, tendency to blend feelings with thought, and preference for hands-on, real-world connections. • Examples of curricular approaches matched to traits are problem-based learning (hands-on; real-world; openness; oral communication; independence), which engages students in real-world problem solving, and independent study (creativity, blending feelings with thought, openness) when teachers personalize learning by offering choices. • Plan opportunities for exposure and enrichment to people, places, and things. • Offer leadership development and provide academic support through extracurricular opportunities (i.e., school clubs, summer enrichment programs, cultural opportunities, and mentors).

Table 7.2, continued

Guideline	What Can be Done in Schools and Districts	Examples of How Each Guideline Can be Addressed
Family Involvement	• Build strong relationships with parents and guardians, based on the belief that they are interested and want the best for their children. • Support low-income families and the culture they bring to school as essential in building relationships. • Provide opportunities for their involvement in the educational process on the parents' timeframes and turf. • Dispel misperceptions about their children's abilities.	• Devise creative ways to involve parents in the educational process of their children that involve fun, food, and fellowship. Community-based student events are one way to highlight students' academic talents and accomplishments and enable parents to better understand the purpose and benefits of the gifted program. • Home visits or conferences in the parent's workplace are two options to explore. These outreach efforts help teachers learn more about the family and demonstrate a willingness to meet parents where they are most comfortable. • Student work samples and/or videotaped classroom performances provide methods by which teachers might show parents what their children do well.
Teacher Development	• Expose and change educators' widely held assumptions and biases about low-income children and their parents. • Shift teacher practice to focus on strengths as a way to develop areas of weakness.	• Use case studies, book studies of biographies of eminent persons from low-income backgrounds, cinematherapy, coursework, and action research to help teachers understand their biases and assumptions about students based on social class.
Continuum of Program Services and Supports	• Plan for ways to address the lack of resources and skills that accompany gifted students of poverty because they often experience social and emotional issues related to the combination of their poverty and their giftedness. • Extend services beyond the gifted classroom to offer low-income gifted students opportunities for enrichment and exposure, for skill development and leadership development.	• Provide specific supports such as exploration of careers and counseling related to planning for college. • Ensure specialized guidance and counseling to address the unique social and emotional issues of these students. • Offer before- and afterschool programs and summer programs that focus on both academics and social skills. • Involve students with mentors who come from similar backgrounds.

Community Supports

The school needs to act as a conduit for existing community support systems that link low-income parents and students with the services and social supports available locally. Free and low-cost healthcare, early childhood education and quality childcare, safe and affordable housing, and parental sources providing training, jobs, and educational opportunities are areas where low-income families need assistance. The knowledge of what exists can be used as a guideline so that we may assist low-income children and their families to navigate through the various systems.

Identification Routes

The second guideline ensures that schools and districts have identification pathways that reveal these hard-to-identify gifted youngsters. Clearly both traditional and nontraditional measures are necessary tools in finding the gifted students in this special population. Utilizing approaches described by VanTassel-Baska et al. (2002) and Piirto (2007) are absolutely critical. Including "try-outs" (Jatko, 1995) and trial placement for students with evidence of high potential to further reveal and develop potential is necessary.

Curriculum

The third guideline is knowledge of the traits low-income gifted learners possess and utilization of best practice to design challenging and intellectually engaging curriculum that matches their traits. The primary learning characteristics of low-income and minority gifted students include "openness to experience, nonconformity and independence in thinking, creativity and fluency in thinking, preference for oral expression, tendency to blend feelings with thought, and a preference for hands-on and real-world connections" (VanTassel-Baska & Stambaugh, 2006, p. 223). Beyond intellectual needs are the affective needs of these youngsters discussed earlier. A curricular example, the use of bibliotherapy to study eminent persons who came from poverty themselves, helps low-income gifted students to gain a vision of future possibilities.

Family Involvement

Building strong relationships with parents and guardians with opportunities for involvement in the educational process is the fourth guideline. Low-income parents care deeply about their children, and they strongly influence their children's attitudes toward education. An issue for low-income Caucasian gifted students is parents who may not understand the gifted program's benefits for their child. Low-income parents may work two or three jobs, so building the traditional PTA relationship is very unlikely. Schools and districts must devise creative ways to involve parents in the educational process of their children on the parents' timeframes and turf. Home visits and community-based student events are ways to build trust and establish relationships with parents and to help them gain understanding of and hope for their child's future.

Teacher Development

The fifth guideline is to explore educators' widely held assumptions and biases about low-income children and their parents. Much work is essential to help those who come from middle-class backgrounds to understand this special population and how to differentiate for these youngsters in ways that promote their learning and achievement. Many teachers lack awareness of the cultural lens through which they see low-income students. Awareness of bias is a first step in dispelling it.

Continuum of Program Services and School Supports

The values and beliefs held by those in poverty may create inner conflict for many low-income gifted students. Planning for ways to address the unique issues and the lack of resources and skills that gifted students of poverty experience is a key element in their development (Slocumb & Payne, 2000). Low-income Caucasian gifted students may experience a number of social and emotional issues related to the combination of their poverty and their giftedness. For example, some students may feel they have to give up their nongifted friends. They may feel unaccepted by middle-class gifted students. They may lack awareness of the hidden rules of the middle class (Slocumb & Payne, 2000). To address these issues, the sixth guideline ensures that these students have specialized guidance and counseling, before- and afterschool programs, and summer programs. This continuum of services extends beyond the gifted classroom and offers low-income gifted students opportunities for enrichment and exposure, skill development, and leadership development.

Conclusion

This group of gifted students has much resilience, creativity, and intelligence and deserves our continued attention. It is not clear that being White affects student performance to any degree; the important factor creating obstacles for members of this group appears to be their poverty rather than their race. In fact, the idea that White privilege operates in any meaningful way for this group is challenged by the stories of these 13 students. Many promising practices exist that need to be implemented more often and more consistently for positive impact on these learners. Actively working to reduce the number of children in poverty through means that extend beyond the classroom door is one underlying solution. At the school level, educators can make certain they seek to find more low-income gifted learners. They can educate themselves about ways to develop the potential of these students. They can design and implement programs that provide the academic and affective development and support these promising learners need.

References

Barone, D., & Schneider, R. (2003). Turning the looking glass inside out: A gifted student in an at-risk setting. *Gifted Child Quarterly, 47*, 259–271.

Begoray, D., & Slovinsky, K. (1997). Pearls in shells: Preparing teachers to accommodate gifted low income populations. *Roeper Review, 20,* 45–49.

Borland, J. (2004). *Issues and practices in the identification and education of gifted students from underrepresented groups.* Storrs: University of Connecticut, The National Research Center on the Gifted and Talented.

Brewer, E. (2005). A longitudinal study of the talent search program. *Journal of Career Development, 31,* 195–208.

Brown, E., Avery, L., & VanTassel-Baska, J. (2003). *Gifted policy analysis study for the Ohio Department of Education.* Williamsburg, VA: The College of William and Mary, Center for Gifted Education.

Burney, V. H., & Beilke, J. R. (2008). The constraints of poverty on high achievement. *Journal for the Education of the Gifted, 31,* 295–321.

Burney, V. H., & Cross, T. L. (2006). Impoverished students with academic promise in rural settings: 10 lessons from Project Aspire. *Gifted Child Today, 29,* 14–21.

Dusek, J. B., & Joseph, G. (1983). The bases of teacher expectancies: A meta-analysis. *Journal of Educational Psychology, 75,* 327–346.

Frasier, M. M., Hunsaker, S. L., Lee, J., Finley, V. S., Frank, E., & Garcia, J. H. (1995). *Educators' perceptions of barriers to the identification of gifted children from economically disadvantaged and limited English proficient backgrounds.* Storrs: University of Connecticut, The National Research Center on the Gifted and Talented.

Griffith, J. (1998). The relation of school structure and social environment to parent involvement in elementary schools. *The Elementary School Journal, 99,* 53–81.

Hébert, T. (2002). Educating gifted children from low socioeconomic backgrounds: Creating visions of a hopeful future. *Exceptionality, 10,* 127–138.

Hodgkinson, H. (2007). Leaving too many children behind: A demographer's view on the neglect of America's youngest children. In J. VanTassel-Baska & T. Stambaugh (Eds.), *Overlooked gems: A national perspective on low-income promising learners* (pp. 7–20). Washington, DC: National Association for Gifted Children.

Hunsaker, S. (1995). *Family influences on the achievement of economically disadvantaged students: Implications for gifted identification and programming.* Storrs: University of Connecticut, The National Research Center on the Gifted and Talented.

Jatko, B. P. (1995). Action research and practical inquiry: Using a whole class tryout procedure for identifying economically disadvantaged students in three socioeconomically diverse schools. *Journal for the Education of the Gifted, 19,* 83–105.

Jimerson, S. R., Egeland, B., & Sroufe, L. A. (2000). A prospective longitudinal study of high school dropouts: Examining multiple predictors across development. *Journal of School Psychology, 38,* 525–549.

Kitano, M. K., & Lewis, R. B. (2005). Resilience and coping: Implications for gifted children and youth at risk. *Roeper Review, 27,* 200–205.

Moon, T. R., & Callahan, C. M. (2001). Curricular modifications, family outreach, and a mentoring program. *Journal for the Education of the Gifted, 24,* 305–321.

Newberg, N. A. (2006). *The gift of education: How a tuition guarantee program changed the lives of inner-city youth.* New York: State University of New York Press.

Olszewski-Kubilius, P., Grant, B., & Seibert, C. (1994). Social support systems and the disadvantaged gifted: A framework for developing programs and services. *Roeper Review, 17,* 20–25.

Piirto, J. (2007). *Talented children and adults: Their development and education* (3rd ed.). Waco, TX: Prufrock Press.

Robinson, A., Shore, B. M., & Enersen, D. (2007). *Best practices in gifted education: An evidence-based guide.* Waco, TX: Prufrock Press.

Robinson, N. (2003). Two wrongs do not make a right: Sacrificing the needs of gifted students does not solve society's unsolved problems. *Journal for the Education of the Gifted, 26,* 251–273.

Robinson, N. M., Lanzi, R. G., Weinberg, R. A., Ramey, S. L., & Ramey, C. T. (2002). Factors associated with high academic competence in former Head Start children at third grade. *Gifted Child Quarterly, 46,* 281–294.

Sennett, R., & Cobb, J. (1972). *The hidden injuries of class.* New York: Knopf.

Shumow, L. (1997). Daily experiences and adjustment of gifted low-income urban children at home and school. *Roeper Review 20,* 35–39.

Slocumb, P. D., & Payne, R. K. (2000). *Removing the mask: Giftedness in poverty.* Highlands, TX: Aha! Process.

Swanson, J. D. (2006). Breaking through assumptions about low-income, minority gifted students. *Gifted Child Quarterly, 50,* 11–25.

VanTassel-Baska, J., & Feng, A. (2006). *Project STAR two year research study* (Unpublished report). Columbia, SC: South Carolina Department of Education.

VanTassel-Baska, J., Feng, A., & deBrux, E. (2007). A longitudinal study of identification and performance profiles of Project STAR performance task–identified gifted students. *Journal for the Education of the Gifted, 31,* 7–34.

VanTassel-Baska, J., Feng, A., & Evans, B. (2007). Patterns of identification and performance among gifted students identified through performance tasks: A three year analysis. *Gifted Child Quarterly, 51,* 218–231.

VanTassel-Baska, J., Feng, A., Swanson, J. D., Quek, C., & Chandler, K. (2009). *The benefits of performance-based gifted identification approaches on middle school students' academic and affective profiles.* Manuscript submitted for publication.

VanTassel-Baska, J., Feng, A., Quek, C., & Struck, J. (2004). A study of educators' and students' perceptions of academic success for underrepresented populations identified for gifted programs. *Psychological Science, 46,* 363–378.

VanTassel-Baska, J., Johnson, D., & Avery, L. (2002). Using performance tasks in the identification of economically disadvantaged and minority gifted learners: Findings from Project STAR. *Gifted Child Quarterly, 46,* 110–123.

VanTassel-Baska, J., Olszewski-Kubilius, P., & Kulieke, M. (1994). A study of self-concept and social support in advantaged and disadvantaged seventh and eighth grade gifted students. *Roeper Review, 16,* 186–191.

VanTassel-Baska, J., Patton, J., & Prillaman, D. (1991). *Gifted youth at risk: A report of a national study.* Reston, VA: Council for Exceptional Children.

VanTassel-Baska, J., & Stambaugh, T. (2006). *Comprehensive curriculum for gifted learners* (3rd ed.). Boston: Pearson.

The Patterns and Profiles of High Nonverbal, Low Verbal Gifted Learners

Julie Dingle Swanson

Introduction

This chapter focuses on students with a unique profile of being strong in nonverbal areas but much lower in verbal abilities, a group that is surfacing with some regularity now that nonverbal tests are being used more frequently in schools. This particular group is included in the discussion of low-income gifted because of the prevailing view that strong nonverbal aptitudes are found in culturally different youngsters (e.g., Native Americans, African Americans, English language learners). We know that culturally different children often are found in poverty at higher rates, so discussion of this subset of gifted learners offers the opportunity to learn more about how to recognize and nurture giftedness in underserved groups. A literature review exploring aspects relevant to this special population opens the chapter. Aspects of the review include a working definition of high nonverbal, low verbal giftedness; identification route influences; student performance; and learning needs and supports, styles, and preferences. Drawing on case study findings of special needs gifted learners, this chapter discusses unique characteristics, educational needs, learning opportunities, and similarities/differences in student, parent, and teacher perspectives found in this special needs group. Examples and quotations from student vignettes illustrate these perspectives. Through integration of the literature and the case study findings, this chapter then provides ideas for school-based practitioners and gifted coordinators in the development of gifted high nonverbal, low verbal children.

What Research Tells Us

New, broader conceptions of giftedness (e.g., Gardner, 1983; Sternberg, 1986) have led to new ways of identifying gifted learners. This shift in thinking about the nature of giftedness and how it manifests itself is partly the result of the quest for inclusion of gifted students historically underrepresented in gifted programs and partly the result of new and evolving theories of intelligence. Past identification of the gifted focused primarily on students who performed well verbally, whether on an IQ or aptitude test or an achievement test based on a high level of verbal competency. As our understanding about the nature of intelligence has grown, many identification protocols have expanded to include assessments that provide evidence of domain-specific talent and nonverbal strengths.

This evolution in practice has increased diversity in the pool of identified gifted students. The archetype of the general intellectually gifted student—the one who reads extensively, has an extraordinary vocabulary, and is highly adept in any task using language—is no longer the norm in many gifted programs. Use of multiple criteria for identification, supported in research as a best practice (Robinson, Shore, & Enersen, 2007), contributes to the diversity we now see in our gifted learners. Student diversity leads to the need for deeper understanding of the strengths, preferences, and learning styles of these varied gifted learners so that well-designed programs may develop their potential. Discussion in this chapter centers around one prototype of these diverse gifted learners, the high nonverbal, low verbal student.

High Nonverbal, Low Verbal Gifted Learner: A Working Definition

High nonverbal, low verbal gifted learners are students with "uneven" profiles, who demonstrate evidence of strong and specific abilities in the areas of mathematical and spatial reasoning and average or lower abilities in verbal reasoning (VanTassel-Baska & Feng, 2006). Generally, their traits and behaviors include strong reasoning and logic, creativity, desire for active, hands-on engagement in learning, and high mathematical and science performance. Some exhibit low confidence and self-efficacy in their abilities and may have perfectionistic tendencies. A minority in the gifted population, the high nonverbal, low verbal gifted youngster's strengths are neither easily recognizable in school settings nor are his or her talents always assessed in identification procedures. High nonverbal, low verbal gifted learners often have domain-specific talent (e.g., mathematical, scientific, and/or spatial abilities). Research on specific characteristics and traits of high nonverbal, low verbal gifted learners is sparse (VanTassel-Baska & Feng, 2006; VanTassel-Baska, Feng, Swanson, Quek, & Chandler, 2009).

Students gifted in the visual-spatial domain can be considered a subgroup of the high nonverbal learners, and some research on this subgroup is reported in the literature. Lohman (1994) described common characteristics of "high spatial" children:

> Potential for visual-spatial creativity of a high order seems most likely to be revealed and/or fostered in a child: (a) who is kept home from school during the early school years and, perhaps, is relatively isolated from agemates as well, (b) who is, if anything, slower in language development, and (c) who is furnished with and becomes unusually engrossed in playing with concrete physical objects, mechanical models, geometrical puzzles, or simply wooden cubes. (p. 256)

Silverman (2005) identified similar traits in what she termed "defining characteristics of visual-spatial gifted learners" (p. 11). She stated that they:

> . . . do extraordinarily well on tasks with spatial compo-
> nents: solving puzzles, tracing mazes, duplicating block
> designs, counting three-dimensional arrays of blocks,
> visual transformations, mental rotations . . . Their
> learning is holistic and occurs in an all-or-none fashion.
> They are most likely to experience the "Aha!" phenom-
> enon, when all of a sudden they "see it." Many have a
> photographic visual memory: they can visually recall
> anywhere they have ever been and how to get there . . .
> These children like to see how things work, and they
> enjoy pulling things apart to see if they can reconstruct
> them. They enjoy novelty and challenge . . . [They]
> have talent in fields such as mathematics, science, com-
> puter science, architecture, engineering. [They] may
> dislike school because of the overemphasis on lecturing,
> rote memorization, drill and practice exercises, and the
> lack of sufficient stimulation of their powerful abstract
> visual reasoning abilities. (p. 11)

Some of the traits are like those of many gifted youngsters (e.g., strong recall, desire for challenge, and dislike of drill and practice). The known difference between the high nonverbal, low verbal gifted youngster and the "traditional" gifted young-ster is the uneven profile, with the high nonverbal, low ver-bal gifted learner exhibiting strong abilities in one domain and average or lower abilities in other domains related to language and linguistic abilities.

Bracken and McCallum (1998) made a distinction between nonverbal assessment, nonverbal intellectual assessment, and nonverbal intelligence. Nonverbal assessment has been defined as a "test administration process in which no receptive or expres-sive language demands are placed on either the examinee or the examiner" (Bracken & Naglieri, 2003, p. 246). Nonverbal intellectual assessment is a process of assessing ability, or gen-eral intelligence, in ways that "do not require examinees to understand spoken language or to express themselves verbally" (Bracken & Naglieri, 2003, p. 246). Bracken and Naglieri contended that what many refer to as nonverbal intelligence is more accurately described as "general intelligence measured nonverbally" (p. 246). Bracken and Naglieri argued that traditional, "language-loaded" IQ tests and nonverbal intellectual assessments "measure essentially the same construct" (p. 247). Their theoretical position on nonverbal intelligence matches the reality: the high nonverbal, low verbal gifted students studied by VanTassel-Baska and colleagues (under review) exhibited many traits and characteristics common to gifted learners. Results from the longitudinal study of Lubinski and Benbow (2006; Wai, Lubinski, & Benbow, in press) of spatially gifted learners found a clear preference for such students toward careers in the physical sciences and engineering. These researchers would argue that many highly gifted students with predominant spatial abilities are overlooked for gifted programs because they do not meet verbal cutoff scores.

Identification Route Influences

For more than a decade, in attempts to find underserved students, more nontraditional approaches to identification have been utilized (Hunsaker, 1994). Because many identification protocols depend on mainstream language skills, thinking and problem-solving abilities of nonverbal gifted youngsters are not necessarily evident in more traditional identification methods (i.e., IQ scores, aptitude testing, and achievement testing). Nonverbal assessment, dynamic assessment, and performance tasks have helped to make gifted learners from different backgrounds more identifiable (Angelelli, Enright, & Valdes, 2002; Ford, 1995; Kirschenbaum, 1998; Naglieri & Ford, 2003; Spicker, Fletcher, Montgomery, & Breard, 1993; VanTassel-Baska, Johnson, & Avery, 2002). Nonverbal assessments reveal students' ability to recognize patterns and relationships and to solve problems, so their use has enabled identification of students who may differ from the mainstream culturally or linguistically (Lewis, 2001). Cattell Culture Fair Intelligence Test (Cattell & Cattell, 1965), the

Naglieri Nonverbal Ability Test (Naglieri, 1997), and the Raven Standard Progressive Matrices (Raven, 1947) are commonly recommended nonverbal assessments used in identifying gifted learners (Robinson et al., 2007). Lohman (2008) cautioned educators "to be skeptical about national norms [of nonverbal assessment tools], especially when they administer tests normed on populations different from the population of interest" (p. 7). For example, he stated that norms of the Cattell Culture Fair Intelligence Test ". . . were woefully inadequate when the test was published" (p. 2) and offered further discussion of potential problems with the norms of the Raven Standard Progressive Matrices (Raven) and the Naglieri Nonverbal Ability Test (NNAT). The Raven is a nonverbal ability test with figural reasoning and analogies. Lohman (2008) noted that the Raven's 1986 U.S. norms ". . . are markedly easier than the 2000 CogAT (Cognitive Abilities Test) and the 1995–96 NNAT norms" (p. 2). The NNAT tests nonverbal reasoning and problem solving through pattern completion, reasoning by analogy, serial reasoning, and spatial visualization.

In his discussion of research comparing CogAT, the Raven, and the NNAT, Lohman (2008) laid out clear evidence of flaws in often-used nonverbal assessments and advised that "it is wrong to assume that nonverbal tests level the playing field for children who come from different cultures or who have had different educational opportunities" (pp. 6–7). He asserted that using a "good nonverbal reasoning test" as part of a more comprehensive assessment of potential "can help identify bright children, especially those who come from low-SES families or who are not fluent in the language of the dominant culture" (p. 7).

There is disagreement about the effectiveness of nonverbal intellectual assessment as a means to identify culturally different gifted learners. Lohman (2005) took issue with results of Naglieri and Ford's 2003 study of the use of the NNAT, which claimed identification of gifted students from varied ethnic groups at proportionate rates. Further, Lohman (2008) presented data analyses from two studies that indicated that there are issues with the norms of both the Raven and the NNAT. He provided evidence that the NNAT scores can be much more variable (i.e., higher and lower scores). Lohman's concerns appear grounded in evidence presented thus far and remind us of the importance of utilizing reliable and valid assessment tools to find bright students.

Naglieri and Ford (2005) strongly rebuffed Lohman's view that nonverbal ability tests should be part of a more comprehensive approach when they wrote, "We reject an emphasis on 'academically gifted' children that excludes the identification of 'intellectually gifted' children who happen to have poor academic skills" (p. 29). They believed that the perceived difference between ability and achievement is muddy at best among many educators, and that lack of distinction between the two "has corrupted the very concept of ability in such a way that any child who does not have an adequately enriched educational experience will be at a disadvantage when assessed with a so-called 'ability' test like the CogAt" (Naglieri & Ford, 2005, p. 33). Naglieri and Ford were concerned with this "theoretical blurring of lines" between achievement and ability and agreed with Bracken and McCallum's (1998) position that nonverbal intellectual assessment is a process for assessing general intellectual ability, not academic achievement. Naglieri and Ford (2005) believed that nonverbal assessment is "more appropriate, or fair, for culturally and linguistically diverse students" (p. 32) and contended that their 2003 study provided data to support that assertion. Other researchers have not been able to replicate the evidence from Naglieri and Ford's 2003 study. Clearly, there is not agreement on the reliability of some nonverbal ability tests nor on sole reliance of these tests to identify giftedness.

Nasca's (1998) study on the use of nonverbal instruments in combination with verbal instruments showed that the use of both favored identification of high nonverbal, low verbal youngsters as gifted. Lewis (2001) concurred that a need exists for the use of nonverbal assessments as part of screening and identification of gifted students. She noted that more research needs to be done on the use of nonverbal assessments, but agreed with others that the combination of verbal and nonverbal assessment is the best approach at this time.

Although not a type of nonverbal assessment, dynamic assessment shows promise as a tool to find gifted students who are difficult to identify. Dynamic assessment (Kirschenbaum, 1998), or assessment of student ability after teaching students strategies they will need to use on specific cognitive tasks, has been used successfully in finding underrepresented gifted students. This tool provides insight into how students learn to think through and solve a problem. For youngsters whose talents and abilities may have not yet been revealed, it provides the teacher with a tool to reveal those talents and abilities.

In an effort to develop a nontraditional assessment protocol to enhance a statewide identification procedure, Project STAR (VanTassel-Baska et al., 2002) utilized dynamic assessment as part of performance tasks that made up the nontraditional assessment. Dynamic assessment in Project STAR is noteworthy because domain-specific protocols were developed to "tap into verbal, mathematical, and spatial abilities" (VanTassel-Baska et al., 2002, p. 115). Domain-specific assessment in this study was an effective way to find high nonverbal gifted youngsters even though they had average or lower verbal ability.

What are performance tasks and how do they relate to high nonverbal, low verbal gifted students? The performance tasks developed through Project STAR (VanTassel-Baska et al., 2002) were designed to enhance the identification of low-income and minority gifted students by "trying to tap into fluid, rather than crystallized abilities" (p. 114). The development and use of performance tasks in combination with preteaching proved to be successful in finding more diverse gifted learners (e.g., from low-income backgrounds and African American students; VanTassel-Baska et al., 2002). Performance tasks included elements of good curriculum for gifted students, such as open-endedness, higher level thinking and problem solving, and metacognition. In addition to finding more underrepresented gifted learners, more students with uneven profiles (i.e., students with strengths either in the verbal domain or the nonverbal domain) were identified as gifted in this study.

Project STAR's performance tasks included both verbal and nonverbal tasks. The nonverbal performance tasks began as two categories of tasks: mathematical thinking and reasoning and spatial thinking and reasoning. During the development of the performance tasks, these separate categories evolved into one, the nonverbal domain (VanTassel-Baska et al., 2002). Nonverbal performance tasks included (VanTassel-Baska et al., 2002):

   a. arithmetic problem solving, advanced problem solving with number facts and place value;

   b. number concepts, utilizing number relationships;

   c. logic, emphasizing quantitative reasoning;

   d. proportional reasoning, based on ratio and proportion;

   e. patterns, including "recognition, extension, description, and analysis";

   f. number theory, involving factors and multiples;

   g. spatial reasoning and visualization, thinking about, moving, and representing figures;

   h. spatial patterning, drawing conclusions from patterns; and

   i. geometry, utilizing concepts of area, perimeter, and parts of the whole. (pp. 115–116)

Nonverbal performance tasks were developed in the areas above, with preteaching, the use of manipulatives in solving the task, and drawing upon "contextual performance" with "no assumption of prior learning" (VanTassel-Baska et al., 2002, p. 115). High scores on the nonverbal performance tasks were one indicator of strong nonverbal abilities.

In a follow-up study of performance task-identified students, one of several student prototypes studied was the high nonverbal, low verbal gifted student (VanTassel-Baska et al., 2009). This research revealed some patterns and traits in this group of gifted learners; those findings will be explicated in the second part of this chapter. This group of high nonverbal, low verbal students was of interest for two reasons. First, these students had an "unbalanced profile." The data reported indicated that the majority of identified gifted students in South Carolina (where the study was conducted) qualified as gifted through a combination of verbal and nonverbal assessment on two of the three state-required dimensions (ability, achievement, and performance tasks). Their profiles were unbalanced because rather than a combination of verbal and nonverbal strengths, their strength was in the nonverbal area only. The second reason this subpopulation was of interest was that data indicated that the high nonverbal, low verbal gifted students were a minority in the state gifted population. Understanding more about this particular subpopulation, their learning needs, and similarities and differences with other subgroups within the gifted population was another basis for further study.

Student Performance

Analysis of achievement data in the Project STAR longitudinal study (VanTassel-Baska & Feng, 2006) revealed higher performance on state language arts tests of verbally identified gifted students over nonverbally identified gifted students. Although there was a difference in mathematics performance of the nonverbal gifted students over the verbally gifted, the difference was small. Also significant was that a "higher percentage of low income African American students who had one strength area qualified through the nonverbal/quantitative dimension" (VanTassel-Baska & Feng, 2006, p. 22).

In a study of high school students gifted in spatial ability, Gohm, Humphreys, and Yao (1998) compared these students with students gifted in mathematics. The sample was drawn from a data bank of high school students first tested in the 1960s. Their findings indicated that the gifted spatial group was underachieving in comparison to the gifted mathematics group. Gohm and colleagues stated:

> Results indicate that, relative to the students gifted in mathematics, the students high in spatial ability were not fully utilizing their academic capabilities, had interests that were less compatible with traditional coursework, received less college guidance from school personnel, were less motivated by the education experience, and aspired to, and achieved lower levels of academic and occupational success. (p. 515)

These results suggest that teachers and counselors might do more to encourage gifted spatial learners to take more rigorous courses and expose them to professions related to their high abilities.

Learning Needs and Supports, Styles, and Preferences

West (1997) investigated how visual talent and verbal weakness played out in the lives of eminent persons (e.g., Albert Einstein, Thomas Edison, and Leonardo da Vinci). He cited research in neuroscience and the possibility that visual-spatial strength and low verbal ability may be connected. In Bloom's (1985) study of talent development, a third of the eminent mathematicians studied did not learn to read easily or before they entered school. In a review of research, von Karolyi and Winner (2004) reported evidence that visual-spatial talent and reading difficulties "can co-occur" (p. 98).

In a longitudinal study of participants in the Study of Mathematically Precocious Youth (SMPY), Webb, Lubinski, and Benbow (2002) explored achievement relative to high school course-taking patterns and undergraduate coursework, preferences, and future plans. The study followed approximately 1,100 students over a 20-year period, from age 13 to age 33. The study had two phases. First, researchers wanted to find out what differentiates mathematically gifted students planning to major in math and/or science as they began their undergraduate studies from others (also mathematically gifted) who majored in other disciplines. In the study's second phase, researchers investigated what happened to the persons who moved out of math/science (called the "non-math-science group") and those who stayed in math/science (called the "math-science group"). Of particular interest to researchers in this study was how gender contributed (or did not) to the educational and vocational choices and outcomes of the individuals. Data indicated more males than females followed the path of a math/science undergraduate degree and a vocation in a math/science field. Related to this finding was that individual interest was the main basis of choices made on whether to pursue math/science studies or studies in other areas. Webb et al. inferred that a possible reason for the gender differences may be that more males in their study had uneven profiles. Referring to an independent study conducted in 2001 by Lubinski, Webb, Morelock, and Benbow, Webb et al. observed that the students in the 2001 study with "high-math tilted profiles (math scores at least 1 SD above their verbal scores) were much more likely to pursue math-science degrees than those with high-flat profiles (more uniform math and verbal scores)" (p. 790). The 2001 study findings were consistent with the 2002 findings in that the males did have "high-math tilted profiles" (p. 791) more often than the females, who had more even profiles. Webb at al. concluded that attention focused on individual differences reflected in the profiles instead of gender differences would enable more effective guidance of gifted students.

Brain research on mathematical talent synthesized by Sousa (2003) indicated that "[e]xact computation seems related to verbal language skills, while approximate computation is related to visual-spatial skills" (p. 138). Based on this research, Sousa hypothesized that exact, precise mathematical computation and verbal language skills are connected. On the approximation skills, he speculated that the area of the brain called the "Einstein area" active in approximation may allow "neural networks the freedom to focus on holistic relationships and patterns rather than to get bogged down in handling discreet numbers" (p. 138). From a study on Einstein's brain, researchers quoted Einstein's description of his thinking: "Words do not seem to play a role," but there is "associative play" of "more or less clear images" of a "visual and muscular type" (Witelson, Kigar, & Harvey, 1999, p. 2149).

Silverman and others at the Gifted Development Center in Denver, CO, have studied visual-spatial learners for more than 20 years. Silverman (2005) made a distinction between two learning styles—auditory-sequential and visual-spatial. For example, the auditory-sequential learner "thinks primarily in words, has auditory strengths, relates well to time, [and] is a step-by-step learner" (Silverman, 2005, p. 3). In contrast, the visual-spatial learner "thinks primarily in pictures, has visual strengths, relates well to space, [and] is a whole-part learner" (p. 3). Silverman's research indicated that about 30% of the school population is strongly visual-spatial in preferred learning style. She recommended effective teaching strategies to use with visual-spatial learners. Those strategies and possible applications to high nonverbal, low verbal gifted students will be discussed in the last part of the chapter under recommendations.

Beyond the work done through Project STAR research (VanTassel-Baska, Feng, & deBrux, 2007; VanTassel-Baska, Feng, & Evans, 2007) and Silverman's (2005) study of gifted learners who are visual-spatial, relevant literature on the high nonverbal, low verbal gifted student is primarily comprised of research on nonverbal assessments utilized as identification tools. Studies on the brain present some evidence of different patterns of brain functioning with individuals who have low verbal abilities and visual talent. The lack of research raises questions about whether we are doing as much as we can to find and develop talent in mathematics, scientific reasoning, and visual-spatial fields such as architecture, technology, and engineering.

In the next section, we explore case findings to better understand the uniqueness of this gifted learner (VanTassel-Baska et al., 2009). The reader is cautioned not to generalize these case findings to other high nonverbal, low verbal gifted students.

Case Study Findings

Unique characteristics, educational needs, and learning strengths and preferences of this particular population of youngsters are drawn from a larger longitudinal study of 37 special needs gifted learners (VanTassel-Baska et al., 2009). In the larger study, cases were developed on five different gifted student prototypes: low-income African American, low-income Caucasian, low-income other minority, twice-exceptional, and high nonverbal, low verbal gifted students. The cases were developed from extensive interviews of middle school students, their parents, their gifted teacher, and their science teacher. At the time of the study, students were in the seventh and eighth grades. The students were enrolled in four school districts that employed varied gifted program service models. Table 8.1 provides an overview of the nine high nonverbal, low verbal gifted students in the study. Gender, identification, school performance, and strengths and weaknesses were included in the demographic data; income level was not included.

Table 8.1
High Nonverbal, Low Verbal Gifted Students

Students (n = 9)	Gender	Traditional Identification	Nontraditional	School Performance	Strengths/ Weaknesses
Adele	Female		Yes	GPA = 3.9	Perfectionist
Alex	Male		Yes	GPA = 3.5	Reading difficulties addressed in IEP
Barry	Male		Yes	Not reported	Underachieving
Butler	Male		Yes	ELA = A Math = F	Nonconformist; creative thinker
Elizabeth	Female	Yes		ELA = C Math = B Science = A	Strong mathematical abilities
Melody	Female	Yes		GPA = 3.0	Self-esteem issues; perfectionist
Violet	Female	Yes		Math = A ELA = B	High in algebra; low motivation
Savannah	Female		Yes	Has all A's and B's	Leadership; perfectionist
Bronwyn	Female		Yes	ELA = A Math = B Science = A	Creativity and leadership; perfectionist

Note. GPA = grade point average; ELA = English/language arts.

Of the nine students, the majority (n = 6) were identified through nontraditional measures, the STAR performance tasks in combination with aptitude or achievement scores, and the remaining students were identified through traditional means. Traditional means of identification were defined in this study as aptitude and achievement testing and school performance as indicated by grades. All of these students perceived participation in gifted programs positively. They recognized the benefits of being identified as gifted and placed in gifted classes and at the same time were keenly aware of the increased expectations. Butler, an eighth grader in a suburban middle school stated,

The [gifted program] is for gifted people, and it lets people do things their own way. At home I skateboard. There's this newspaper article where a guy said [skateboarding is] better than a team sport because you can express your talents without a coach telling you what to do. I think that's the same way the [gifted program] is because you can do your stuff like that without being told to do it in certain terms. (VanTassel-Baska & Feng, 2006, p. 129)

The majority of these high nonverbal students were female (*n* = 6). Almost all of the high nonverbal, low verbal students' school performance was above average. The one exception was Butler, who was failing mathematics but had A's in all other subjects. Most of the nine youngsters were served in both English/language arts and mathematics gifted classes. Program placement was of note, because even though students had average ability in verbal areas, they were placed in gifted language arts classes and most were performing well. Several were described as perfectionists, underachieving, or unmotivated in some area. All but one was Caucasian. As a group, these students were perceived as creative learners who enjoyed hands-on and active engagement.

Common strengths and favorite subjects cited by these youngsters were mathematics and/or science, and they preferred hands-on, creative, and active learning in classroom activities. Parents concurred with what students said about their strengths and preferences. Several teachers noted the strong reasoning, problem solving, and high level of creativity they observed in these students. The cases provide a snapshot of each student at a particular point in time, and data from the cases offer evidence and further details on these students' lives.

Identification Route

The disparity between verbal and nonverbal ability mentioned previously about this group of high nonverbal, low verbal gifted students is an important facet of this profile. Table 8.2 shows the identification data on Alex, Barry, and Violet to illustrate the uneven profiles of high ability in nonverbal mea-

Table 8.2
Identification Data to Illustrate Uneven Profiles

Student	Aptitude Dimension	Achievement Dimension	Performance Dimension
Alex	N/A	MAT: Math Concepts subtest = 95%ile	STAR Performance Tasks: Nonverbal Score = 17 (85%) Verbal Score = 8 (40%)
Barry	TCS: Total aptitude = 91%ile Verbal aptitude = 68%ile Nonverbal aptitude = 95%ile	N/A	STAR Performance Tasks: Nonverbal Score = 16 (80%) Verbal Score = 8 (40%)
Violet	OLSAT: Verbal aptitude = 57%ile Nonverbal aptitude = 94%ile	MAT: Math Concepts subtest = 97%ile Reading subtest = 67%ile	N/A

Note. TCS = Test of Cognitive Skills; MAT = Metropolitan Achievement Test; OLSAT = Otis-Lennon School Ability Test; N/A = not applicable sures and of average or below ability in verbal measures that were characteristic of this group of students.

Both Alex and Barry were identified through a combination of traditional measures of aptitude and achievement (e.g., tests such as Test of Cognitive Skills [TCS], Otis-Lennon School Ability Test [OLSAT], Metropolitan Achievement Test [MAT]) and nontraditional measures of performance assessment (STAR). Data in Table 8.2 on Alex's identification show a high level of mathematical achievement in combination with a high performance on the nonverbal tasks of STAR. His performance on the verbal tasks of STAR is below average. In Table 8.2, Barry's high performance in the 95th percentile on the nonverbal portion of the TCS and a score of 80th percentile on the nonverbal portion of STAR stand in contrast to his TCS verbal aptitude in the 68th percentile and his score of 40% on the verbal portion of the STAR performance tasks.

The third example shown in Table 8.2 is Violet, a student identified through aptitude and achievement. Violet exemplifies a traditionally identified gifted student. Her unbalanced profile shows how domain-specific ability in mathematics might create the perception that she is not "truly gifted," a phrase sometimes used to describe gifted learners who do not fit the commonly held stereotypical notion that gifted students are strong in all academic areas.

An issue related to the lopsided abilities of these students is what teachers may not see. Teacher perceptions may impact the student's confidence and self-esteem, either positively or negatively. Adele's gifted program teacher commented on the support provided as she worked with Adele, a nontraditionally identified student, to help Adele realize her strengths:

> We helped [Adele] to gain confidence. If she were in a classroom with someone who didn't get to know her, that would be a problem for her. [A teacher] with a flippant "You're in [the gifted program]?" attitude would cause Adele to stop asking questions. (VanTassel-Baska & Feng, 2006, p. 120)

Data from Elizabeth's case illustrate the very different perceptions of her held by significant adults in her life. Elizabeth's mother saw her giftedness clearly and at an early age, but her science teacher saw Elizabeth as "ordinary" and stated, "She's nothing exceptional but is a good kid" (VanTassel-Baska & Feng, 2006, p. 134).

Clearly the identification route is key in finding high nonverbal, low verbal gifted students because teachers may not always recognize student potential, especially when the student's abilities are uneven. Rather than using traditional measures alone, the use of multiple measures, combining traditional measures and performance-based measures, enabled identification of more gifted youngsters with uneven profiles.

Strength Areas, Preferences, and Learning Style

Not surprisingly, the majority of these gifted learners preferred mathematics and science as their favorite subjects. Barry said, "I am not that great of a writer . . . Math is pretty easy for me. I play piano and it helps out in math" (VanTassel-Baska & Feng, 2006, p. 125). Alex's teacher commented on his academic strength in mathematics and science and his love for research and use of technology. She stated, "He could see solutions of problems before questions were even asked" (VanTassel-Baska & Feng, 2006, p. 123). Melody was more comfortable in mathematics and said her strength is science. She noted, "I know I can do better in math and I want to learn everything . . . I like [science because I like] learning about what we live in and the world around us" (VanTassel-Baska & Feng, 2006, p. 136).

Teachers and parents noticed students' strength in reasoning, problem solving, and creativity; active learning also was observed as a preferred style. The cases of most of these youngsters provided evidence that active, hands-on learning was the preferred style. The following excerpts provide evidence from the cases of strong reasoning, critical thinking, and problem solving and predilection for active engagement in learning.

An illustration of the strong creative abilities observed in this group of youngsters is Butler whose teacher described him as a "sleeper" who would surprise her and his classmates with his original thinking. "He seemed so introverted but would 'wow' us. He would be so dramatic and creative." [His teacher] also noted that he "thinks outside the box" and is not afraid to be different (VanTassel-Baska & Feng, 2006, p. 131). For example, Butler won the poet laureate award for his class because he "wrote from his heart" (p. 131).

Alex's teacher observed how his ideas were unique and different. She discussed some of his learning preferences (i.e., his need for active, hands-on learning):

> During the 2 years she taught Alex, [his gifted class teacher] found him to be a "very creative child" who often came up with ideas that other students never thought of, noting that ". . . he could figure out different ways to solve a problem. He looked at a different perspective and used a variety of lenses." She saw him as a tactile learner, noting that he had very strong problem-solving ability and learned better with his hands. "When I teach him, I better have manipulatives. When something was broken, my students always came to get help from Alex." (VanTassel-Baska & Feng, 2006, p. 123)

One of Elizabeth's teachers commented on her strengths. Her teacher stated, "Elizabeth learns quickly and works well with spatial tasks, and is above average on creativity. She will expand, do a lot with project work" (VanTassel-Baska & Feng, 2006, p. 134). Elizabeth's mother observed that hands-on, active learning was important to Elizabeth and noted that Elizabeth was strong in creativity and logical thinking. The strengths exemplified above show that creativity and reasoning were evident in the students studied.

Adele's teacher discussed how she utilized Adele's learning preference in her class. "Adele is more of a hands-on type of student. In our classroom, the thinking skills activities were very challenging to her. On her contract, I always try to put one hands-on activity" (VanTassel-Baska & Feng, 2006, p. 120). This active style is consistent with Silverman's (2005) research on gifted visual-spatial learners. The example below of building in a hands-on project further illustrates the point that high nonverbal, low verbal students' learning is enhanced with hands-on, active engagement as part of the process.

In responding to a question about what she likes best about her gifted program, Melody made distinctions between her elementary program and the middle school one: "I like using my hands. I'm not so good at writing. I like using my hands to learn. We would build bridges in elementary school" (VanTassel-Baska & Feng, 2006, p. 136).

Alex's comment provides additional evidence of "using hands" and combining visual cues and auditory cues to "learn easily":

> [Alex] desired better teachers who can make the class activities more interesting, saying, "I wish to have a wood class or workshop where I can use my hands." He summarized his learning strengths succinctly, "I learn easily by seeing and hearing it, and I remember a lot easier than just from reading it. I learn a bit faster in math than other students." Alex aspired to become an automobile or car designer some day. (VanTassel-Baska & Feng, 2006, p. 124)

Other traits, such as leadership, were noticed in some students. Leadership was a strong suit in Savannah and Bronwyn. Bronwyn's leadership was evident in her work on the school yearbook. Both of Savannah's teachers observed her leadership in classroom group work (e.g., science lab settings). Her mother commented on the strong leadership and creative abilities she saw in her daughter (e.g., Savannah's recent election to student council and selection as a school cheerleader; VanTassel-Baska & Feng, 2006, p. 142). Her science teacher observed the same talents, stating, "[Savannah's] leadership abilities also emerge in lab settings where she takes the responsibility for verbalizing questions and recording the group's responses" (VanTassel-Baska & Feng, 2006, p. 143).

With a clear idea in mind of the strengths, preferences, and styles of these high nonverbal, low verbal gifted students, the cases offer evidence that several of these students have social and emotional issues that should be taken into account. The next section discusses some of these issues.

Learning Needs and Supports: Perfectionism and Underachievement

Most of the high nonverbal, low verbal gifted students in the study demonstrated solid performance in school subjects, but they showed evidence of some of the common social and emotional issues and achievement problems that gifted learners face. Those issues include underachievement, perfectionism, and low motivation.

Using reported grades as an indicator of school performance, all of the high nonverbal, low verbal gifted students in this study were making A's and B's with the exception of Butler, already mentioned. Grades for Barry, a student described as underachieving, were not reported, but both of his teachers interviewed see him as not working up to his potential. Barry's English/language arts gifted teacher said,

> "I have not seen a gift in my classroom. He is easily distracted. I have to pull him back into focus often." In his regular science class, the teacher notes Barry is "hands-on." She, too, comments that he is easily distracted and does better in a small group setting . . . In his gifted English/language arts class, Barry is late and slow in turning in work. The teacher says, "He is a reluctant learner, an underachiever, and is not working up to potential." His science teacher comments, "He is not living up to his ability." (VanTassel-Baska & Feng, 2006, p. 127)

Barry's mother echoed what the teachers said about some of her son's skills; study skills and time management were definite areas of weakness that she saw in Barry.

Alex, an eighth grader, was not in the language arts strand of the gifted program because of an IEP resulting from problems he had in reading. The reading difficulty impacted his performance, as related below by Alex's mother.

> The mother noted Alex was at ease in learning audio-visually, noting that his preferred way of absorbing information was through watching and hearing rather

than reading and writing . . . She [stated,] "Alex had difficulty in putting down his ideas on paper. He could write a storybook but had no time for punctuation. He would like to tell you in every detail about the book he read rather than write it down." (VanTassel-Baska & Feng, 2006, p. 122)

Several students exhibited perfectionistic tendencies, and some suffered from related issues of self-esteem and lack of confidence. Melody, a seventh-grade African American female, articulated some of the challenges she faced. "I have trouble with reading, not understanding what I am reading. Compared to others in the [gifted] class, I'm in the middle. I'm an A-B-C student. In the regular classes, I'm good in social studies" (VanTassel-Baska & Feng, 2006, p. 136). Melody's mother described the change in her daughter's attitude toward the gifted program over the years. The mother noticed a change when she found Melody, upon return to her regular classroom after her pull-out gifted class, making up all of the work she missed in regular class while in gifted class. Melody's mother stated,

"They (the gifted learners) were taken out of the class for the program (from the regular class). [Melody] had the class work to make up. She couldn't go [to gifted class] because she hadn't finished the class work. That made her upset, and she would come home crying." In spite of the experiences in fifth grade, her mother felt that overall, the changes had been good. "[The gifted program] made her more positive about what she was doing. She has a cheery disposition. Melody is her own worst critic. She tears herself apart even though she did well." (VanTassel-Baska & Feng, 2006, p. 137)

Adele's mother commented on her daughter's perfectionism as being both a strength and weakness, saying,

"If it's not natural for her, she'll work on it until it's natural. She's never had anything below a 96 in middle school so far." Remarking about the negative aspects of perfectionism, [her mom] said, "She's gonna burn out, or she'll have high stress problems. She's not going to be able to put in perspective what's important." (VanTassel-Baska & Feng, 2006, p. 120)

Bronwyn's teachers saw the positive side of her desire for excellence.

Both [Bronwyn's] teachers see her as a lovely student who is artistically creative, highly motivated, strong in task management and organization, and a perfectionist. The language arts teacher found Bronwyn a straight A student and an excellent writer, elaborating that she is "meticulous" in that "she doesn't finish tasks as quickly as others . . . It takes her time. Things must be complete and done well." The science teacher echoed the gifted class teacher that Bronwyn is a perfectionist and very resilient. "She has been persistent in making sure that work is well done." (VanTassel-Baska & Feng, 2006, p. 83)

Research indicates that perfectionism is more common in gifted students than average achieving students (Schuler, 2002). These examples show both the positive and negative sides of perfectionism.

Lack of motivation and effort was a concern of Violet's teachers and her mother. They recognized her ability, but they observed that she appeared to have low self-esteem.

The middle school teacher cites her for not having the drive to succeed unless she is interested in the task, noting, "Motivation affected [Violet] not doing homework. There are times she would not turn things in . . . She would do minimal work to get by." Despite the minimal effort, she was able to do well on tests, suggesting a strong aptitude . . . [Her teachers notice] Violet appears to have low self-esteem, and has some difficulty in doing presentations in front of people . . . She prefers to do work alone, and has had some difficulty with group work. (VanTassel-Baska & Feng, 2006, p. 139)

Violet's mother stated, "Violet has a low motivation in learning, and would rather stay with a B as long as she does not have to put much effort into it" (VanTassel-Baska & Feng, 2006, p. 138). Examining the roots of Violet's low motivation and lack of effort could lead to interventions before the pattern of underachievement is established.

Creative Outlets: Hobbies and Interests

An aspect that stood out with these high nonverbal, low verbal gifted students was the creativity expressed through numerous hobbies and interests. Hobbies included skateboarding, Japanese cartoon animation, athletics, music, drawing, and collecting. Extracurricular activities included cheerleading, student council, and work on the school yearbook. Creative outlets such as these provided students with a focus other than academics. These hobbies were of particular importance to Violet, the student described above who has exhibited boredom and low motivation in her schoolwork. Her mother observed that she is much more relaxed at home and described her interest in nature study. Violet's mother and her teachers all commented on her other interest in Japanese cartoon animation.

Her mother notes that her daughter has been fascinated by Japanese cartoon animation since third or fourth grade to the extent that everything in her bedroom has been of Japanese style; she still has the hobby today without sign of decreasing interests. [Her mother] shares that Violet even taught herself Japanese and checked out books related to Japan from the library. (VanTassel-Baska & Feng, 2006, p. 139)

Barry's mother mentioned her son's hobbies: piano, basketball, tennis, and robotics. Butler loved skateboarding, drawing, and building. Butler's mother described his hobbies, stating,

Butler liked to do something visually and to do something with his hands . . . At about ten years of age, he started doing more drawing; he could figure things out; and he was always with my husband doing stuff. I realized he was very creative . . . He likes to skateboard and therefore he has developed ramps and things and built them in the backyard [all by himself]. He could build a skate park. (VanTassel-Baska & Feng, 2006, p. 130)

These vignettes offer an eye into the preferences and strengths of this group of special needs gifted learners. Although not generalizable beyond the students studied, their stories tell about their creativity, reasoning, and preference for active engagement in learning. We see examples of their complexity and unevenness of abilities as well as the specific issues they face and the resulting need for supports. The vignettes show different perceptions of the same student. Recognizable patterns and similarities and differences of high nonverbal, low verbal gifted students to other gifted students also are evident in these excerpts. The final section of the chapter explores some guiding principles for educators.

Key Points to Guide Practice

Based on a review of relevant literature and case study findings, what are guideposts for recommended practice relative to gifted high nonverbal, low verbal children? Four key points may guide school-based practitioners and gifted coordinators in the development of programs for this special needs population of gifted youngsters. The four major areas for consideration are (1) identification routes that enable these youngsters to be included in gifted programs; (2) optimal educational placement that allows for talent development; (3) teacher development that builds understanding and knowledge of them; and (4) program services and supports for both learning and social/emotional needs. These key areas are discussed below, then synthesized with the case study findings in recommended programmatic and curricular interventions.

Identification

The first guidepost for teachers, administrators, and counselors is to look systematically for these atypical gifted learners. Do identification routes allow high nonverbal, low verbal gifted learners to be identified? Comprehensive approaches to identification utilize multiple pathways and include verbal and nonverbal assessments. Naglieri and Ford (2005) wrote, "It is our contention and conviction that nonverbal tests offer much promise in initiating and otherwise supporting the process of finding intellectually gifted students" (p. 35). We see in the cases that the irregular profiles of the high nonverbal, low verbal gifted students may result in a masked or hidden strength, much like the gifted student with a learning disability. We also see in the cases that the uneven abilities did not always fit with educators' ideas of giftedness. Recognizing how these students' strengths may be manifested as well as how they process and learn differently will enable the unmasking of student talent.

A caution is not to paint all high nonverbal, low verbal gifted learners with the same brush. For example, all high nonverbal, low verbal gifted learners are not visual-spatial learners. We see some similarities in strengths and learning preferences from the vignettes of these youngsters, but additional research needs to be done to more fully understand the patterns of this special needs learner. Paying attention to the individual's learning profile is key.

Developing Strengths

By definition, high nonverbal, low verbal gifted learners are strong in one domain and average or below average in another domain. Are we providing programs that develop these gifted students' talent? Matching students with mentors in their talent areas and encouraging participation in clubs and extracurricular interest-based groups such as Odyssey of the Mind illustrate approaches to building on strengths. In their study of mathematics and science graduate students from SMPY with highly regarded talent, Lubinski, Benbow, Shea, Eftekhari-Sanjani,

& Halvorson (2001) found that these students took advanced coursework but went beyond the "prescribed curricula" by "[participation] in research, special programs, and many other out-of-school or informal learning opportunities" (p. 315). In the classroom, using a diagnostic-prescriptive method to accelerate individual students' learning in the areas they already have mastered is another way to build upon strengths. Acceleration can buy time for special projects designed with student growth in mind. For example, Alex aspired to design cars. Compacting his curriculum could "buy time" for Alex to explore aspects of automobile design and production. As he explores an area of interest, his creativity and talent in building could be tapped. Such an individualized project could include attention to Alex's weakness in reading and putting his ideas down on paper, in essence building on his strength to develop areas of weakness. A focus on development of strength areas means gifted program placement will provide opportunities for talent development. Teachers must have knowledge of the uneven profile of the high nonverbal, low verbal gifted learner, so that they are able to differentiate based on these students' learning needs. The second guidepost then is utilizing knowledge of strength areas to determine optimal educational placement for high nonverbal, low verbal gifted learners.

Research has offered some evidence of different ways of cognitive functioning (Silverman, 2005; Sousa, 2003; Witelson et al., 1999) and suggested that there may be a link to learning difficulties in highly visual learners (von Karolyi & Winner, 2004; West, 1997). Notable was that much of the literature on nonverbal ability (not necessarily high nonverbal ability) relates to disability (e.g., von Karolyi & Winner, 2004). Several of the students illustrated in the cases had some learning challenges, and although there was not evidence of identified disabilities in these youngsters with the exception of Alex, possible negative consequences of their uneven development may be something to watch for as students progress into middle and high school. Learning difficulties experienced by the students in these cases may be related to gifted program placement or lack of understanding of their giftedness on the part of the teacher. For example, what academic and emotional supports might high nonverbal gifted students who have average or lower verbal abilities need if they are placed in a gifted English/language arts class? Is it possible that students who have these uneven profiles may be perceived by educators as learning disabled? Obviously, from the vignettes presented here, high nonverbal, low verbal gifted learners are able to perform well in gifted classes, perhaps because the teachers are differentiating curriculum based on students' learning needs. Designing learning opportunities to optimize talent development is critical for special needs gifted learners.

Curriculum and Instruction

How do you design learning opportunities to maximize talent development for these high nonverbal, low verbal gifted students? Guidepost three is to add curricular approaches and instructional methods to one's teaching toolkit that match the preferences and strengths of this group of gifted students. The vignettes provide many examples of the desire of these youngsters for active, hands-on learning. Creativity and strong reasoning were strengths these students possessed. Problem- and inquiry-based learning techniques are congruent with these traits and preferences and consistent with research-based practices in the field (Robinson et al., 2007; VanTassel-Baska & Brown, 2007). Silverman (2005) advocated for discovery and inquiry teaching because many visual-spatial gifted students learn holistically. Designing curricular units that are inquiry-driven and problem-based will engage and motivate high nonverbal, low verbal gifted learners. A diagnostic prescriptive approach, allowing for acceleration, faster pacing, and more abstract and complex content (Silverman, 2005; VanTassel-Baska & Sher, 2003), is effective in building on student strengths and developing weaker areas. Silverman (2005) strongly suggested that teachers utilize visual aids, visual imagery, and manipulatives in teaching youngsters with high spatial abilities.

Some high nonverbal, low verbal gifted students may be gifted in mathematics. Sousa (2003) stated, "One reason that mathematically gifted students are not identified may be that the method of teaching mathematics in the classroom does not evoke the type of thinking processes associated with high mathematical ability" (p. 141). He argued that much of mathematics teaching focuses on rules, formulas, and step-by-step learning. He suggested abstract mathematical reasoning, faster pacing, use of thought-provoking problems, and multiple approaches to problem solving in teaching mathematically gifted students.

Program Services and Supports

The final guidepost is to examine the match between program services and supports and students' learning and social/emotional needs. The uneven development evident in high nonverbal, low verbal gifted learners likely means uneven development in other areas (i.e., time management, study skills, organization, and goal setting). "Challenges to emotional peace can also come from within when a student's intellectual abilities are out of sync" (Delisle & Galbraith, 2002, p. 67). Do program provisions offer the support these students may need to develop their emotional potential fully? The examples from student vignettes provided evidence of perfectionism, underachievement, and low motivation. Naglieri and Ford (2005) pointed out that when nonverbal or other nontraditional measures are used to find gifted students who are not working up to their potential, educators must do different things for them: "These gifted underachievers or potentially gifted students will require additional support to reach their potential" (p. 34). Naglieri and Ford (2005) stated that some may need help with basic academic skills, particularly skill development related to language and literacy. Provisions for gifted students who struggle with these issues are essential in program service and support.

Synthesis Based on Findings: Programmatic and Curricular Interventions

From the case study data (VanTassel-Baska et al., 2009) of high nonverbal, low verbal gifted students (*n* = 9), we know that most were identified through Project STAR performance tasks. Almost all perceived their participation in the gifted program positively. The students had an awareness of the increased

Case Study Findings	Programmatic Interventions
• Identified through STAR performance tasks • Perceived program participation positively • Aware of increased expectations • Strong in math/science • Preference for active, hands-on experiences • Strong reasoning, problem solving, and high creativity • Balanced in social relationships, academics, and creative activity • Evident family support	1. Identification routes that enable identification and placement of high nonverbal, low verbal gifted students 2. Systematic teacher development to build understanding and knowledge of the high nonverbal, low verbal student and building an instructional toolbox to teach these youngsters 3. Continuum of program services and supports (e.g., academic needs such as time management, study skills, and organization as well as affective needs, such as perfectionism and self-efficacy)
	Curricular Interventions
	1. Awareness of student profile (i.e., strengths and talents of these students, and how they process information and learn) 2. Differentiation is based on individual's learning needs, styles, and preference (e.g., use of visual imagery and manipulatives) 3. Problem-based learning, inquiry, diagnostic-prescriptive instruction, and abstract, complex content are utilized. 4. Attention to and support for uneven development and possible learning challenges.

Figure 8.1. Synthesis: Programmatic and curricular interventions for high nonverbal, low verbal gifted students.

expectations once they were identified and placed in the gifted program. As a group, these youngsters were strong in mathematics/science. They preferred hands-on, active experiences. These students exhibited strong reasoning, problem-solving skills, and high creativity. They were balanced in their social relationships, academics, and creative activity. Family support of these youngsters was evident.

The synthesis shown in Figure 8.1 organizes recommendations for practice into programmatic and curricular interventions. Programmatically, identification processes that utilize multiple measures of assessing student potential and performance allow pathways to find high nonverbal, low verbal gifted students. Systematically planning for teacher development that builds understanding and knowledge of diverse gifted learners is fundamental. Teachers who better understand diverse gifted learners will need to expand their instructional expertise, increasing the likelihood that they will make the teaching-learning connection with this special population of gifted students. Gifted program coordinators will need to be certain a continuum of services is available to address academic needs as well as provide the supports critical to creating an environment where these students will be successful.

The curricular interventions in Figure 8.1 provide more specifics about what teachers need to know and be able to do at the classroom level. Knowledge of student strengths and talents and how these youngsters process information and learn best will enable teachers to differentiate curriculum and instruction more effectively. Utilizing problem-based learning, inquiry, diagnostic-prescriptive instruction, and abstract, complex content is key to successful differentiation for these gifted students. A watchful awareness of potential learning difficulties created by the uneven skills as well as planning for and providing the necessary supports for students who need them are critical elements.

Conclusion

How much talent has gone unrecognized and undeveloped due to our lack of understanding of this special needs population of gifted learners? What mathematical and scientific breakthroughs could happen if we do more with these students? What discoveries and inventions might occur if we approach the development of this special population's talent in a careful and systematic way? How might we increase the educational opportunities for these youngsters? Much more study is needed to better understand the similarities and differences of high nonverbal, low verbal gifted students and other gifted students. We have some knowledge of their special needs, but we need to know more about programs and curriculum that develop the talent of these students with uneven profiles. Recommendations to guide practice draw from a limited research base and focus on the uniqueness of these learners. These recommendations included systematic approaches that enable identification of the high nonverbal gifted student, development of talents and strength areas through optimal educational placement, curricular and instructional techniques that fit learners' strengths and preferences, and program services and supports that match students' learning and social/emotional needs.

References

Angelelli, C., Enright, K., & Valdes, G. (2002). *Developing the talents and abilities of linguistically gifted bilingual students: Guidelines for developing curriculum at the high school level* (Research Monograph 02156). Storrs: University of Connecticut, The National Research Center on the Gifted and Talented.

Bracken, B. A., & McCallum, R. S. (1998). *Universal Intelligence Test.* Itasca, IL: Riverside.

Bracken, B. A., & Naglieri, J. A. (2003). Assessing diverse populations with nonverbal tests of general intelligence. In C. R. Reynolds & R. W. Kamphaus (Eds.), *Handbook of psychological and educational assessment of children* (2nd ed., pp. 243–273). New York: Guilford.

Bloom, B. S. (1985). *Developing talent in young people.* New York: Ballantine.

Cattell, R. B., & Cattell, K. S. (1965). *Manual for the Culture-Fair Intelligence Test, Scale 2.* Champaign, IL: Institute for Personality and Ability Testing.

Delisle, J., & Galbraith, J. (2002). *When gifted kids don't have all the answers.* Minneapolis, MN: Free Spirit.

Ford, D. Y. (1995). *A study of achievement and underachievement among gifted, potentially gifted, and average African-American students* (Research Monograph 95128). Storrs: University of Connecticut, The National Research Center on the Gifted and Talented.

Gardner, H. (1983). *Frames of mind: The theory of multiple intelligences.* New York: Basic Books.

Gohm, C. L., Humphreys, L. G., & Yao, G. (1998). Underachievement among spatially gifted students. *American Educational Research Journal, 35,* 515–531.

Hunsaker, S. L. (1994). Adjustments to traditional procedures for identifying underserved students: Successes and failures. *Exceptional Children, 61*(1), 72–76.

Kirschenbaum, R. J. (1998). Dynamic assessment and its use with underserved gifted and talented populations. *Gifted Child Quarterly, 42,* 140–147.

Lewis, J. D. (2001). *Language isn't needed: Nonverbal assessments and gifted learners.* San Diego: Conference Proceedings of the Growing Partnerships for Rural Special Education.

Lohman, D. F. (1994). Spatially gifted, verbally inconvenienced. In N. Colangelo, S. G. Assouline, & D. L. Ambroson (Eds.), *Talent development: Proceedings from the 1993 Henry B. and Jocelyn Wallace National Research Symposium on Talent Development* (Vol. 2, pp. 251–264). Dayton: Ohio Psychology Press.

Lohman, D. F. (2005). Review of Naglieri and Ford (2003): Does the Naglieri Nonverbal Ability Test identify equal proportions of high-scoring White, Black, and Hispanic students? *Gifted Child Quarterly, 49,* 19–28.

Lohman, D. F. (2008, Winter). Comparing CogAT, NNAT, and the Raven. *Cognitively Speaking, 6,* 1–8.

Lubinski, D., & Benbow, C. P. (2006). Study of Mathematically Precocious Youth after 35 years: Uncovering antecedents for the development of math-science expertise. *Perspectives on Psychological Science, 1,* 316–345.

Lubinski, D., Benbow, C. P., Shea, D. L., Eftekhari-Sanjani, H., & Halvorson, M. B. J. (2001). Men and women at promise for scientific excellence: Similarity not dissimilarity. *Psychological Science, 12,* 309–317.

Lubinski, D., Webb, R. M., Morelock, M. J., & Benbow, C. P. (2001). Top 1 in 10,000: A 10-year follow-up of the profoundly gifted. *Journal of Applied Psychology, 86,* 718–729.

Naglieri, J. A. (1997). *Naglieri Nonverbal Ability Test.* San Antonio, TX: The Psychological Corporation.

Naglieri, J. A., & Ford, D. Y. (2003). Addressing underrepresentation of gifted minority children using the Naglieri Nonverbal Ability Test (NNAT). *Gifted Child Quarterly, 47,* 155–160.

Naglieri, J. A., & Ford, D. Y. (2005). Increasing minority children's participation in gifted classes using the NNAT: A response to Lohman. *Gifted Child Quarterly, 49,* 29–36.

Nasca, D. (1998). *The use of non-verbal measures of intellectual functioning in identifying gifted children.* (ERIC Document Reproduction Service No. ED296551)

Raven, J. C. (1947). *Raven Standard Progressive Matrices.* London: H. K. Lewis.

Robinson, A., Shore, B. M., & Enersen, D. (2007). *Best practices in gifted education: An evidence-based guide.* Waco, TX: Prufrock Press.

Schuler, P. (2002). Perfectionism in gifted children and adolescents. In M. Neihart, S. M. Reis, N. M. Robinson, & S. M. Moon (Eds.), *The social and emotional development of gifted children: What do we know?* (pp. 71–79). Waco, TX: Prufrock Press.

Silverman, L. K. (2005). *Effective techniques for teaching highly gifted visual-spatial learners.* Retrieved July 16, 2008, from http://www.gifteddevelopment.com/Articles/vsl/v05.pdf

Sousa, D. A. (2003). *How the gifted brain learns.* Thousand Oaks, CA: Corwin Press.

Spicker, H., Fletcher, R., Montgomery, D., & Breard, N. (1993). *Rural gifted education in a multicultural society.* (ERIC Document Reproduction Service No. ED359005)

Sternberg, R. J. (1986). A triarchic theory of intellectual giftedness. In R. J. Sternberg & J. E. Davidson (Eds.), *Conceptions of giftedness* (pp. 223–243). Cambridge, England: Cambridge University Press.

VanTassel-Baska, J., & Brown, E. (2007). Towards best practice: An analysis of the efficacy of curriculum models in gifted education. *Gifted Child Quarterly, 51,* 342–358.

VanTassel-Baska, J., & Feng, A. (2006). *Project STAR two year research study* (Unpublished report). Columbia, SC: South Carolina Department of Education.

VanTassel-Baska, J., Feng, A., & deBrux, E. (2007). A longitudinal study of identification and performance profiles of Project STAR performance task–identified gifted students. *Journal for the Education of the Gifted, 31,* 7–34.

VanTassel-Baska, J., Feng, A., & Evans, B. (2007). Patterns of identification and performance among gifted students identified through performance tasks: A three year analysis. *Gifted Child Quarterly, 52,* 1–4.

VanTassel-Baska, J., Feng, A., Swanson, J. D., Quek, C., & Chandler, K. (2009). *The benefits of performance-based gifted identification approaches on middle school students' academic and affective profiles.* Manuscript submitted for publication.

VanTassel-Baska, J., Johnson, D., & Avery, L. (2002). Using performance tasks in the identification of economically disadvantaged and minority gifted learners: Findings from Project STAR. *Gifted Child Quarterly, 46,* 110–123.

VanTassel-Baska, J., & Sher, B. (2003). Accelerating learning experiences in core content areas. In J. VanTassel-Baska & C. Little (Eds.),

Content-based curriculum for high-ability learners (pp. 27–46). Waco, TX: Prufrock Press.

von Karolyi, C., & Winner, E. (2004). Dyslexia and visual spatial talents: Are they connected? In T. Newman & R. J. Sternberg (Eds.), *Students with both gifts and learning disabilities: Identification, assessment, and outcomes* (pp. 95–117). New York: Kluwer Academic/Plenum Publishers.

Wai, J., Lubinski, D., & Benbow, C. P. (in press). Spatial ability for STEM domains: Aligning over fifty years of cumulative psychological knowledge solidifies its importance. *Journal of Educational Psychology*.

Webb, R. M., Lubinski, D., & Benbow, C. P. (2002). Mathematically facile adolescents with math-science aspirations: New perspectives on their educational and vocational development. *Journal of Educational Psychology, 94,* 785–794.

West, T. G. (1997). *In the mind's eye: Visual thinkers, gifted people with dyslexia and other learning difficulties, computer images and the ironies of creativity* (Updated ed.). Amherst, NY: Prometheus Books.

Witelson, S. F., Kigar, D. L., & Harvey, T. (1999). The exceptional brain of Albert Einstein. *The Lancet,* 2149–2153.

Curriculum Development for Low-Income and Minority Gifted Learners

Joyce VanTassel-Baska

Planning and developing curricula for low-income and minority gifted learners must consider developmental discrepancies in the profiles of these learners that may call for adjustments in the curriculum landscape. These developmental discrepancies lead us to think about special populations of gifted learners as possessing uneven profiles, with peaks and valleys that require special accommodation in the curriculum development process. To address the strengths in curriculum areas for these gifted learners is a necessary but insufficient action in nurturing their development over time. We also need to develop value-added curriculum opportunities that address the relatively weaker aspects of their profiles, some of them in noncognitive areas. Current identification and programming practices for the gifted have not been sensitive to these uneven profiles; consequently, potential giftedness has been overlooked.

Several issues surrounding these special populations of learners need to be addressed. One of the most obvious is to involve other professionals who may have greater expertise than we do in understanding these students from social-cultural and psychological perspectives. This book and others (see VanTassel–Baska & Stambaugh, 2007) represent a collaborative effort with colleagues whose backgrounds are in social psychology, multicultural education, and other domains (see Chapters 2 and 3 of this book). If we are to progress as a field in working with special populations, we must engage and collaborate more with professionals from other relevant disciplines.

A second issue relates to choices in school program delivery systems. As the need to understand both individual and group differences among gifted learners becomes greater, our resource capacity becomes more stretched, and we are forced to rely on existing school organizational structures to deliver curriculum services. Consequently, we are experiencing a movement to provide for gifted learners in the regular classroom, toward cooperative teaching strategies and away from pull-out programs that use a resource teacher to work directly with small groups of gifted learners. While instructional grouping and regrouping are the hallmark of effective teaching, less separate and distinct grouping of gifted learners is likely to occur under this model. Although it is counterintuitive and rather impolitic, more grouping of low-income gifted learners together is likely to enhance their growth and development rather than patchy approaches that do not allow sustained periods of intervention to occur across years.

Finally, we must acknowledge the importance of working with these learners over time in a well-developed curriculum that allows authentic growth to take place. Too often, we give up and think the student is not capable of higher level thinking at a stage of development rather than persisting in using high-level material. Several studies have documented that persistent use of high-level scaffolds yields positive results, across multiple years (VanTassel-Baska, Feng, & deBrux, 2007; VanTassel-Baska, Johnson, & Avery, 2002).

Intervention Issues

Whether we are talking about minority students from urban areas or poor White students from rural areas, one factor remains common to each group: These students reside outside the mainstream networks that provide access to educational advantage. This knowledge is crucial to converting high aspirations into creative, productive achievement at various stages of development. The role of key interventions is a critical conversion process.

At their best, in-school programs have provided rigorous coursework comparable to what advantaged learners in the best school settings would receive. Other school programs have set out to remediate skill deficits or offer programs in nonacademic areas, such as the performing arts. A national survey identified programs for the disadvantaged gifted at the local level across the United States in 100 districts (VanTassel-Baska, Patton, & Prillaman, 1991). Most of these programs, however, were not differentiating service delivery for the low-income or culturally diverse gifted learner, even though they did include these learners in programs for the gifted.

United States Department of Education (1996) statistics revealed that during the 1993–1994 school year, 9% of the learners receiving gifted services were from the bottom quartile of family income whereas 47% of the students in gifted programs were from families whose income was in the top quartile. A recent update of these findings, based on state self-report data, suggested that fewer than 20% of states are providing any alteration in instructional plans for these learners (Brown, Avery, VanTassel-Baska, Worley, & Stambaugh, 2006).

The literature on low-income gifted learners has tended to emphasize the following intervention strategies:

1. attention to cognitive strengths, particularly in creativity and other domains (see Kitano chapter);
2. creation of programs that enhance motivation and reduce psychosocial stressors (see Worrell chapter); and
3. value-added programs that provide access to advanced work and increase learning time (College Board, 1998; Johnsen, Feuerbacher, & Witte, 2007).

Economically disadvantaged minority students who are gifted also are at risk for attending college. They may be poorly prepared for college because their schools often fail to recognize their abilities or place them in programs to develop them (Alamprese & Erlanger, 1989; VanTassel-Baska et al., 1991). They may receive negative messages about the value of college for their future from peers and others (McIntosh & Greenlaw, 1986; Passow, 1972) or mixed messages because their families fear losing them as a result of advanced education and upward mobility. Often, the message is one of nonachievement in order to maintain cultural identity (Ogbu, 1994). Students also may have difficulty setting long-term educational or career goals and conducting the planning and investigation needed to prepare for college entrance, given the immediate and often overwhelming demands of everyday life (Jones & Jones, 1972; Lindstrom & VanSant, 1986; McIntosh & Greenlaw, 1986). In addition, economically disadvantaged, academically gifted minority students may make inappropriate choices because they fear the isolation resulting from increasing disparities between their future world of college and work and their present homes and communities (Frasier, 1989; Lindstrom & VanSant, 1986).

School psychologists and/or counselors need to assist students in improving skills that are critical for academic success in college including test-taking skills, study strategies, and managing time effectively (Ford & Thomas, 1997). Students also need to be supported in developing aspirations for their careers (McIntosh & Greenlaw, 1990). Many students who are poor also are ethnically diverse, and it is important for professionals and parents to help foster career aspirations by using strategies to support self-esteem and to develop racial identity within multicultural curricula (Ford, 2000).

Program interventions geared to address psychosocial stressors may need to involve counselors in the process to construct meaningful interventions and serve as small-group discussion facilitators (Peterson, 2008). Selecting students for the group who represent similar backgrounds may aid in student articulation of concerns, as would the selection of a group leader of shared culture and/or SES level.

Learner Characteristics of Low-Income and Minority Students: The Basis for Differentiation

Low-income students who are not members of minority groups tend to exhibit similar characteristics to those who are members in several respects. Both groups may appear socially marginalized in school settings due to their socioeconomic backgrounds in respect to clothing, mannerisms, and circle of friends. Often these students have difficulty penetrating the inner circle of popularity or even the circle of "nerds" because their behaviors are not really aligned with either group. Rather it is more likely that they become independent in their mode of operation and thereby limited in opportunities for learning from productive social interactions. By the same token, their mode of learning tends to be pragmatic, focused on what is necessary to get by and close to the ground in respect to the day-to day existence their circumstances compel them to lead. This pragmatic outlook thus encourages their preference for concreteness in learning, for practical applications of knowledge in their world, and for examples that both come from and harken back to that world.

For these students, the world of the arts is more freeing, both psychologically from their deprived circumstances but also in modes of expression that do not require verbal explanation. In the arts, these students can revel in being. Thus activities that simulate and use the world of the arts are more likely to reach them because of the compelling affective forces they provide. Use of the visual arts, dance, music, and theater all have their special pull for these students.

Because fluid intelligence often is the prominent type of cognition of these students, they gravitate well to real-world thinking and problem-solving situations, especially those that are highly open-ended and require the use of fluency and flexibility in attempting solutions. Many also like to verbalize their thinking and use this technique to develop elaborative skills orally. Transference of this process to written form is much more difficult and often takes many more years of practice to develop proficiency.

These students have all learned disappointment early, whether in their single-parent family constellation or the denial of material possessions taken for granted by other students, or by the impoverished nature of their lives, lived without the richness of learning resources such as private lessons, special summer programs and camps, and other opportunities afforded those of greater means. Such learning early from adverse circumstances propels these students to want to make their world better, for which metacognitive skills are essential. Thus these students can be deeply influenced by self-help algorithms that

focus on ways to achieve upward mobility. The skills of planning, monitoring, and assessing one's progress are central to
them as is serious reflection upon goals and strategies to accomplish them.

In such lives, the role of individuals who take a special
interest is central to keeping their dream of a better life alive.
Sometimes it is a family member but many times it is an educa-
tor who sees a spark and encourages its ignition. Low-income
students disproportionately need these individuals to teach
them informally what they need to know to be successful, thus
serving as role models extraordinaire. Although mentors can be
a wonderful resource to such students, the likelihood of mentor
matches for all of the promising low-income students who need
them appears limited. Therefore, the educational community
needs to find other means for encouraging and nurturing such
students on a less formal basis.

Many times these students have skill gaps in learning, especially in core areas of the curriculum. A targeted tutorial, using
good diagnostic-prescriptive approaches, can go a long way in
improving student performance. If the tutor also is an older student of similar background or an adult of the same gender and ethnicity, the informal message is even more strongly communicated.

If the foregoing discussion provides a psychological profile
of low-income students, it also provides a blueprint to the central learning characteristics they possess, which typically include:
- openness to experience;
- nonconforming, independence in thinking;
- creativity and fluency in their thinking;
- preference for oral expression;
- quickness to blend feelings with thoughts;
- responsiveness to multiple modes of learning as displayed
  in the arts;
- preference for hands-on applications;
- preference for real-world connections; and
- responsiveness to individual learning patterns.

A curriculum that is responsive to such learners will need
to possess enough flexibility to address these characterological
needs to a great extent.

Intervention Approaches That Work

Interventions that have been documented to be successful with learners who are economically disadvantaged include early attention to needs, family involvement, use of effective instructional and leadership strategies in the school, experiential learning approaches, encouragement of self-expression, community involvement, counseling efforts, and building on strengths (VanTassel-Baska, 2003b). It also is important to be sensitive to cultural values that may repress giftedness in students from impoverished backgrounds, including the high importance of social acceptance and the rejection of solitary activities (Ford & Thomas, 1997), because researchers have stressed the importance of understanding cultural value systems when working with gifted students (Ford, 2007; Ford & Harris, 1995).

As we examine effective interventions, several directions seem promising:

1. *Separate instructional opportunities for students with the same developmental profile.* Data across special populations suggest the importance for within-group instructional time that allows for interaction based on similar conditions whether it be gender, social background, or other adverse conditions such as poverty.

2. *The use of technology, especially microcomputers, to aid in transmission of learning for many special population learners.* Although new technology has been used most predominantly with disabled gifted learners, it holds promise for targeted use with other learners who evidence discrepant learning patterns and can profit from compensatory intervention.

3. *Small-group and individual counseling, mentorships, and internships for special population learners.* These interventions all constitute individual attention to affective as well as cognitive issues of development.

4. *A focus on the arts as a therapeutic intervention as well as a creative and expressive outlet.* Through the arts, the dissynchronies of one's experience can be reduced and absorbed into a higher pattern of integration. Thus, the arts can enhance higher level functioning.

5. *Use of materials rich in ideas and imagination coupled with emphasis on higher level skills.* Both self-concept and motivation are in jeopardy if prolonged use of compensatory strategies and basic-level materials are maintained in the educational process of these learners. Challenging content with attention to ideas and creative opportunities is essential to combat further discrepant performance.

The potential positive effects of peers and teachers on the achievement and motivation of low-income and minority students also has been well-documented in the literature (Olszewski-Kubilius, 2007; VanTassel-Baska, 2007; VanTassel-Baska, Olszewski-Kubilius, & Kulieke, 1994; Worrell, 2007). For minority students, the need for teacher support and understanding is a critical variable in their success (Ford, Wright, Grantham, & Harris, 1998; Struck, 2002; Tucker, Harris, Brady, & Herman, 1996). Engagement with peers who share similar values and interests also has been shown to be facilitative in keeping these students focused on academics and motivated to achieve (Ford, 1993, 1996).

Studies also have documented the importance of advanced curriculum content and the use of higher order processes in serving gifted learners from low-income circumstances (Fields, 1997; McIntosh, 1995; Tomlinson, Callahan, & Lelli, 1997; VanTassel-Baska, Johnson, et al., 2002). Successful content-based interventions in reading for all disadvantaged learners, regardless of ability, have stressed a tutorial or small-group intensive approach where students are grouped according to instructional level (Hurley, Chamberlain, Slavin, & Madden, 2001; Sensenbaugh, 1995). More recently, the use of a specialized reading curriculum that moves students from lower level reading comprehension to higher level thinking has been successful in enhancing skills in both (Stambaugh, 2007).

In teaching mathematics, studies have found that the use of direct instruction coupled with an emphasis on math concepts delivered by math and science specialists impacts learning significantly (Fields, 1997; Webster & Chadbourn, 1992). Grouping these students together also appears to produce important benefits. The more homogeneous the grouping context over time,

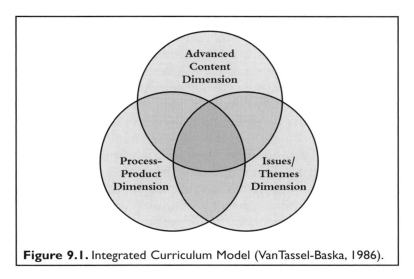

Figure 9.1. Integrated Curriculum Model (VanTassel-Baska, 1986).

the more likely disadvantaged gifted learners will show significant and long-term gains in achievement in all areas of learning
measured (Howells, 1992; Rito & Moller, 1989; Struck, 2002).

Application of a Conceptual Framework for Curriculum for Low-Income Gifted Learners

Earlier work has explicated in detail the Integrated
Curriculum Model (VanTassel-Baska, 1986, 1992, 1998,
VanTassel-Baska & Little, 2003), on which 20 years of Javits
curriculum projects have been constructed. Briefly, its components are based on a review of literature on what approaches
work with gifted students in schools and involve the combina-
tory dimensions of (a) advanced content; (b) the higher level
processes of thinking, problem solving, and research linked to
a quality product; and (c) the use of a central concept, issue, or
problem to guide the unfolding of student understanding. This
model has proven effective in conceptualizing and organizing
exemplary curriculum units of study in science, language arts,
mathematics, and the social studies (see Figure 9.1).

For students from low-income and minority backgrounds,
the model is flexible enough to accommodate a curriculum tailoring process these students need to make curriculum more

appropriate to their characterological profiles. For example, in both the language arts and social studies units, the use of multicultural materials is standard. In language arts, selections by different ethnic groups in the United States (i.e., African American, Hispanic American, Asian American, and Native American) are carefully woven into each unit of study. The texts selected have been carefully chosen to reflect the contributions of each minority group and avoid cultural stereotyping.

In the social studies units, there is a major emphasis on building multiple perspectives and recognizing alternative points of view on many social and political issues. Not only does this aid critical thinking, it also promotes tolerance and understanding of diversity. Students have the opportunity to explore major historical events through the lens of the victims as well as the oppressors, the losers as well as the winners. In this way, they can come to appreciate different assumptions about the world, different beliefs and values, and differing understanding about what events of history mean and represent to different groups in this country and abroad.

In the science units, students come to see the complexity of the world through problem-based learning. Beginning in kindergarten and extending through eighth grade, promising learners explore an acid spill on the highway or a long lost set of scientist notes on a discovery for alternative fuel or the discovery of an artifact from the past on a school construction site. Working in small investigatory teams, students begin to work through the scientific research process, using a metacognitive tool called the Need to Know Board. In the process of this protracted investigation over 6 weeks or more, students reach a resolution on what the problem really is and ways to resolve it, given the restriction of time and resources.

In the mathematics units, geared to primary, intermediate, and middle school learners, students again encounter real-world problems, one in the form of animal overpopulation, and must confront the seriousness of the problem and generate alternative approaches to solve it through the use of mathematical models that project various scenarios or hypotheses. In these units students use the mathematical tools of estimation, probability, logic, and statistics to address the unit's problem and learn to appreciate the role of mathematics as an important augmentation to real-world problem solving in any domain.

The use of constructivist approaches in all of the units encourages safe risk-taking. Discussion in small collaborative groups, group research, concept mapping, and metacognitive strategies all address the research-based needs of this population for tailored curriculum. The special features of curriculum that especially match learning characteristics and research on these populations are the following:

- use of creative expressive activities;
- use of open-ended activities;
- concept mapping;
- metacognition;
- use of multicultural readings and materials;
- use of multiple perspectives;
- use of real-world applications;
- use of hands-on approaches;
- use of community; and
- use of inquiry approaches, promoting student question asking.

The William and Mary units not only have been used with low-income and minority learners to enhance achievement with successful results (see VanTassel-Baska, 2008; VanTassel-Baska, Bass, Ries, Poland, & Avery, 1998, VanTassel-Baska & Stambaugh, 2006; VanTassel-Baska, Zuo, Avery, & Little, 2002), they also have been used as models for creating new curriculum units tailored to these students' needs (Swanson, 2004).

Curriculum Prototypes

Several approaches to adapting curriculum for low-income learners have been found to be successful. A few of these are enumerated below, along with examples to highlight their use in classrooms.

Nonverbal Curriculum Interventions

There is a need to create strong nonverbal curriculum that can be effectively employed with students whose profiles may be more nonverbal in orientation. Several approaches may be taken to ensure that the curriculum is well-balanced. One obvious way is to ensure that there are more math and science activities included that are project-based and hands-on. One middle school math project follows that exploits spatial reasoning abilities (see Figure 9.2).

In the science area, the use of an investigation wheel (see Figure 9.3) can help students focus on the reiterative nature of science as they conduct their own experiments based on student-generated designs. Whether testing the effects of certain variables like water, air quality, or light on flowers or plants or animals, students can experience real science in classrooms and the intellectual thrill of finding out what works.

Use of Divergent Thinking Models

Teaching the skills of creativity to these learners also is an important emphasis in the curriculum. It responds directly to their learning preferences for open-ended tasks and associative thinking patterns and their fluency and flexibility in addressing real-world problems. One example model to consider is Creative Problem Solving, illustrated in Figure 9.4 with a sample problem.

Another model that may be useful to include would be metaphor development, a process that enhances these students' communication abilities in written and oral forms. The example template that follows in Figure 9.5 allows students to approach the task systematically and then move to more creative applications.

Creative writing is another application of creative skills that may aid in the development of talent among these students. Providing them with a scaffold like the one in Figure 9.6 may prove useful in structuring their ideas for narrative writing.

Use of Art

For these students, the use of art can be an additional motivator to participate in gifted programs, especially if the art form and project is left up to the choice of the student. Teachers may provide ideas, however, so that students can decide how to

Lesson	Parallel City Planner
Task Demand	It is your job to plan and draw the street map for a city according to the guidelines given below. Your next promotion is dependent on how well you complete this assignment for your boss. You remember learning these topics from your geometry class, so let's impress your boss and get to work!
Design Rules	*Required Items Your Map Must Include:* • All streets must be labeled • 6 parallel streets • 2 transversal streets that are NOT parallel • 2 traffic lights and 2 stop signs located at 4 different intersections • A gas station and a restaurant located at *congruent alternate exterior* angles • Your house and school located at *supplementary consecutive interior* angles • Courthouse and bank located at *noncongruent alternate interior* angles • Department store and police station located at a *linear pair* of angles • Structures/objects (relevant to a city) of your choice that use *vertical* angles *Appearance:* • Project must be presented on poster board • Buildings, roads, and structures must be placed according to the directions • Appropriate names must be placed on signs on or near the buildings • Must be drawn neatly (STRAIGHTEDGE!!!) and with color • Print your name in the lower right corner on the back of the project • Allow your creativity to shine through *Written Reflection:* Upon completion of your project, you need to write a reflection paragraph. It should answer the following questions: • What geometry skills are used for the project? • Who would use these skills outside of class? • How does the project demonstrate your knowledge of geometry as well as a paper-pencil test for the chapter? • Explain why or why not you enjoyed the project.

Figure 9.2. Sample lesson using spatial reasoning abilities.

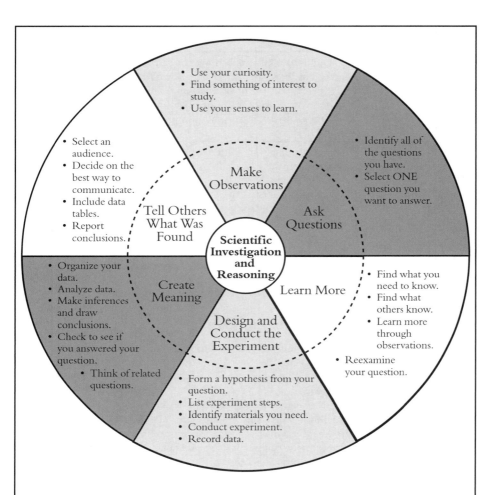

- Use your curiosity.
- Find something of interest to study.
- Use your senses to learn.

- Select an audience.
- Decide on the best way to communicate.
- Include data tables.
- Report conclusions.

Make Observations

Tell Others What Was Found

Ask Questions

- Identify all of the questions you have.
- Select ONE question you want to answer.

Scientific Investigation and Reasoning

- Organize your data.
- Analyze data.
- Make inferences and draw conclusions.
- Check to see if you answered your question.
  - Think of related questions.

Create Meaning

Learn More

- Find what you need to know.
- Find what others know.
- Learn more through observations.
- Reexamine your question.

Design and Conduct the Experiment

- Form a hypothesis from your question.
- List experiment steps.
- Identify materials you need.
- Conduct experiment.
- Record data.

Phase of Investigation	Steps
What you do before the experiment . . .	• Make observations • Ask questions • Learn more
	• Design and conduct the experiment
What you do after the experiment . . .	• Create meaning • Tell others what was found

Figure 9.3. Wheel of Scientific Investigation and Reasoning.

Note. Adapted from Kramer (1987).

Creative Problem Solving

Brainstorm:
- What are all of the ways that unhealthy emotions manifest themselves in school and home settings?
- What are illustrations and examples of this?
- What are the three most critical aspects of the problem? What is the most critical?

Restatement of the problem:
- How can students _____?

Solution finding:
- What are all of the approaches we might use to solve the problem of unhealthy emotions?

Develop a comprehensive solution:
- What are the best solutions proposed and how could they be synthesized to create a comprehensive approach?

Create a plan of action to address the issue:
- What objectives need to be addressed?
- Who will be responsible?
- What should they do?
- On what timeline?
- How will they know the plan worked?

Figure 9.4. Sample Creative Problem Solving activity.

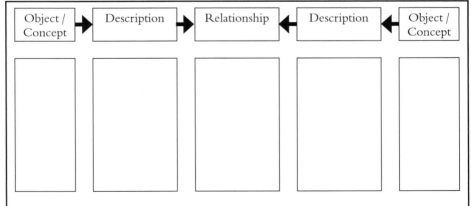

Figure 9.5. Metaphor chart.

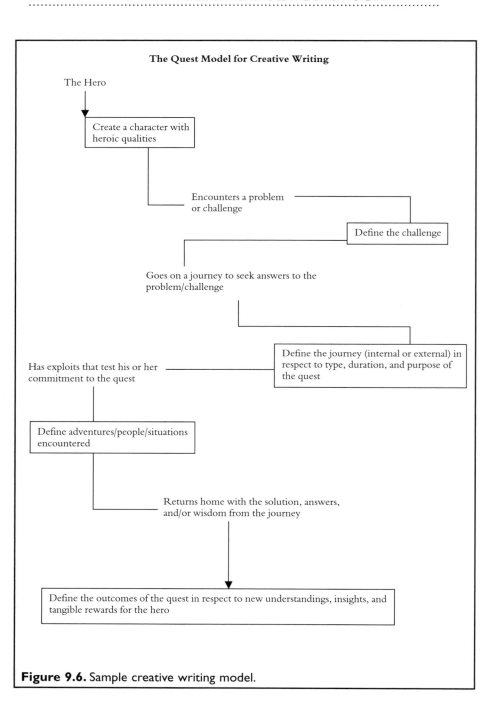

Figure 9.6. Sample creative writing model.

proceed in making intelligent choices among options in which they may be interested. Models for art appreciation projects follow:

- Analyze a selected poem, art object, and musical work (i.e., songs, instrumental pieces). Answer the following questions about each:
  - o What is the theme or major ideas of the work?
  - o What mood does the work convey?
  - o How is the work organized? What is its structure?
  - o How would you describe the form of the work?
  - o What is the purpose of the work?
  - o What are aspects of the work that you most enjoy? Why?

- Write critical reviews of plays, movies, and other performances. Analyze the performance via characterizations, storyline, and theme expressed.
- Design relevant objet d'art, using key design specifications such as the following: rhythm, tone, color, theme, subject matter, perspective, symmetry/balance, and value.

Use of Conceptual Learning Tools

Students from underprivileged backgrounds many times revel in the world of ideas, especially when those ideas are linked to relevant aspects of their own lives. Focusing curriculum at the level of big ideas while providing illustrations they can relate to is an excellent way to energize the curriculum for these students. Figure 9.7 is an assignment that uses the theme of oppression to elevate students' comparative analysis skills in literature.

Model Interventions Over Time

Several programs, using differentiated curriculum and/or curriculum prototypes, have been successful over multiple years in serving low-income and minority learners. These programs are examples of the value-added options needed by this population to advance to higher levels of educational attainment, including gifted program membership.

Multicultural Author Study

- Read a short story, essay, or poetry by an African American, Hispanic American, and Asian American author on the theme of oppression. How are the stories/poems similar yet different?

- Here is a list of possible authors to choose from:

African American	Hispanic American	Asian American
Gwendolyn Brooks	Sandra Cisneros	Carlos Bulosan
Langston Hughes	Isabel Allende	Peter Ho Davies
Lorraine Hansberry	Julia Alvarez	Anita Desai
Toni Morrison	Rudolfo Anaya	David Henry Hwang
Maya Angelou	Oscar Hijuelos	Maxine Hong Kingston
James Baldwin	Maria Hinojosa	Chang-Rae Lee
Phyllis Wheatley	Geraldo Rivera	Amy Tan
	Luis Santeiro	Lin Yutang
	Gary Soto	

- Write in your journal what you learned about each culture from your readings.

- Read the biography or autobiography of one author you have read. How does the author's life influence his or her writing?

Figure 9.7. Sample lesson incorporating comparative analysis skills.

Many programs use whole-class interventions in problem-solving skills to stimulate latent abilities in poor and minority learners (McIntosh, 1995). Project LEAP in Hampton, VA, is an archetype of such programs (VanTassel-Baska, 2003a). It uses an experiential approach to the identification and assessment of gifted and talented primary students by exposing students to differential educational experiences designed to expand problem-solving abilities and creative thinking. Multiple disciplines are integrated in encouraging the development of productive, abstract, and higher level thinking skills.

Observation of PROJECT LEAP activities in both second and third grade revealed a heavy emphasis on higher level thinking in the context of traditional content domains. These activities were hands-on and required students to make pre-

---

Grade Two: Session Three

I. General Introductory Activities

II. Content Area: Science and Mathematics
  a. Objective: To develop the ability to generate relations between figural items, relations which must be arrived at uniquely and organized constructively.
  b. Activity: "Marble Roll"—Generating mathematical data to be recorded in a consistent manner.

III. Content Area: Creative Problem Solving and Mathematics
  a. Objective: To develop the ability to deduce meaningful information implicit in given information.
  b. Activity: "Magic squares"—Using deductive reasoning to determine the method and mathematical operations used in the "number trick."

IV. Content Area: Language Arts
  a. Objective: To develop the ability to judge which objects or ideas could best be transformed or redefined to meet new requirements.
  b. Activity: "Creative Application"—Sponge stories

V. Content Area: Language Arts
  a. Activity: "Reflective Writing"—Journal entries

VI. Structured Assessment Activity (Human Figure Drawings)

Figure 9.8. Sample LEAP session.

---

dictions, to deduce, and to problem solve in small groups and individually. Activities changed about every 20 minutes. Each session contained activities in mathematics, language arts, and creative problem solving, and, in the third-grade session, journal writing activities. Figure 9.8 provides insight into the nature and extent of LEAP sessions.

A multiyear project, sponsored by Northwestern University, was focused directly on gifted disadvantaged students in the city of Chicago (Olszewski-Kubilius, Grant, & Seibert, 1994; Olszewski-Kubilius & Scott, 1992). It emphasized family empowerment by providing seminars for junior high students and their parents regarding college choices, how to obtain scholarships, and academic planning. The second and third years of the program were directed toward student mentorships and internships, resulting in greater gains in college success and adjustment.

A College of William and Mary program and curriculum, entitled *Libraries Link Learning* (Boyce, Bailey, & VanTassel-Baska, 1990), was designed to serve at-risk gifted primary students in the language arts. Multicultural literature was a central aspect of the program. Each session featured a different book whose characters represented the diverse cultural backgrounds of African Americans, Hispanic Americans, Native Americans, and Asian Americans. The literature used in the program reflects key criteria for selecting books for the intellectually gifted (Baskin & Harris, 1980), affective criteria (Halsted, 2002), and criteria for appropriate multicultural literature (Hernandez, 1989). Classroom activities were structured to address discussions utilizing higher level thinking skills and the writing process. Extension activities were developed as a link to the family as well as a reinforcement for each lesson.

Conclusion

This chapter has explored the world of intervention for gifted students from low-income and culturally diverse backgrounds. It has delineated both general and specific approaches to curriculum development practices that can be used in classrooms. It has applied our understanding of what works in curriculum for these learners to deliberate prototypical models that can be used as scaffolds for developing new curriculum. In the process, it has illustrated activities that can be applied to project-based work and to skill sets in content areas that will elevate the learning of these students over time. Affective and conative concerns also have been addressed, and readers are encouraged to access the third book in this series, *Social-Emotional Curriculum With Gifted and Talented Students*, for more explicit direction on providing interventions in these domains.

References

Alamprese, J. A., & Erlanger, W. J. (1989). *No gift wasted: Effective strategies for educating highly able, disadvantaged students in mathematics and science.* Washington, DC: Cosmos Corporation.

Baskin, B., & Harris, K. (1980). *Books for the gifted child.* New York: Bowker.

Boyce, L., Bailey, J., & VanTassel-Baska, J. (1990). *Libraries link learning resource guide.* Williamsburg, VA: The College of William and Mary, Center for Gifted Education.

Brown, E., Avery, L., VanTassel-Baska, J., Worley, B., Stambaugh, T. (2006). A five-state analysis of gifted education policies: Ohio policy study results. *Roeper Review, 29,* 11–23.

College Board. (1998). *Equity 2000: A systematic education reform model.* Retrieved May 21, 2009, from http://www.ecs.org/clearinghouse/15/10/1510.htm

Fields, C. D. (1997). An equation for equality: Maryland's Prince George's County puts Equity 2000 to the test. *Black Issues in Higher Education, 13,* 24–30.

Ford, D. Y. (1993). Support for the achievement ideology and determinants of underachievement as perceived by gifted, above-average, and average Black students. *Journal for the Education of the Gifted, 16,* 280–298.

Ford, D. Y. (1996). *Reversing underachievement among gifted Black students: Promising practices and programs.* New York: Teachers College Press.

Ford, D. Y. (2000). *Infusing multicultural content into the curriculum for gifted students* (ERIC Digest #E601). Arlington, VA: ERIC Clearinghouse on Disabilities and Gifted Education.

Ford, D. Y. (2007). Teacher referral as gatekeeping: Cultural diversity training is one key to opening gifted education doors. *Gifted Education Press Quarterly, 21*(3), 2–5.

Ford, D. Y., & Harris, J. J., III. (1995). Underachievement among gifted African-American students: Implications for school counselors. *School Counselor, 42,* 196–203.

Ford, D. Y., & Thomas, A. (1997). *Underachievement among gifted minority students: Problems and promises* (ERIC Digest #E544). Arlington, VA: ERIC Clearinghouse on Disabilities and Gifted Education.

Ford, D. Y., Wright, L. B., Grantham, T. C., & Harris, J. J., III. (1998). Achievement levels, outcomes, and orientations of Black students in single- and two- parent families. *Urban Education, 33,* 360–384.

Frasier, M. (1989). Identification of gifted Black students: Developing new perspectives. In J. Maker & S. Schiever (Eds.), *Critical issues in gifted education: Defensible programs for cultural and ethnic minorities* (Vol. II, pp. 213–225). Austin, TX: Pro-Ed.

Halsted, J. W. (2002). *Some of my best friends are books: Guiding gifted readers from preschool to high school.* Scottsdale, AZ: Great Potential Press.

Hernandez, H. (1989). *Multicultural education.* Columbus, OH: Merrill.

Howells, R. F. (1992). Thinking in the morning, thinking in the evening, thinking at suppertime. *Phi Delta Kappan, 74,* 223–225.

Hurley, E. A., Chamberlain, A., Slavin, R. E., & Madden, N. A. (2001). Effects of Success for All on TAAS reading scores: A Texas statewide evaluation. *Phi Delta Kappan, 82,* 750–756.

Johnsen, S., Feuerbacher, S., & Witte, M. M. (2007). Increasing the retention of gifted students from low-income backgrounds in university programs for the gifted: The UYP Project. In J. VanTassel-Baska (Ed.), *Serving gifted learners beyond the traditional classroom* (pp. 55–80). Waco, TX: Prufrock Press.

Jones, J. H., & Jones, M. C. (1972). The neglected client. In R. Jones (Ed.), *Black psychology* (pp. 195–204). New York: Harper & Row.

Kramer, S. P. (1987). *How to think like a scientist.* New York: HarperCollins.

Lindstrom, R. R., & VanSant, S. (1986). Special issues in working with gifted minority adolescents. *Journal of Counseling & Development, 64,* 583–586.

McIntosh, S. (1995). Serving the underserved: Giftedness among ethnic minority and disadvantaged students. *School Administrator, 52*(4), 25–29.

McIntosh, M. E., & Greenlaw, M. J. (1986). Fostering the postsecondary aspirations of gifted urban minority students. *Roeper Review, 9,* 104–107.

McIntosh, M. E., & Greenlaw, M. J. (1990). *Fostering the post-secondary aspirations of gifted urban minority students* (ERIC Digest #E493). Arlington, VA: ERIC Clearinghouse on Disabilities and Gifted Education.

Ogbu, J. U. (1994). Understanding cultural diversity and learning. *Journal for the Education of the Gifted, 17,* 355–384.

Olszewski-Kubilius, P. (2007). Working with promising learners from poverty: Lessons learned. In J. VanTassel-Baska & T. Stambaugh (Eds.), *Overlooked gems: A national perspective on low-income promising learners* (pp. 43–46). Washington DC: National Association for Gifted Children.

Olszewski-Kubilius, P., Grant, B., & Seibert, C. (1994). Social support systems and the disadvantaged gifted: A framework for developing programs and services. *Roeper Review, 17,* 20–25.

Olszewski-Kubilius, P. M., & Scott, J. M. (1992). An investigation of the college and career counseling needs of economically disadvantaged minority gifted students. *Roeper Review, 14,* 141–148.

Passow, A. (1972). The gifted and the disadvantaged. *The National Elementary Principal, 61*(5), 24–41.

Peterson, J. (2008). Focusing on where they are. In J. L. VanTassel-Baska, T. L. Cross, & R. F. Olenchak (Eds.), *Social-emotional curriculum with gifted and talented students* (pp. 193–226). Waco, TX: Prufrock Press.

Rito, G. R., & Moller, B. W. (1989). Teaching enrichment activities for minorities: T.E.A.M. for success. *Journal of Negro Education, 58,* 212–219.

Sensenbaugh, R. (1995). *Reading recovery* (Report No. RR93002011). Bloomington: Indiana University. (ERIC Document Reproduction Service No. ED386713)

Stambaugh, T. (2007). *An exploratory study of Jacob's Ladder Reading Comprehension program.* Unpublished doctoral dissertation, The College of William and Mary.

Struck, J. M. (2002). A study of talent development in a predominantly low socio-economic and/or African American population. (Doctoral dissertation, The College of William and Mary, 2002). *Dissertation Abstracts International, 63,* 560.

Swanson, H. (2004). Working memory and phonological processing as predictors of children's mathematical and problem solving at different ages. *Memory and Cognition, 32,* 648–661.

Tomlinson, C. A., Callahan, C. M., & Lelli, K. M. (1997). Challenging expectations: Case studies of high potential, culturally diverse young children. *Gifted Child Quarterly, 41,* 5–18.

Tucker, C. M., Harris, Y. R., Brady, B. A., & Herman, K. C. (1996). The association of parent behaviors with the academic achievement of African American children and European American children. *Child Study Journal, 26,* 253–277.

U.S. Department of Education. (1996). *Nature of the reforms.* Washington, DC: Author.

VanTassel-Baska, J. (1986). Effective curriculum and instructional models for talented students. *Gifted Child Quarterly, 30,* 164–169.

VanTassel-Baska, J. (1992). *Planning effective curriculum for gifted learners.* Denver, CO: Love.

VanTassel-Baska, J. (1998). Disadvantaged learners with talent. In J. VanTassel-Baska (Ed.), *Excellence in education gifted & talented learners* (pp. 95–114). Denver, CO: Love.

VanTassel-Baska, J. (2003a). *Content-based curriculum for low income and minority gifted learners* (Research Monograph 03180). Storrs: University of Connecticut, The National Research Center on the Gifted and Talented.

VanTassel-Baska, J. (2003b). *Curriculum planning and instructional design for gifted learners.* Denver, CO: Love.

VanTassel-Baska, J. (2007). Introduction. In J. VanTassel-Baska & T. Stambaugh (Eds.), *Overlooked gems: A national perspective on low-income promising learners* (pp. 1–5). Washington, DC: National Association for Gifted Children.

VanTassel-Baska, J. (2008). Curriculum development for gifted learners in science at the primary level. *Revista Espanola de Pedagogia, 66*(240), 283–295.

VanTassel-Baska, J., Bass, G., Ries, R., Poland, D., & Avery, L. (1998). A national study of science curriculum effectiveness with high ability students. *Gifted Child Quarterly, 42,* 200–211.

VanTassel-Baska, J., Feng, A., & deBrux, E. (2007). A longitudinal study of identification and performance profiles of Project STAR performance task-identified gifted students. *Journal for the Education of the Gifted, 31,* 7–34.

VanTassel-Baska, J., Johnson, D., & Avery, L. D. (2002). Using performance tasks in the identification of economically disadvantaged and minority gifted learners: Findings from Project STAR. *Gifted Child Quarterly, 46,* 110–123.

VanTassel-Baska, J., & Little, C. A. (2003). *Content-based curriculum for high-ability learners.* Waco, TX: Prufrock Press.

VanTassel-Baska, J., Olszewski-Kubilius, P., & Kulieke, M. (1994). A study of self-concept and social support in advantaged and disadvantaged seventh and eighth grade gifted students. *Roeper Review, 16,* 186–191.

VanTassel-Baska, J., Patton, J., & Prillaman, D. (1991). *Gifted youth at risk.* Reston, VA: Council for Exceptional Children.

VanTassel-Baska, J., & Stambaugh, T. (2006). Project Athena: A pathway to advanced literacy development for children of poverty. *Gifted Child Today, 29*(2), 58–63.

VanTassel-Baska, J., & Stambaugh, T. (2007). *Overlooked gems: A national perspective on low-income promising learners.* Washington, DC: National Association for Gifted Children.

VanTassel-Baska, J., Zuo, L., Avery, L. A., & Little, C. A. (2002). A curriculum study of gifted-student learning in the language arts. *Gifted Child Quarterly, 46,* 30–42.

Webster, W. J., & Chadbourn, R. A. (1992). *The Evaluation of Project SEED, 1990–91* (Report Number DISDEPSS910432). Dallas, TX: Dallas Independent School District, Dept. of Evaluation and Planning Services. (ERIC Document Reproduction Service No. ED371101)

Worrell, F. (2007). Identifying and including low-income learners in programs for the gifted and talented: Multiple complexities. In J. VanTassel-Baska & T. Stambaugh (Eds.), *Overlooked gems: A national perspective on low-income promising learners* (pp. 47–51). Washington, DC: National Association for Gifted Children.

Teacher Development to Work Effectively With Diverse Gifted Learners

Julie Dingle Swanson

What do teachers need to know and be able to do to help diverse gifted learners? What are common preconceptions and assumptions educators hold about diverse gifted learners? How can those assumptions be revealed and challenged when inaccurate? How might teachers bridge understandings about who these diverse gifted learners are with what needs to be done in the classroom to better develop their talents?

This chapter describes current knowledge of effective teacher development practices, beginning with national standards and what data show about professional development in gifted education. The chapter also examines what the research says relative to diversity and teaching gifted learners. Next, what works (i.e., effective models) in planning for and structuring teacher development are presented. Research based on key principles of how people learn (Bransford, Brown, & Cocking, 2000) provides the framework for helping educators consider how to plan for and offer systematic teacher development based on key principles of how people learn. Finally, utilizing case study to understand the nature of these diverse gifted students, how to accommodate their learning needs, how to differentiate instruction, and how to plan for necessary programming is illustrated. Suggestions for parent education and involvement are included in the discussion.

Current Knowledge

National Standards and Teacher Development

Any discussion of current knowledge of effective professional development for gifted educators begins with the National Staff Development Council (NSDC; 2001) standards. These standards are relevant to the discussion because they explain in a comprehensive way important aspects of planning for teacher development. The NSDC standards are grouped into context standards, or how staff development impacts creating a context for learning; process standards, focused on skills and knowledge necessary to improve learning; and content standards, centered around deep content knowledge combined with knowledge of students and their families. Consideration of NSDC's context, process, and content standards is critical in planning effective teacher development. Specific information can be accessed at http://www.nsdc.org.

Another important resource in planning is the *Pre-K–Grade 12 Gifted Program Standards* (Landrum & Shaklee, 2000). This resource includes a programming criterion on professional development that outlines key principles about professional development for teachers of the gifted. Each of the key principles shows minimum and exemplary standards to guide the teacher development component of programming.

Joint work of the National Association for Gifted Children (NAGC) and the Council for Exceptional Children's The Association for the Gifted (CEC-TAG) provides a third resource, the *NAGC-CEC Teacher Knowledge and Skill Standards for Gifted and Talented Education* (Council for Exceptional Children, 2006). This set of standards specifies the essential knowledge and skills educators of the gifted and talented need. In particular, "Standard 3: Individual Learning Differences" explicates teacher knowledge and skill related to diverse gifted learners.

The significant efforts of these and other professional organizations have helped to clarify the knowledge and skills important for teachers of gifted learners (Robinson, Shore, & Enersen, 2007). NAGC's (1995) *Standards for Graduate Programs in Gifted Education* offers other important guidelines. These sets of standards are excellent starting points for understanding the content of teacher development in gifted education and in guiding planning.

In addition to these standards, knowledge of the research on teacher development is foundational. Research in three relevant areas is explored next: Where are gaps in preparation and development of teachers of gifted students? What is known about effective teaching of diverse gifted learners? What works effectively in teacher development?

What Research Shows

Preparation and Development Gaps

Although evidence exists that gifted education coursework makes a difference in the classroom for bright learners, many colleges and universities have limited study of gifted learners in their preservice teacher preparation and in graduate coursework. Gifted education courses in teacher preparation are sometimes offered, but almost all courses are at the graduate level (Lindsey, 1980). Even when offered, however, many graduate-level courses do not lead to a degree or credential in gifted education (Clark, 2007). Lack of opportunity for gifted education coursework is particularly relevant in studies of teacher education candidates: Findings indicate that when undergraduate students' beliefs about gifted learners were challenged, their attitudes about the nature and learning needs of gifted students became more positive and accurate (Bangel, Enersen, Capobianco, & Moon, 2006; Goodnough, 2000). As evidenced in a study of preservice teachers, those in preservice recognize and believe in student differences but do not know how to meet the needs of their diverse students (Tomlinson et al., 1994). Moon, Callahan, and Tomlinson (1999) reported new teachers' attitudes toward differentiation for gifted students were more positive when workshops were used in combination with coaching to apply learning how to meet diverse needs. These studies suggest that much more is called for at both the preservice level of preparation and in opportunities for advanced study leading to a degree or credential at the graduate level.

Not only is there little preservice training in gifted education, but there also is lack of funding for teacher development. In a national study to determine practices around the country in gifted education professional development, Westberg et al. (1998) found on average that state-level dollars were only allocated for gifted education at 4% of the total teacher development budget. In states with mandates, more teacher development on gifted education was provided. The study (Westberg et al., 1998) showed that development was rarely offered to educators who did not teach gifted students. Other data provided evidence that most teachers do not have training in how to teach gifted students (Westberg, Archambault, Dobyns, & Salvin, 1993).

Knowledge on Effective Teaching: What Works

Relevant research on teachers already working with gifted students indicates that training makes a difference. In Hansen and Feldhusen's (1994) study of the difference between trained and untrained teachers of the gifted, the trained teachers created a better classroom environment for their gifted students' learning. They also utilized higher level thinking and discussion more than those without training.

Extending teacher development beyond gifted educators is important. In a Javits project study to train general education teachers to differentiate for gifted students in their classrooms, researchers found evidence of change in classroom practice (Johnsen, Haensly, Ryser, & Ford, 2002). Further, teachers said they benefited from project support (i.e., the workshops and learning activities, the resources, and the mentoring). The study's data indicated almost all involved in the project changed their practice. Johnsen et al. advocated for involvement of all stakeholders affected by the change. In their project, professional development activities included simulated instructional practices and clear communications to teachers of desired classroom changes. Teachers could decide, from the suggested changes, what they would change and to what degree. Along with typical professional development approaches, the teacher development in this project used peer coaches and mentors, provided support in materials and leadership, and allowed time for implementation.

Matthews and Foster (2005) reported on a teacher development model that utilizes some similar elements (e.g., choice, options, coaching, mentors) to the study above. The Dynamic Scaffolding Model (Matthews & Foster, 2005) uses resource teachers/gifted education consultants through a three-tiered approach to help teachers learn. The first tier of the model offers optional professional development workshops on gifted youngsters' nature and needs. Teachers have the choice to participate or not. This tier builds foundational knowledge for teachers and stimulates their interest in and attention to the differences of gifted learners. The model's second tier provides individual consultation with teachers on their gifted students and how to assist those students. As teachers have questions and seek ideas and input on particular students, they are able to confer with an expert through a mentoring/coaching approach. The third tier connects like-minded teachers with opportunities to network and additional resources and services.

Guskey's (2000) model offered an effective planning tool for teacher development promoting change in practice. In planning, the first step is specification of knowledge and skills teachers will gain about gifted youngsters and the resulting learning from the planned development. Then, decisions about the most effective delivery modes are made, based on what teachers should know and be able to do. For example, delivery modes could be book study groups or workshops. A workshop might be followed up with in-class demonstration and coaching; a book study may lead to action research. As teachers learn about new practices, they need support for that change. Consideration of organizational structures necessary to support change in teacher practice is critical. For example, do teachers have the necessary curriculum materials to use with their students? Is there a conduit for communication of questions, ideas, and concerns that allows teachers to clarify their understanding as they use new curriculum and instructional approaches in their classrooms? How will fidelity of implementation be monitored? The fourth consideration is assessment. How will the program coordinator (or person directing the teacher development) assess the degree to which desired knowledge and skills have been acquired and applied in the classroom? Assessment is the final step in this planning model: impact on students. In what ways have the newly acquired knowledge and skills impacted gifted learners? This model provides a systematic approach to designing teacher development that promotes change.

Effective Teaching of Diverse Learners: Teacher Development

What are characteristics of the effective teacher in a classroom with diverse gifted youngsters? According to Ford and Trotman (2001), teacher characteristics that enable diverse gifted students to be well taught include the skills to develop materials and learning approaches useful to these students; the skills to recognize and address individual and cultural differences; and the ability to see students' talents, strengths, and needs.

Attitudes about diversity and giftedness are an important consideration in planning teacher development. How does training in gifted education impact teacher attitudes about gifted students? McCoach and Siegle (2007) observed that research on the impact of gifted education training on teacher attitudes has been mixed and reported findings suggesting that gifted education training has no effect on teachers' attitudes toward gifted students. McCoach and Siegle suggested that a critical, often omitted step in teacher development planning is preassessment of teacher attitudes toward the gifted. They cautioned against assuming that attitudes are positive or negative without preassessment of teachers.

How have less than positive teacher attitudes toward gifted students been changed? Research on a Javits project called U-STARS~PLUS (Coleman, Coltrane, Harradine, & Timmons, 2007) showed that when teachers utilized higher end teaching and learning in their classes, they began to see students differently (i.e., they saw the potential that students have rather than what students did not have). This project advocated that, for children from poverty in particular, "high quality content and curriculum" are essential (Coleman et al., 2007, p. 60). These researchers found that preparation to teach high-poverty students requires teacher support in the form of coaching, reflection, and study through seminars and institutes to develop necessary knowledge and skills.

What do diverse gifted students say they want in a teacher? Abel and Karnes (1994) examined the preferences of low-income gifted students from a rural setting compared to those in a middle- to upper class suburban setting. They reported the personal and social behaviors of teachers made more of a difference to the low-income youngsters than other teacher behaviors. This finding suggests that teacher-student relationships and social interactions are especially important to low-income students.

Previous chapters in this book make clear many of the challenges faced by gifted students from underrepresented groups. The numerous examples and multiple perspectives show that often students from these groups are at a disadvantage educationally. Thus successful programs and interventions for these diverse gifted learners are critical to their talent development and future possibilities.

There is little preparation to teach gifted students and the opportunities for teachers to advance knowledge and skills through graduate programs are quite limited. Training of teachers improves education for gifted learners; several effective models are available to use in designing such training. Studies suggest that attention to individual and cultural differences and attitudes and beliefs are essential if educators are to develop the teaching and learning relationships that low-income gifted students say they want.

This review directs attention to the need for teacher development that builds better understanding of the nature and learning needs of diverse gifted learners as well as how to teach these youngsters. Without conscious effort and resources targeting teacher development, these students may continue to be misunderstood and lack opportunities to advance.

Teacher Learning: Working With Diverse Gifted Students

Returning to the central questions posed at the beginning of this chapter allows the reader to think carefully about key aspects of teacher development: how people learn and how the knowledge, understanding, and recognition of aptitude and talent in diverse gifted learners might be conveyed. What do teachers need to know and be able to do to help diverse gifted learners? This question is best addressed through examination of the *NAGC-CEC Teacher Knowledge and Skill Standards for Gifted and Talented Education* (Council for Exceptional Children and National Association for Gifted Children, 2006) and foundational coursework in the nature and needs of gifted students along with a study of curriculum for gifted learners. The foundational knowledge is simply a starting point upon which to build. Inquiry-based learning is one way to build on the foundational knowledge and get at a deeper understanding of diverse gifted learners.

Learning through inquiry applies techniques such as learning by design, projects, problems, and cases (Donovan, Bransford, & Pellegrino, 1999). This section explores the use of cases or vignettes as the basis of inquiry learning to better understand diverse gifted learners. These vignettes, or short descriptive stories, were developed as part of a longitudinal study (VanTassel-Baska, Feng, Swanson, Chandler, & Quek, 2009) conducted on 37 special needs gifted youngsters from four underrepresented groups: low-income African Americans, low-income Caucasians, twice-exceptional students, and high nonverbal, low verbal students. The profiles and patterns illustrated in the vignettes enable professional educators to consider individual student needs and to think through what they can do in the classroom to support low-income and nontraditional gifted students.

Drawing Upon Knowledge About Learning

Three principles central to how people learn (Donovan et al., 1999) are discussed and applied to the use of cases to understand diversity of gifted learners. Table 10.1 outlines ways in which each principle might be used to deepen teacher learning.

The first principle is related to preexisting beliefs, knowledge, and assumptions of the learner. Application of this principle means that educators' preconceptions and misconceptions are revealed, challenged, and replaced with accurate understandings (Donovan et al., 1999). The teaching-learning process involves drawing out and working with preexisting understandings teachers hold about gifted students from underrepresented populations. An illustration might be a teacher who believes

Table 10.1
Research on Learning Applied to Teacher Learning on the Diversity of Giftedness

Central Principles to Guide Learning (Donovan et al., 1999)	Sample Ideas for Application to Teacher Learning
Preexisting beliefs, knowledge, and assumptions: The learners' preconceptions and misconceptions are revealed, challenged, and replaced with accurate understandings.	• Influences of poverty, race, ethnicity, and class on who is and is not gifted. • Deficit model thinking (focus on student weaknesses rather than strengths) as an obstacle for advancement.
Key ideas, concepts, and principles: Deep coverage of fewer key concepts and ideas through multiple examples builds stronger foundational knowledge and understanding, and application of ideas and concepts enables transfer of new knowledge to other contexts.	• Identification route as it relates to the diverse gifted learner. • Social and emotional issues experienced by the diverse gifted learner (e.g., the impact of confidence gained through gifted program placement on motivation). • Coaching and classroom demonstration to test out new ideas and strategies.
Metacognitive thinking: Explicit use of metacognitive instruction enables the learner to self-monitor understanding and engage in reflective assessment.	• Teacher self-assessment: Beliefs and attitudes about students through reflection. • Reflective practice: What have I changed and what are the results?

that lack of print materials in the home means that parents do not really value education. Further, this teacher may assume that because parents do not attend meetings during the school day, they do not think school is important. The teacher's hidden belief that low-income children cannot be "truly" gifted could be uncovered through discussion. Using this misconception to build accurate understanding of aspects of poverty and how middle-class persons may view these aspects is one example of this principle in action.

The second principle promotes in-depth coverage of fewer key concepts and ideas through multiple examples as the way to build stronger foundational knowledge and understanding. Discussion of the concepts and ideas is not enough. Application of ideas and concepts is necessary to transfer new knowledge to other contexts (Donovan et al., 1999). For example, teachers must understand how the newly gained knowledge applies in their classroom, with their students. They need to try the ideas out. Trying new strategies and techniques requires ongoing, sustained forms of support such as coaching, demonstration teaching by master teachers, curriculum materials, and opportunities to network. Teachers are able to deepen their understanding when provided with formative feedback and offered the opportunity to ask questions and get answers (Donovan et al., 1999). A teacher may learn that bibliotherapy is an effective strategy to use with gifted students who come from poverty as a way to help students envision future possibilities as they read about eminent persons from poverty. Trying out the approach with a student or a small group of students, with a peer coach assisting during student discussion, increases the likelihood that this teacher will understand the power of the approach and use it again to address the same or a different issue.

The third principle encourages the explicit use of metacognitive instruction, because use of such strategies enables the learner to self-monitor and engage in reflective assessment and practice. Teachers are busy persons with full days, so engaging in reflective practice and talking with colleagues about their work must be deliberately scheduled (Donovan et al., 1999). To illustrate the third principle, consider a low-income gifted student struggling to fit in with other students in a self-contained gifted class. The student is newly placed in the program, has left his friends behind in his regular classes, and has yet to make new friends. His teacher has been engaged in a book study of *Removing the Mask: Giftedness in Poverty* (Slocumb & Payne, 1998), so she can utilize new understandings gained from the book study and put some of the ideas into practice as she provides transitional support to this student. Her plan is to keep a brief, daily reflection for a week about how the student is responding to the planned intervention. She will take those reflective observations, along with how she monitored and adjusted during the week, and share insights with her book study group.

The section that follows walks the reader through an example of how to apply the three principles central to how people learn using a case-based inquiry approach. Important to note is that Donovan et al. (1999) suggested that professional development for teachers needs to be "learner-centered" (p. 24), which means assessment of where teachers need help is the starting point. The development needs to be "knowledge-centered," ensuring clarity around why, when, where, and how some new strategy or understanding is valuable and important, particularly in the context of the classroom (Donovan et al., 1999, p. 24). Development activities need to be "assessment-centered," providing teachers with opportunities to test out approaches and new ideas, and to get and use feedback in a formative way to understand what is and is not working (Donovan et al., 1999, p. 24). Incorporating "community-centered" activities into teacher development combats the isolation teachers experience and allows opportunities to learn from others with similar challenges (Donovan et al., 1999, p. 24). The use of networks and Internet discussion groups allows teachers to apply new knowledge with ongoing support (Donovan et al., 1999).

Using Cases to Understand the Diversity of Giftedness

Several studies (Gilbert, 2003; Glynn, Koballa, Coleman, & Brickman, 2006; Kaste, 2004; Van Den Berg, Jansen, & Blijleven, 2004) described successful use of case study with undergraduate and graduate students to bridge theory and practice. Evidence suggests that the use of cases helps students better understand real-world situations and strengthens transfer of learning into classroom practice.

The chapters in this book profiling particular special needs gifted learners (see Chapters 6–8) provide rich information, examples, and multiple perspectives for understanding these youngsters. A way to deepen understanding of a specific group of students is to read, analyze, and discuss a vignette or a group of vignettes, depending on the particular needs of teachers. For example, if teachers are working with large numbers of low-income students, a study of profiles of low-income Caucasian and African American gifted students would be beneficial. This section guides the reader through a scenario illustrative of how case analysis (i.e., using a vignette in combination with other strategies) might be utilized to build teacher understanding.

Case Analysis: An Example

Prior to beginning case analysis, steps will have been taken to preassess educators' knowledge, so that the "learner-centered" approach is utilized (Donovan et al., 1999, p. 24). Selecting readings and forming study groups based on needs and the context each teacher faces touches on "knowledge-centered" and "community-centered" approaches to learning (Donovan et al., 1999, p. 24). In this scenario, the professional development coordinator may choose to use one or more vignettes, and plan for follow-up to enable "assessment-centered" learning (Donovan et al., 1999, p. 24).

Using the vignette in Figure 10.1 on Blair Clancy, a seventh-grade girl who is a low-income Caucasian gifted student, the reader will explore how case analysis might be utilized to build understanding.

Blair, described physically as "overweight and carelessly dressed" (VanTassel-Baska, Feng, Swanson, Chandler, & Quek, 2007, p. 49), has uneven performance in school subjects, but is a strong student in English/language arts (ELA). Although Blair says she does not like writing, her mother and her teachers note that her writing is one of Blair's talents. Her gifted ELA teacher states, "She comes out with the most beautiful writing . . . [Her] 'adult' maturity is not only evidenced in her insightful writing but also in the books she selects to read" (VanTassel-Baska et al., 2007, p. 51). Her teachers have noticed some instances of perfectionism, and Blair has shown some defiant behaviors from time to time. Her mother is proud of her and states, "[Blair] is very driven. She has BIG goals, dreams. She knows what she wants to do in life. I am very proud of her. She is going in the right direction" (VanTassel-Baska et al., 2007, p. 50). The complete case is provided in Figure 10.1.

Blair Clancy, a Caucasian seventh grade female in a suburban middle school in South Carolina, was identified as gifted in fourth grade. She was selected on Dimension B, Achievement, with a score of 97%ile in Reading on the Metropolitan Achievement Test-7, and Dimension C, Star Performance Tasks, with a score of 17 on the verbal portion. She fits the profile of low income, Caucasian identified through performance tasks. Blair's current placement is in the language arts portion of the middle school gifted program. Her grades at the end of last year were 74 in Math, 81 in English/Language Arts, 93 in Science, and an overall grade point average of 2.75.

In physical appearance, Blair was overweight and carelessly dressed. She was reserved, and her responses were short and abrupt. Blair did not offer much elaboration even with probing. Asked how she felt about being identified as gifted, Blair stated, "When I got in, I was excited. I would be doing things that required more thinking. When doing projects for another class, I think, 'I am in [GT]. I can do this. I'm smart enough to do this.'" Identification affected her self confidence and made her feel special. She felt more a sense of belonging in her [GT] class, saying, "most of my friends were already in [GT]classes." She said in 5th grade [GT], they worked on word stems and book reports. To Blair, the more interesting learning activities were word games, e.g., jeopardy with word stems, and mystery word, with a sentence on the board and a missing word. She talked about a project where students picked an invention that affected their lives and researched it. She indicated a preference for different types of work, commenting that she would like to have the same amount of group work as independent work in [GT]. Interestingly, Blair said she did not like writing, which was opposite of what her current teacher noted as her strength. She stated that [GT] "does not really help with other subjects, because they ([GT]and other subjects) don't really connect."

Mrs. Clancy, Blair's mother, said her daughter was speaking in complete sentences early, and she could have conversations with her as a two year old. "When Blair was born, I could tell from very young she was brighter than most kids. It only took two days to potty train her." Her mother observed by age 5, Blair was reading at a 2nd grade level. She continued with a high level of school performance through age 10 with "straight A's on her report card and homework that we (parents) could not understand." Now, Blair's mother says that she relies on her daughter to help her understand things sometimes. "I'm 36. I ask her things. Last night, I had a project. I asked her how to do it." At this time, Blair's school performance is uneven. Mrs. Clancy stated, "Blair has the capability to do well but sometimes doesn't. She is not afraid to ask questions; she's very inquisitive."

Blair has a younger brother who is also smart according to Mrs. Clancy. Blair's mom notes that brother and sister are different in that Blair procrastinates yet she persists in a way her brother does not. Mrs. Clancy said that most of her daughter's friends are not in Gate. This observation indicates a change from when Blair first began in Gate where most of her friends were at that time. Her mother describes Blair and her friends as "tom boys, tough girlfriends. She has lots of friends; she gets along with all types of people."

Figure 10.1. Vignette on Blair Clancy.

Note. From *Vignettes of Project Star Students* (pp. 49–51) by J. VanTassel-Baska, A. X. Feng, J. D. Swanson, K. Chandler, & C. Quek, 2007, Columbia, SC: Department of Education. Copyright © 2007 by Department of Education. Reprinted with permission.

Figure 10.1, continued

Blair is a "night owl" who enjoys doing computer research. She has extensive knowledge about music, sings in a band, and plays an instrument. Blair likes horses and is an avid reader. Mrs. Clancy sees Blair's strengths as reading and spelling, and believes that math is her weakness. "She likes it (math), but it is not her cup of tea." Her mother notes that Blair has increased her reading and has more homework, especially in language arts, as a result of the gifted program. "She reads more at 13 than her parents." Mrs. Clancy stated that her daughter has become a procrastinator. "She puts it (schoolwork) off, does it at last minute, and still pulls off a good grade." The most significant change Mrs. Clancy has noticed is that "[Blair] became more articulate. I talk to her as an adult. My friends enjoy talking with her. She relates well with them and knows what they are talking about." Her mother is proud of her. She said, "[Blair] is very driven. She has BIG goals, dreams. She knows what she wants to do in life. I am very proud of her. She is going in the right direction."

Without hesitation, Blair's language arts teacher, Ms. Tyler, said Blair's strength was her writing. Tyler stated, "Being in tune to her topic, her writing, her surroundings, the beautiful words that come from her hand—that is her talent. Her mind is incredible and wonderful." Her creativity and thinking ability is evident in class. "You don't think she is paying attention—but she is on top of it." Blair's science teacher, Ms. Rupert, has noticed her deep understanding; "She operates much like other gifted students. She understands material on a deeper level." Other strengths noted in science class were good vocabulary, strong oral communication and leadership. "[Blair] is good academically, [displays] good graphing techniques, and is very creative and funny." Ms. Rupert commented on Blair's distractibility; "She may get halfway through work and go to another task or play with something. She is easily distracted and likes to play sometimes." In language arts, Blair's attention to details or rules that have an academic basis are problematic. "If [students] have to meet a certain type of requirement, she leaves things out—partly due to her lack of organization and partly to her personality. Guidelines are not always followed. An example was doing an MLA citation—something out of the ordinary. She did not do that; she left it off from the assignment. Her weakness seems to be attention to detail—but definitely not mind weakness."

A special learning characteristic observed by Blair's language arts teacher is her insightful writing. Ms. Tyler stated. "[Blair] surprised me. When you look at her—a white middle class kid—you wouldn't expect the type of writing from her. [She is a] big girl [with] kind of a gruff attitude. She knows more about life than the average 13 year old. She comes out with the most beautiful writing. [She's] not a pleasure, [but is] just the type of character who does what she wants to do. She is making connections, asking questions like 'I wonder why? What would happen if . . .' " Blair's "adult" maturity is not only evident in her insightful writing but also in the books she selects to read. Her science teacher sees Blair as a good student, who is a visual learner and who can quickly master words.

As for Blair's social-emotional development, her [English/Language Arts] teacher sees her development as normal except that Blair is more direct than the typical middle schooler. "She tells it like it is. It may be a control issue in some group interactions. She does not want to share power. She[can be] unbending with others, not to an extreme where it is causing problems. She does not comprise much on group work. [Blair] may have self-esteem issues [that] may be linked to control. [She] has

> **Figure 10.1, continued**
>
> friends—not a problem there." Her science teacher believes Blair has good self-esteem and commented that while she likes science, Blair may not work on projects in which she is not interested. She "doesn't like to be corrected and may be perfectionist at times." Ms. Rupert has observed some defiant behaviors and noted that Blair at times displays an attitude of superiority. For example, she has refused to say the Pledge of Allegiance and has talked during the daily "moment of silence."
>
> Blair is a young woman with strong self esteem, independent spirit, and apparent maturity for her age. She is aware of the skill development that she has experienced in the gifted program in vocabulary study and literacy analysis. She has noticed that the program is challenging sometimes, although she denies liking writing, a perceived strength by others. Clearly, her language skills of speaking, writing, and reading are strong as are her creative skills. However, her procrastination, lack of attention to detail, and distractibility contribute to uneven performance in school.

Analyze

After reading the vignette on Blair, a graphic organizer provides the framework for teachers to use in case analysis. Based on concepts and ideas relevant to understanding the diverse learner, this format includes learner characteristics evident in the profile; curriculum, instruction, and/or assessment modifications suggested from the vignette; program delivery modifications that may be indicated; social/emotional issues/needs, both apparent and inferred; and possible extracurricular options to provide additional support for this student and her family. A completed analysis using the graphic organizer illustrates aspects of Blair's case and is found in Table 10.2.

Discuss

Whole-group discussion is an effective way to share ideas, note similarities and differences in responses, and debrief following individual analysis of the vignette. During the discussion, the teacher development leader would ask teachers to think about several questions. Examples of discussion questions follow. Based on the student's learning needs, what appropriate differentiation is already occurring for this student? What further differentiation is indicated by the case? What are risk factors, issues, or problems related to social and emotional needs that are evident or might be inferred from Blair's profile? What are recommendations for interventions and/or supports

Table 10.2
Vignette Analysis Format: Analysis of Vignette on Blair Clancy

Ideas and Concepts Relevant to Understanding the Diverse Gifted Learner	Evidence From Vignette
Learner characteristics evident in the profile	• Early language development • High reading and verbal ability • Average to above-average performance in school subjects • Inquisitive • Creative • Sense of humor • Visual learner who learns quickly • Insightful writer
Curriculum, instruction, and/or assessment modifications suggested by the vignette	• Examples of learning in elementary school pull-out enrichment gifted class include engaging challenge activities with language and a research project utilizing choice • Special class model in middle school gifted program; Blair is in the language arts gifted class, indicated to be her strength area in her identification profile • Lack of challenge in elementary school suggested by "straight A's" indicates Blair may need work on study skills, time management, and organizational strategies • Distractibility and lack of attention to details indicates a need for strategies to improve focus • Mathematics is a gateway to many high-level professions; Blair may need tutoring or afterschool work to develop her math skills and knowledge
Program delivery modifications indicated	• Stronger connections between regular education classes and gifted education classes needed • Guidance and counseling support needed

Ideas and Concepts Relevant to Understanding the Diverse Gifted Learner	Evidence From Vignette
Social/emotional issues/ needs	• Procrastination indicates time management may be an issue • Has many friends and enjoys interactions with adults • Blair's teacher offered observations that may indicate self-esteem and control issues • Perfectionism appears to be an issue with Blair
Extracurricular options	• Debate team • Book club • Summer programs sponsored by the Talent Identification Program
Additional supports for this student and her family	• Scholarship sources for summer programs • Blair's aspirations for the future may need financial support; assisting the family with finding scholarship sources and selecting potential colleges is indicated

to address the risk factors, issues, or problems discussed? What data/information are missing from this case? What steps would help to locate missing data/information?

Apply

Next, the designated leader would ask teachers to connect new understandings from the case and discussion to their students and classroom. The following summary questions would focus teachers' thinking on new insights, remaining questions, and how to apply what has been learned in the classroom. When considering this case, what students with similar profiles come to mind? What has happened in the classroom with those students? What is known and understood that was not previously? What questions still remain? How will classroom practices change as a result of new insights? What necessary supports are needed to make the identified changes?

Follow-Up and Assess

Finally, the leader would ask teachers to list specific actions (resulting from their new understandings) to implement in their classrooms. As teachers take action, they will track the results of their actions. In other words, when a teacher tests out a specific idea, such as afterschool tutoring, he or she will reflect on how the idea addressed the issue of concern. As teachers test out new ideas with their students, providing a format for discussion of challenges, obstacles, and successes established via interschool technology, such as E Chalk, assists in building a network supportive of idea exchange. The teacher development leader's next step is scheduling the follow-up session that will be based on postassessment and centered on the results of planned teacher actions.

The results of the postassessment serve as a basis for planning future professional development sessions. Do teachers need more time to explore other vignettes? Is a book study exploring a practical strategy, such as how to motivate underachieving students, indicated by the postassessment results? Is there a particular curricular approach (e.g., culturally responsive teaching) that teachers need to learn about now? Are family issues of diverse gifted students the next key area for exploration? This scenario shows the reader a concrete example of how to begin to deepen teacher understanding of a diverse gifted learner using case study.

Teacher development focused on diverse gifted students builds on foundational knowledge of who the gifted learner is and how his or her learning needs differ. The next section offers key points to be mindful of in planning for teacher development for diverse gifted learners.

Key Points to Guide Practice

Guidelines for school-based practitioners and gifted education coordinators synthesize important considerations in planning for teacher development for diverse gifted learners. Practical ideas and suggestions offer a place to start. The guidelines discuss support and resources for learning, learning about culture, and parent education and involvement.

Necessary Supports and Resources for Learning

Essential to effective professional development is consistent application of key principles of how people learn (Bransford et al., 2000; Donovan et al., 1999). Creating a community of learners, with support in terms of time to learn, the resources with which to learn, and opportunities to apply learning are all part of the first guideline. Necessary supports and resources include the time and opportunity to learn, experts to facilitate learning, and varied strategies and materials. One example of a district-based practice of how to offer time and opportunity is a regularly scheduled, bimonthly meeting for middle school gifted teachers. This district has used selections from the *Practical Strategies Series* (published by Prufrock Press) for afterschool book study. Food is provided for the group, and teacher leaders from the group facilitate discussion. The meeting is open, not required, and teachers attend because it is beneficial for them.

Research (Clark, 2007; Lindsey, 1980; Westberg et al.,1993) has indicated a necessary support missing in many places around the country: gifted education coursework at the preservice and advanced levels. Advocating for inclusion of gifted education in teacher preparation and supporting certificate and master's programs in gifted education in the local/state college or university are actions that will significantly enhance resources for learning. Funding for gifted education teacher development is limited. Partnering with general education in planning mutually beneficial experiences creates a source of funding and expands gifted education learning to others.

Learning About Different Cultures

Guideline two is the will to build self-awareness and understanding while developing knowledge of other cultures. Educators must know and understand themselves and the lens through which they see the world. They must resolve to understand in what ways their background influences how they view and interact with the students in their classrooms. Cash (2007) stated,

[E]ducators of the gifted must continually challenge themselves to learn more about cultures different from their own; understand the range of perspectives various cultures have on the meaning of giftedness/talent and or creativity; and acknowledge that many children coming from diverse backgrounds may not have a historically supportive environment toward advanced education. (p. 100)

Cash (2007) stated that some families ". . . may consider advanced classes that single students out as discriminatory and/ or culturally insensitive" (p. 100). Teachers need the knowledge to recognize perspectives such as this that may differ from their own perspective. Cash believed cultural differences underline the importance of helping families understand the benefits of participation in gifted programs and advanced classes. Barbara Clark (2007) stated,

Research suggests that some of the important intellectual skills that parents, counselors, and teachers need to help racially and ethnically diverse students learn are questioning skills, introspective attitudes, and the ability to remediate any areas of skill that [students] are lacking, especially limited language skills. As [students] begin to succeed, they will need help coping with peer pressures not to succeed, when they exist, and learning how to align their cultural values with those of the dominant culture, when they choose. As [students] become more independent and mature, they will need help exploring opportunities in a variety of career options, understanding and exploring the problems they may face as they become upwardly mobile, and developing their own individuality and personal cultural identity. (p. 337)

Understanding and awareness are the first steps in bridging cultural differences often seen in diverse gifted learners. The examples above link closely with the third and final guideline.

Parent Education and Involvement

The third guideline is planning for and including parents in development activities that build their understanding of gifted learners. Parents and teachers are partners in educating children. Parents can help educators to understand and gain insight into their children's special needs. The importance of understanding multiple perspectives about diverse gifted learners is illustrated in Blair's case. Evidence that goes beyond the school setting, and provides a different point of view assists teachers in establishing a clearer picture of students.

On the flip side, parents need educators, too. They need teachers to help them understand why their gifted students need challenge, study skills, and planning skills. Parents need school-based personnel to offer ideas and guidance about how they can involve themselves in their child's learning process and schooling to promote success. For example, VanTassel-Baska's (1989) research on low-income families found that successful low-income students' families have high expectations and standards for their children's achievement in school. The families encourage their children, keep track of their progress, and believe that economic status is part of motivation for success.

Building strong relationships with parents, seeking them out as partners, and helping them understand issues related to giftedness will assist in developing teachers' knowledge of diverse gifted students. Home visits and conferences where teachers meet with parents in the workplace are ideal in building a relationship with parents that allows teachers to educate and learn from parents. PowerPoint presentations, Web sites, and DVDs are examples of media-based approaches to reaching parents of diverse gifted learners.

Conclusion

Planning and implementation of effective development has been described and exemplified in the chapter through the discussion of standards, current knowledge of research, effective teacher development models, principles on how people learn, and the case study example. Teacher development does make a difference for gifted students, and as the population of gifted students grows more diverse, keeping abreast of current knowledge and research of who these youngsters are and how to teach them is essential. This chapter offers guidelines for key considerations in planning and implementing effective teacher development.

The research from earlier chapters is clear: Diverse gifted learners are underrepresented in gifted programs and misconceptions about these students are widely held by both educators and parents. To continue to dispel these misconceptions, the diversity of gifted learners requires special attention to increased efforts in teacher development and expansion of useful resources to guide that development. Educators are not serving their students well when they paint all gifted learners with the same brush. The lost potential of these young people can be averted through a strong emphasis on what teachers need to know and be able to do. A focus on more and deeper teacher development should result in brighter prospects for diverse gifted learners and their families, enabling these youngsters to develop their potential, advance their learning, and ultimately, contribute in positive ways to society.

References

Abel, T., & Karnes, F. A. (1994). Teacher preferences among low socioeconomic rural and suburban advantaged gifted students. *Roeper Review, 17,* 52–57.

Bangel, N., Enersen, D., Capobianco, B., & Moon, S. (2006). Professional development of preservice teachers: Teaching in the Super Saturday Program. *Journal for the Education of the Gifted, 29,* 339–361.

Bransford, J. D., Brown, A. L., & Cocking, R. R. (Eds.). (2000). *How people learn: Mind, brain, experience, and school.* Washington, DC: National Academy Press.

Cash, R. M. (2007). The local school district focus . . . Recognizing emergent potential of low-income promising learners. In J. VanTassel-Baska & T. Stambaugh (Eds.), *Overlooked gems: A national perspective on low-income, promising learners* (p. 100). Washington, DC: National Association for Gifted Children.

Clark, B. (2007). *Growing up gifted: Developing the potential of children at home and at school.* Upper Saddle River, NJ: Pearson Education.

Coleman, M. R., Coltrane, S. S., Harradine, C., & Timmons, L. A. (2007). Impact of poverty on promising learners, their teachers, and their schools. In J. VanTassel-Baska & T. Stambaugh (Eds.), *Overlooked gems: A national perspective on low-income, promising learners* (pp. 59–61). Washington, DC: National Association for Gifted Children.

Council for Exceptional Children. (2006). *NAGC-CEC teacher knowledge and skill standards for gifted and talented education.* Retrieved from http://www.nagc.org/uploadedFiles/Information_and_Resources/NCATE_standards/final%20standards%20(2006).pdf

Donovan, M. S., Bransford, J. D., & Pellegrino, J. W. (Eds.). (1999). *How people learn: Bridging research and practice.* Washington, DC: National Academy Press.

Ford, D. Y., & Trotman, M. F. (2001). Teachers of gifted students: Suggested multicultural characteristics and competencies. *Roeper Review, 23,* 235–239.

Gilbert, J. (2003, April). *Transformative learning process of one teacher.* Paper presented at the Home Economics Special Interest Group Business Meeting at the Annual American Educational Research Association Conference, Chicago.

Glynn, S., Koballa, T., Coleman, D., & Brickman, P. (2006). Professional development cases. *Journal of College Science Teaching, 36,* 10–12.

Goodnough, K. (2000). Fostering liberal views of giftedness: A study of the beliefs of six undergraduate education students. *Roeper Review, 23,* 89–90.

Guskey, T. R. (2000). *Evaluating professional development.* Thousand Oaks, CA: Corwin Press.

Hansen, J., & Feldhusen, J. (1994). Comparison of trained and untrained teachers of gifted students. *Gifted Child Quarterly, 38,* 115–124.

Johnsen, S. K., Haensly, P. A., Ryser, G. R., & Ford, R. F. (2002). Changing general education practices to adapt for gifted students. *Gifted Child Quarterly, 46,* 45–63.

Kaste, J. (2004). Scaffolding through cases: Diverse constructivist teaching in the literacy methods course. *Teaching and Teacher Education: An International Journal of Research and Studies, 20,* 31–45.

Landrum, M., & Shaklee, B. (Eds.). (2000). *Pre-K–Grade 12 gifted program standards.* Washington, DC: National Association for Gifted Children.

Lindsey, M. (1980). *Training teachers of the gifted and talented.* New York: Teachers College Press.

Matthews, D. J., & Foster, J. F. (2005). A dynamic scaffolding model of teacher development: The gifted education consultant as catalyst for change. *Gifted Child Quarterly, 49,* 222–230.

McCoach, D. B., & Siegle, D. (2007). What predicts teachers' attitudes towards the gifted? *Gifted Child Quarterly, 51,* 246–255.

Moon, T. R., Callahan, C. M., & Tomlinson, C. A. (1999). The effects of mentoring relationships on pre-service teachers' attitudes towards academically diverse students. *Gifted Child Quarterly, 43,* 56–62.

National Association for Gifted Children. (1995). *Standards for graduate programs in gifted education.* Washington, DC: Author.

National Staff Developmental Council. (2001). *NSDC's standards for staff development.* Retrieved September 14, 2007, from http://www.nsdc.org/standards/index.cfm

Robinson, A., Shore, B. M., & Enersen, D. (2007). *Best practices in gifted education: An evidence-based guide.* Waco, TX: Prufrock Press.

Slocumb, P., & Payne, R. (1998). *Removing the mask: Giftedness in poverty.* Highlands, TX: Aha! Process.

Tomlinson, C. A., Tomchin, E. M., Callahan, C. M., Adams, C. M., Pizzat-Tinnin, P., Cunningham, C. M., et al. (1994). Practices of preservice teachers related to gifted and other diverse learners. *Gifted Child Quarterly, 38,* 106–114.

Van Den Berg, E., Jansen, L., & Blijleven, P. (2004). Learning with multimedia cases: An evaluation study. *Journal of Technology and Teacher Education, 12,* 491–509.

VanTassel-Baska, J. (1989). The role of the family in the success of disadvantaged gifted learners. *Journal for the Education of the Gifted, 1,* 22–36.

VanTassel-Baska, J., Feng, A. X., Swanson, J. D., Chandler, K., & Quek, C. (2009). *The benefits of performance-based gifted identification approaches on middle school students' academic and affective profiles.* Manuscript submitted for publication.

VanTassel-Baska, J., Feng, A. X., Swanson, J. D., Chandler, K., & Quek, C. (2007). *Vignettes of Project Star students.* Columbia, SC: Department of Education.

Westberg, K. L., Archambault, F. X., Jr., Dobyns, S. M., & Salvin, T. J. (1993). An observational study of classroom practices used with third- and fourth-grade students. *Journal for the Education of the Gifted, 16,* 120–146.

Westberg, K. L., Burns, D. E., Gubbins, E. J., Reis, S. M., Park, S., & Maxfield, L. R. (1998). *Development practices in gifted education:*

Results of a national survey. Storrs: University of Connecticut, The National Research Center on the Gifted and Talented.

Policy and Underrepresented Gifted Students: One State's Experience

E. Wayne Lord

This chapter seeks to set the context for policy changes in gifted education in South Carolina from 1999 through 2004. In addition to discussing the policy changes, the primary implications from these changes for working with underrepresented academically gifted diverse learners are identified and responses to the implications are presented. In South Carolina, the major underrepresented populations include learners of low socioeconomic status (SES), as well as Black and, increasingly, Hispanic children. A review of the 2007 gifted and talented student counts in South Carolina (R. Blanchard, personal communication, August 1, 2008) revealed the following information:

- White students represent 53.3% of the total state enrollment with 14.7% of these students qualifying for gifted services. White students represent 78% of the total students served in gifted programs (61,396 of 78,623).
- Black students represent 38.5% of the total state enrollment with 4.5% of these students qualifying for gifted services. Black students represent 16.6% of the total students served in gifted programs (13,025 of 78,623).
- Hispanic students represent 4.7% of the total state enrollment with 4.4% of these students qualifying for gifted

services. Hispanic students represent 1.9% of the total students served in gifted programs (1,555 of 78,623).

In 1999 when the South Carolina State Board of Education approved sweeping policy changes in the identification process of academically gifted learners, the changes rippled throughout all aspects of gifted programming and services in the state. Unfortunately, as with many policy initiatives, the magnitude of change was not completely foreseen. As the State Department of Education (SDE) monitored implementation of these new policies and practices from 1999 through 2004, issues and challenges for working with gifted diverse learners became clearer. In retrospect, it is now possible to diagnose flaws in the policy development process that was in place; however, the politics of policy development and approval do not always initially allow for perfect and complete understanding.

This uncertainty regarding the "fallout" from policy changes as well as fear of the unknown often serve as a barrier for state program directors as they consider developing initial policy or reworking existing rules and regulations. Why create the turmoil that accompanies change in education? Why risk scrutiny of a program that often is perceived to be nonessential? Why disturb the status quo when present resources are already inadequate?

The answers to these questions are as follows: It is a moral duty to respond to real or perceived policy problems within program areas. It is the responsibility of state program directors to do so. It is a function of being a leader.

Catalyst for Action

The initial regulations for gifted programs in South Carolina were developed in 1986 and guided practice in the state for 13 years. Data suggested that minority and low-income students were not being identified to participate in gifted programs. For example, in 1996–1997, approximately 10% of the state's students in grades 3–12 were enrolled in academically gifted programs. However, 11 districts with high minority demographics reported identifying less than 6% as academically gifted learners (Lee, 1997).

Moreover, policies supporting the referral, screening, and identification of gifted learners from diverse populations were weak, unmonitored, and narrow in their approach. A formal complaint challenging equal access to gifted programs led to a Title VI Resolution Agreement between the South Carolina Department of Education and the Office for Civil Rights (OCR) in August of 1997. In this agreement the SDE identified the need to address state policies related to referrals, screening, and identification of students for the academically gifted program. There were inconsistent statewide practices for accepting referrals, for screening all referrals, and for being responsive to best practices in gifted education.

Although the earliest state gifted policy allowed for trial placement of underachieving gifted students (demonstrating high potential, but low performance), districts had not exercised this flexibility. Also, empowered to develop and submit for approval alternative screening procedures, districts had relied solely on the state identification protocol rather than creating processes congruent with their student population. The use of a weighted profile, obtained through combining intelligence/aptitude, academic achievement, grades, and teacher nomination, failed to acknowledge discrete or domain-specific areas of giftedness (Swanson, 2007).

Thus, changes in state policy were needed not only to increase the likelihood of identifying gifted learners from more diverse student populations but also to reflect the most current thought and work in the field of gifted education (Ford, 1996; Swanson, 2006).

Broaden Access—How?

As Gallagher and Coleman (1992) found, highly motivated individuals willing to persist in both policy development and policy approval efforts are critical to a successful outcome. To guide the 1999 revisions of the regulations governing the state gifted program, the SDE convened a task force of stakeholders. Using research from the field on the use of multiple criteria and nontraditional assessment approaches (Coleman, 2003; Ford, 1994; Ford & Trotman, 2000; Frasier, Garcia, & Passow,

1995; Passow & Frasier, 1996), identification criteria were selected to allow for domain-specific identification of gifted learners: nonverbal, verbal, and quantitative. These domains were applied to three dimensions: aptitude, achievement, and performance. By meeting a standard in two of these three dimensions, a student would qualify for gifted services. Also, the policy continued to allow placement using a composite aptitude score at the 96th national age percentile or higher as a sole criterion for identification.

At the same time, the policy mandated census testing at the grade prior to the beginning of gifted services. In South Carolina this meant that all grade 2 students would be assessed for state-funded gifted programs that begin in grade 3, eliminating the possibility of selective referrals for screening (Frasier et al., 1995). Any student from other grade levels who was referred for screening would be assessed as well.

Districts were required to provide parents with written materials explaining the referral, screening, and identification processes. Additionally, teachers and administrators were to receive professional development in the characteristics of gifted learners in order to assist in the referral of students.

Translating these approaches to traditional assessments of aptitude and achievement was fairly easy, and the state assumed these multiple ways for identifying gifted learners would broaden access when compared to the original policy. However, the task force went further by proposing the use of performance-based assessments that could be administered in addition to traditional assessments. These performance-based assessments hopefully would increase identification of low-income and minority gifted learners (Callahan, Tomlinson, Moon, Tomchin, & Plucker, 1995; Maker, 2001; VanTassel-Baska, Johnson, & Avery, 2002). In addition to performance-based assessments, grade point average was included as an indicator of performance.

A word of caution is appropriate at this point. Often changes in gifted education policy, regardless of how small or large, are made with the best of intentions—to focus on a particular, single program element in response to a problem, issue, or opportunity. Although the catalyst for such a response may

Table 11.1
GT Enrollment and Funding Data 2000–2005

School Year	Served in Academic GT Program	Increase in Number Identified and Served	State Funding for Academic GT
2000–2001	54,817		$27,040,023
2001–2002	60,493	5,676	$24,319,943
2002–2003	64,579	4,086	$25,607,780
2003–2004	67,882	3,303	$25,607,780
2004–2005	71,267	3,385	$25,692,780

be founded on good intentions, there will be a ripple effect on all aspects of a gifted program as a result of even the smallest policy change. As Barker (2008) suggested, the significant implications and unintended consequences reside far away from those that appear immediately as a result of change. Tinkering with the identification protocol affected multiple areas: personnel, curriculum, instruction, assessment, support services, and resources (financial, staff, and space).

The SDE anticipated that these changes in the identification protocol would yield a more diverse gifted population, particularly increasing the identification of minority and low-SES gifted learners. However, the SDE failed to anticipate the impact of domain-specific identification on program services, curriculum, support services, and professional development for teachers. In other words, when the protocol for identification changed, all aspects of gifted programs in districts were affected in ways that were not initially considered.

Suddenly, there were more students qualifying for gifted program services (see Table 11.1). From 2001 to 2005 the number of students identified and served increased by 16,450 while funding decreased (R. Blanchard, personal communication, June 1, 2008). How was additional staff going to be secured? How would districts find the resources to support more students when state financial support for gifted programs was already insufficient?

Well-established (entrenched) and valued gifted curricula were no longer relevant for working with a more diverse gifted population. How would teachers "let go" of traditions that defined gifted programs? Where might curricula for these learners be found to allow their potential to be developed and giftedness to emerge over time? Additionally, how would teachers gain the instructional skills necessary for working with culturally diverse gifted learners as well as twice-exceptional learners in larger proportions? Would guidance counselors be equipped to support the social and emotional needs of the learners?

Requiring graduate work for all teachers in gifted programs made a statement with regard to the specialized preparation required for working with gifted students. How were teachers in a largely rural state going to have access to required courses? With Converse College as the only in-state institution of higher education offering a master's degree in gifted education, how would higher education in South Carolina respond to the overwhelming demand for graduate course work in gifted education?

Approval of 1999 Policy Changes

Acknowledging that considerable thought, research, planning, and discussion precede policy changes, there are always unanticipated effects that emerge and are not identified during the phase of policy preparation (Barker, 2008). Change happens. (Educational practitioners might have an alternative statement for capturing this reality.)

The creation or amendment of policy results in planned change as well as unplanned change. Often with little attention to implementation, policy makers may assume changes will happen as proposed. However, the unplanned changes that either gradually appear or arrive in full force create challenges that must be managed through responsive leadership. Unplanned changes might include not anticipating the wide range of needs that will appear as a result of the policy or not predicting the time or resources required for replacing and adjusting previously institutionalized practices. These unplanned changes should not necessarily be seen as negative factors or barriers appearing because of incompetent policy crafting. Rather, unplanned changes must be worked through, allowing time for learning and successful transitions to occur.

Upon approval of the 1999 policy changes in South Carolina, the SDE faced multiple implementation challenges that Gallagher and Coleman (1992) would label as examples of nonlinear policy implementation—approval of policy preceded development and application.

These were some of the primary challenges that emerged:

- using performance-based assessments as part of the state identification protocol that did not yet exist;
- establishing in regulation a performance standard for these nonexisting assessments in order to qualify for gifted service;
- implementing census testing of students with nationally normed aptitude and achievement measures without consideration of fiscal impact on districts;
- requiring and providing statewide professional development for administrators and teachers;
- outlining elements of curriculum differentiation for gifted programs when previously there had been none; and
- expecting gifted curricula to have content, process, and product standards that would exceed state-adopted standards for all students.

Undoubtedly, educators and administrators from the state would add many other challenges to this list; however, these represent the major "opportunities" inherited as a result of the 1999 policy changes. Each of the bulleted items above required action.

Implications of the 1999 Policy Changes

Performance-Based Assessments

Through collaboration with the Center for Gifted Education at The College of William and Mary and through the tireless effort and support of the South Carolina Consortium for Gifted Education (the NAGC state affiliate), performance-based assessments in the verbal and nonverbal domains at the primary level (grades 2 and 3) and the intermediate level (grades 4 and 5) were developed and introduced. (For a comprehensive summary of this process, see VanTassel-Baska et al., 2002.) Using the research on authentic assessment and being conscious of factors affecting minority and economically disadvantaged learners, the SDE ventured into an assessment area where there was little previous work done in terms of the elementary-level student.

These performance-based assessments, known in South Carolina as Project STAR—Student Tasks and Rubrics, have the following characteristics:

- small-group assessments that are not timed;
- preteaching experiences that engage the student prior to his responding to an assessment prompt of a similar nature;
- separate assessment forms for nonverbal and verbal domains;
- manipulatives for hands-on, concrete learning; and
- paper-and-pencil responses to prompts.

The development of the performance-based assessments represented only one hurdle in their use. The cost of producing these consumable assessments, creating the manipulatives required for administration of the tasks, training test coordinators and teachers to administer the tasks, scoring the assessments, and reporting the results had not been considered. Neither was there a plan for how often and when these performance assessments would be administered as a new component of the statewide testing system. Also, there was no idea of the size of the potential pool of students who would be eligible to participate in performance-based assessments as part of the identification protocol.

Finally, a most significant question remained to be answered: What were the consequences of using performance-based assessment? What would these students look like when compared with "traditionally" identified gifted learners? What educational needs unique to them would be present? How would teachers adapt curriculum and respond with different instructional strategies? What support systems and procedural guidelines would be needed to ensure success for these learners?

Census Testing

A process for partially assisting districts with the costs associated with administering census aptitude and achievement assessments was solved by the SDE providing these assessments. Paying the costs did not diminish concerns from early childhood educators with regard to testing. Neither did it provide a solution to parental concerns that a child was having a bad day when tested. What it did accomplish was that, for the first time, every second-grade child had access to screening for gifted services.

Previous barriers of not being referred for screening by parents or teachers or possible bias in the nomination process were broken down; equal access to the screening process was being realized. Census testing also contributed to the likelihood that gifted learners from more diverse backgrounds would now be identified.

One should not confuse equal access to the state screening process with access to an appropriate screening process. Hurdles were still in place for underrepresented gifted children. Performance on aptitude and achievement assessments was still the primary way the majority of children were identified. Furthermore, the opportunity for performance-based assessments hinged on first meeting the standard in either aptitude or achievement. So, while the system was improving, it still was not as responsive to identifying minority and low-SES students as it could be.

Professional Development Needs

In partnership with Converse College, a "packaged" staff development presentation, "Gifted Students, Who Are They?" was developed and disseminated to each district for use in building the knowledge base of teachers and administrators on the characteristics of gifted students. This resource provided the initial professional development to assist administrators and teachers in making referrals and in understanding the needs of gifted learners. Although this served to build awareness, it did not address solutions for follow-up, ongoing growth, or technical assistance with the target audiences. Also, it did not adequately meet the need for building a knowledge base for teachers in terms of meeting the educational needs of gifted learners from diverse populations with domain-specific strengths.

Curriculum Concerns

Prior to 1999 the curricula used to serve academically gifted learners could best be described as enrichment. In many districts gifted curricula resided in the mind of the teacher, based upon his or her interests and knowledge. Responding to challenges as to why all students should not have access to these enrichment experiences was difficult. Although not denying the relevance of enrichment, the state policy now called for a blending of acceleration and enrichment that must be based upon state academic standards. In fact, language in the regulation called for content, process, and product standards that exceeded the academic standards expected of all students.

This shift in program service expectations and curriculum expectations combined with a dramatically more diverse gifted population was received with mixed feelings. Many veteran teachers were reluctant to turn loose of favorite enrichment experiences. Other teachers complained that the identified students were not on par with previous gifted students. The refrain "These students are not really gifted" was becoming a common theme. In reality, the problem was not providing a curriculum that matched the domain strength of the learner coupled with pressure to teach state academic standards (VanTassel-Baska & Feng, 2004).

In collaboration with the South Carolina Consortium for Gifted Education, the SDE created a *Best Practices Manual* (1999) to clarify the new regulations, to provide districts with research-based best practices in gifted education, and to identify resources that would support implementation of the new policy. In addition to providing this resource, professional development for district gifted coordinators in its use was provided. For the next few years, sessions at the annual state gifted conference were planned to respond to the concerns being expressed by district coordinators, administrators, and teachers.

It is apparent by this point that a nonlinear approach to policy development yields multiple problems that affect the attitudes, beliefs, and commitment of those expected to implement the policy.

Preparing to Respond

Almost immediately upon implementation of the 1999 regulation, the SDE began to collect data and define problems in order to make adjustments in state policy. A common theme heard during implementation was an expression of doubt in terms of meeting the original intention: to increase access, broaden the gifted population, and identify more minority and low-income gifted learners. To understand the actual impact of the policy, the SDE contracted for an external study of the students who qualified for the gifted program—comparing those qualifying through traditional assessments with those qualifying through performance tasks (VanTassel-Baska & Feng, 2004).

Through data collection by the SDE and supported by findings from the external review, it was found that referrals and screenings increased the percentage of students being identified significantly, and minority and low-income students who would not have been identified when relying solely on traditional assessments were being found. For example, in the 1999–2000 and 2000–2001 school years, 9,034 students participated in the administration of Project STAR. Across these 2 years, 2,206 (24.4%) qualified for gifted services through performance assessment. Of these, 15% (1999–2000) and 18% (2000–2001) receive free or reduced lunch. On average, 16% were African American (VanTassel-Baska & Feng, 2004). This increase in the number of students eligible for gifted programs led to the need for more teachers, raised problems with teacher-pupil ratios, and caused budgetary strain in an already under-funded program.

Moreover, the students identified through the 1999 protocols exhibited more uneven profiles of performance, with many of these students having high nonverbal abilities. For example, during the first 2 years of administering Project STAR, 81.3% of the students identified for gifted services had high nonverbal abilities (VanTassel-Baska & Feng, 2004). This increased diversity of giftedness gave rise to teacher perceptions that questioned student abilities and domain-specific giftedness. Issues around performance in the regular classroom, lack of verbal skills, lack of persistence on tasks, inability to manage time, poor organizational skills, and varying motivation were reported. However, site visits revealed that teachers in gifted programs made little to no accommodations in the curriculum or with instructional strategies for students with diverse profiles.

Also, the liberal use of grade point average as a performance indicator contributed to the percentage increase as well as to the differences within the gifted population. As these students entered gifted programs, it became clear that grade point average was not a strong enough indicator of giftedness and had been weighted too heavily in the identification criteria.

In terms of performance on state assessments, a trend appeared to be emerging: Traditionally identified students performed better than performance-based identified students. However, the difference did not appear to be educationally significant (SCEOC, 2006; VanTassel-Baska, Feng, Chandler, Quek, & Swanson, 2007).

Back to the Policy Drawing Board

Cuban (2004) suggested that factors such as knowledge, beliefs, attention, motivation, and capacity influence how school administrators and teachers receive and implement state policy. These factors certainly were active in the response to the first changes in South Carolina gifted policy in 13 years. Although acknowledging the challenges and discomfort of the unanticipated changes, the SDE held its course. Assisting and supporting, listening and learning, the state monitored and evaluated the amended regulations from 1999 until 2004. Then, in 2004, gifted policy again was reworked based upon what had been learned.

Diverse Gifted Learners

As a result of changes in the identification process, a more diverse gifted population was identified with domain-specific strengths and weaknesses (see Table 11.2 and Table 11.3). Also, students identified through performance-based assessments

Table 11.2
Students Taking South Carolina Performance Assessments and Percentage Qualifying 2000–2008 (Carolinian Consultancy, 2008)

Administration	Number of Students	Number Qualified	Percentage
Spring 2000 (William & Mary) Form A	1,699	412	24.5
Fall 2000 (C2) Form A	7,081	1,771	25.4
Spring 2001 (C2) Form B	6,039	1,589	26.3
Fall 2001 (C2) Form B	5,335	1,788	33.5
Spring 2002 (C2) Form A	7,757	1,442	18.6
Fall 2002 (C2) Form A	4,338	1,033	23.8
Spring 2003 (C2) Form B	12,589	3,080	24.5
Spring 2004 (C2) Form A	14,584	3,056 V = 1,090, NV = 1,523 Both = 443	21.0
Spring 2005 (C2) Form B	16,125	3,457 V = 1,642, NV = 1,277 Both = 538	21.4
Spring 2006 (C2) Form C	20,087	5,313 V = 1,642, NV = 2,530 Both = 796	26.4
Spring 2007 (C2) Form D	15,287	4,744 V = 1,567, NV = 2,242 Both = 935	31.0
Spring 2008 (C2) Form A	16,466	3,177 V = 1,999, NV = 962 Both = 216	19.3
Totals	127,387	30,862	26.4 (average)

Note. From Carolinian Consultancy (2008). V = Verbal, NV = Nonverbal.

Table 11.3
Performance Assessments, Primary Level, by Ethnicity

Year		White	Black	Other
2000	#	5,792	2,038	243
	Q	1,724	268	65
	%	29.8	13.2	26.7
2001	#	6,647	2,331	244
	Q	2,266	475	76
	%	34.1	20.4	31.1
2002	#	6,889	2,531	317
	Q	1,679	364	62
	%	24.4	14.4	19.6
2003	#	6,568	2,656	377
	Q	2,074	509	94
	%	31.6	19.2	24.9
2004	#	7,804	2,449	577
	Q	1,902	312	125
	%	24.4	12.7	21.7
2005	#	6,751	1,906	529
	Q	2,365	382	160
	%	35.0	20.6	30.2
2006	#	7,547	2,212	625
	Q	1,966	370	171
	%	26.1	20.6	27.4
2007	#	5,934	1,713	560
	Q	2,667	510	250
	%	44.9	29.8	44.6
2008	#	5,739	1,740	662
	Q	1,124	179	107
	%	19.6	10.5	16.2
Total	#	59,671	19,576	3,757
	Q	17,767	3,369	1,110
	% (average)	29.8	17.2	29.5

Note. From Carolinian Consultancy (2008). Q = qualified for gifted services.

tended to have an unbalanced profile when compared with students who qualified by way of traditional aptitude and achievement assessments.

Performance-Based Assessment

Performance can be used effectively as a dimension for identifying students who will benefit from gifted services. However, the use of performance tasks (Project STAR) rather than grade point average is the more valid and reliable indicator at least for elementary-level students. By not relying solely on traditional and aptitude measures, the state continues to identify a higher proportion of low-income gifted learners and African American gifted learners with the use of performance assessments.

Gifted Program Services

Gifted learners need support and time for adjustment when entering gifted program services. This particularly is true when working with diverse gifted learners and special populations (Briggs & Reis, 2003). Data suggest that there are statistically significant differences in the performance of traditionally identified gifted learners and Project STAR-identified gifted learners. However, size of difference is small, and not educationally important (VanTassel-Baska, Feng, & Evans, 2007).

With the identification of more diverse gifted learners, a shift in models used to support these learners is being observed. There appears to be a movement away from a pull-out (resource room) approach that dominated program service previously to a special class model that matches the strength domain of the learner. At the elementary level, the SDE still promotes use of pull-out programs with differentiated curricula that supports not only state standards but also allows for student interest. Elementary programs moving toward special classes do so most often because of limited resources; efficiency prevails.

Teacher interviews indicate that with support and time in the gifted program, Project STAR students work at a comparable level with traditionally identified gifted students. In response to these findings, the SDE instituted guidelines for removal of students from the gifted program when the policy was revised in 2004. These guidelines foster communication and collaboration with the support systems available to diverse gifted learners and reinforce the state's philosophy that access to gifted services is a right not a privilege. (See Removal of Students From Gifted and Talented Programs at http://ed.sc. gov/agency/Standards-and-Learning/Academic-Standards/old/ cso/gifted_talented/gt.html.)

District Gifted Program Planning

Districts lacked strategic plans for gifted programs that stated clear, explicit goals. The need for action plans was even stronger now in order to be responsive to the needs of diverse gifted learners and to clarify the services offered (Smith, 2006). State policy hinted at the need for district gifted program planning, but there was no mandate for it to occur.

In response to these realities, the SDE went back to the policy drawing board—fine-tuning what was working well, adding language to respond to concerns, and eliminating policy that was ineffective. The lessons learned from 1999–2004 guided the SDE in amending state policy.

For example, the 2004 policy instituted 3-year district gifted plans with annual updates. The 3-year plan must be approved by the local school district board, and the initial plan and annual update must be submitted to the SDE for review. Based primarily on the need to respond to a more diverse gifted population, the initial 3-year district plans were required to focus on the areas of curriculum, professional development, and meeting the social and emotional needs for gifted learners.

The 2004 policy presently guides gifted programs, and the SDE continues to monitor its implementation with a task force presently working on revisions to state policy that will go to the State Board of Education in the fall of 2009 (R. Blanchard, personal communication, June 6, 2008).

Some Final Thoughts

This chapter has identified some of the primary policy implications for identifying and serving a more diverse population of gifted learners in South Carolina. In order to understand the implications of state policy, it is critical to plan for the monitoring and assessment of such policy. Stakeholders, who include legislators, state boards, state education agencies, state affiliates for gifted education, district and local administrators, teachers, students, and parents, will want evidence concerning the results from policy implementation. Do the assumptions upon which the policy changes were made hold true?

There always is a delicate tension between state policy that is comprehensive and complete, and flexibility that is responsive to district and local school needs. The gifted and talented program exists to provide services to identified students that will develop their unique talents and abilities. Participation in an educational program that goes beyond the services provided by the regular classroom/school program should allow these students to achieve their potential.

Because identified students have demonstrated high performance ability or potential, they have an educational right to these services. Moreover, the services provided for identified students must match their area(s) of strength(s)—be domain-specific. Accepting diversity in giftedness, state policy must support these learners, ensuring these students are found; provided with appropriate curriculum; taught by teachers who have the knowledge, skills, and dispositions to work with diverse gifted learners; and supported as necessary to be successful.

A Personal Word

It is difficult to imagine policy change and implementation without the presence of leadership. Although leadership may certainly come from personnel within a state educational agency, it most often is insufficient and ill-equipped for the work of designing, implementing, supporting, and monitoring the policy changes discussed in this chapter. A lesson learned is that policy work requires a broad, dedicated, and committed leadership network. There is no single definition for such a network; it will vary from state to state. It must consist of leaders who will be advocates for gifted programs and exercise their unique gifts and skills to make policies come to life.

A strong, well-defined relationship with the state affiliate for gifted education (in this case, South Carolina Consortium for Gifted Education) allows for outreach and technical assistance that an individual functioning inside a state bureaucracy could never provide. The relationship is held together through mutual respect, mutual trust, and mutual commitment. The state affiliate understands and accepts the role it can appropriately fulfill and does not assume an identity that would create conflict with the state education agency. The members of the state affiliate serve as a cadre of leaders supporting the districts and guiding the SDE—a collective voice while maintaining responsibility for the uniquely individual needs and concerns.

Also, an effective working relationship with higher education is critical to the success of policy design and implementation. Leadership from higher education (in this case, Dr. Nancy Breard, Converse College, and Dr. Julie Swanson, College of Charleston) supports professional development as well as research for understanding the impact of policy. When faced with limited support from higher education within the state, relationships must be established and nurtured with colleges and universities outside of the state. Partnerships with individuals at these colleges as well as with centers located at universities support leadership when strained and provide expertise in areas lacking (in this case, Dr. Joyce VanTassel-Baska and the Center for Gifted Education at The College of William and Mary, and Dr. Jean Gubbins and The National Research Center on the Gifted and Talented at the University of Connecticut).

Lastly, there are always individual leaders whose passion and tireless energy force others to press on and who refuse to surrender even in the most challenging of times (in this case, Dr. Fran O'Tuel, Donna Darby, and Senator Nikki Setzler). Their imagination and inspiration can sustain us when frustration is high and can "shake us up" when our complacent nature begins to appear.

References

Barker, J. (2008). *Scouting the future.* Retrieved August 26, 2008, from http://strategicexploration.com/strategic-exploration/scouting-the-future

Briggs, C. J., & Reis, S. M. (2003). An introduction to the topic of cultural diversity and giftedness. In C. A. Tomlinson, D. Y. Ford,

S. M. Reis, C. J. Briggs, & C. A. Strickland (Eds.), *In search of the dream: Designing schools and classrooms that work for high potential students from diverse cultural backgrounds* (pp. 5–32). Washington, DC: National Association for Gifted Children.

Callahan, C. M., Tomlinson, C. A., Moon, T. R., Tomchin, E. M., & Plucker, J. A. (1995). *Project START: Using a multiple intelligences model in identifying and promoting talent in high-risk students* (Research Monograph 95136). Storrs: University of Connecticut, The National Center on the Gifted and Talented.

Carolinian Consultancy. (2008). *Annual report Project STAR performance tasks.* Columbia: South Carolina State Department of Education.

Coleman, M. R. (2003). *The identification of students who are gifted.* East Lansing, MI: National Center for Research on Teacher Learning. (ERIC Document Reproduction Service No. ED480431)

Cuban, L. (2004). A solution that lost its problem: Centralized policy-making and classroom gains. In N. Epstein (Ed.), *Who's in charge here?* (pp. 104–130). Washington, DC: Brookings Institution Press.

Ford, D. Y. (1994). *The recruitment and retention of African-American students in gifted education programs: Implications and recommendations* (RBDM9406). Storrs: University of Connecticut, The National Center on the Gifted and Talented.

Ford, D. Y. (1996). *Reversing underachievement among gifted Black students: Promising programs and practices.* New York: Teachers College Press.

Ford, D. Y., & Trotman, M. F. (2000). The Office for Civil Rights and non-discriminatory testing, policies, and procedures: Implications for gifted students. *Roeper Review, 24,* 52–58.

Frasier, M. M., Garcia, J. H., & Passow, A. H. (1995). *A review of assessment issues in gifted education and their implications for identifying gifted minority students.* Storrs: University of Connecticut, The National Center on the Gifted and Talented.

Gallagher, J. J., & Coleman, M. R. (1992). *State policies on the identification of gifted students from special populations: Three states in profile.* Chapel Hill, NC: Gifted Education Policy Studies Program.

Lee, S. (1997). [Title VI resolution agreement between the South Carolina Department of Education and the Office for Civil Rights]. Unpublished raw data.

Maker, C. J. (2001). DISCOVER: Assessing and developing problem solving. *Gifted Education International, 15,* 232–251.

Passow, A. H., & Frasier, M. M. (1996). Toward improving identification of talent potential among minority and disadvantaged students. *Roeper Review, 18,* 198–202.

Smith, L. (2006). Strategic planning and gifted programs. In J. Purcell & R. Eckert (Eds.), *Designing services and programs for high-ability learners: A guidebook for gifted education* (pp. 277–291). Washington, DC: National Association for Gifted Children.

South Carolina Department of Education. (1999). *South Carolina gifted and talented best practices manual.* Columbia, SC: Author.

South Carolina Education Oversight Committee. (2006). *A performance analysis of South Carolina's gifted and talented.* Columbia, SC: Author.

Swanson, J. D. (2006). Breaking through assumptions about low-income, minority gifted students. *Gifted Child Quarterly, 50,* 11–25.

Swanson, J. D. (2007). Policy and practice: A case study of gifted policy implementation. *Journal for the Education of the Gifted, 31,* 131–164.

VanTassel-Baska, J., & Feng, A. (2004). *Project STAR follow-up study.* Unpublished report, South Carolina State Department of Education.

VanTassel-Baska, J., Feng, A., Chandler, K., Quek, C., & Swanson, J. (2007). *Project STAR two year research study report: Commission by the South Carolina Department of Education.* Columbia: South Carolina State Department of Education.

VanTassel-Baska, J., Feng, A., & Evans, B. (2007). Patterns of identification and performance among gifted students identified through performance tasks: A three-year analysis. *Gifted Child Quarterly, 51,* 218–231.

VanTassel-Baska, J., Johnson, D., & Avery, L. D. (2002). Using performance tasks in the identification of economically disadvantaged and minority gifted learners: Findings from Project STAR. *Gifted Child Quarterly, 46,* 110–123.

Leveraging Resource Capital to Chart a New Course for Promising Students From Poverty

Joyce VanTassel-Baska

The issues explored in this book regarding poverty and its comingling effects with race, geographic location, family patterns, and gender exemplify the complexity of identifying and providing appropriate programming for gifted learners who exhibit these risk factors. Especially of concern is the need for continuous and comprehensive services across the K–16 span that acknowledge and address the typical transitional shifts in school settings and characteristics of school cultures that can derail such students as new challenges emerge. Equally critical is the need for personal support and nurturance from school people as well as peers. As seen from the case study data presented, these students tend to have families desiring to support them at home albeit in ways not always conducive to academic pursuits. However, they also often do not have sufficient support from teachers and administrators or from peers who share their background.

Thus a model of working with learners from low-income backgrounds clearly is needed in order to understand the issues fully and move forward to ensure the success of these deserving learners.

The Metaphor of Capital

The idea of capital is an intriguing metaphor to use in conceptualizing such a model for low-income students. Capital refers to resources of various types that can be used to advance the development of any venture. In the business world, risk capital is that which is used to expand current efforts in directions where the outcome is not assured. In the case of low-income learners, the capital investment needed would fall into the risk category as currently only 5% of these learners are likely to become socially mobile in their lifetime, less than 1% are likely to get an advanced degree, and many more fall by the wayside earlier in respect to educational attainment. A larger number of these students are likely to become lifetime underachievers, taking jobs commensurate with educational level but not ability (Wyner, Bridgeland, & Dilulio, 2007). If it had not been for the GI Bill post World War II, many more males in our society would have joined this underachieving group.

So, is the idea of investing in this group of individuals to be seen as risk capital or a good long-term investment that will yield important returns to society? Studies of eminent people continue to demonstrate the overrepresentation of individuals who have experienced adversity in their lives, including poverty, yet have risen above these circumstances to achieve at high levels. The real-world examples we have favor the view that such an investment is worthwhile and likely to pay off for the larger society as well as the individual. If we also think about the power of parents as role models in the intergenerational struggle to extricate oneself from poverty, then the investment also makes sense as it may facilitate a break in the chain so that these families can begin to experience upward mobility for the first time through their child.

There are various types of capital that people from poverty need. At the national level, policy might address some universal needs. At a basic level, these students need social and intellectual capital that a rich society has to offer, capital that is housed in its institutions of learning and its institutions of culture, and of social interaction afforded by association with children and youth who come from more advantaged backgrounds. How can social policy provide such capital? For older children of poverty, scholarships to college based on merit and need provide initial entry points. In an age of post-affirmative action, these students will continue to require resources outside their circumstances to elevate the trajectory of their lives. For veterans of the Iraq conflict, the new GI Bill will provide a pathway to these institutions. For very young students in poverty, there is a critical need to identify and nurture promise in early childhood in order to ensure they enter school fully prepared to compete successfully with other promising learners who come from more advantaged backgrounds at home. A policy of universal childcare coupled with preschool options that are educationally enriched is an essential provision to ensure these students are not overlooked early. Currently, only about half of poor children have access to Head Start programs of varying quality (Hodgkinson, 2007). The need for gifted-level opportunities at these ages as a foundation for future excellence cannot be underestimated as crucial for optimal development in adverse circumstances. For elementary and middle school students, there is a real need to provide guaranteed access to appropriate social and intellectual capital through social policy gateways that seek to identify and nurture intellectual, academic, and creative talent. Grants to universities to find and serve these learners in laboratory settings, while an old idea, may have new currency for this purpose. Such policy would augment the fine work done by the Jack Kent Cooke Foundation and others to provide such assistance to promising learners of poverty at middle school level and beyond. Current scholarship programs at talent search universities only begin to scratch the surface of those in need of support. For younger students, the provision of educational vouchers to promising learners that would entitle them to attend full-time gifted programs in their state would be a way to encourage development.

At a state and regional level, these students require the mobilization of organizations including state departments, foundations, and community groups to support their talent development process. At this level, policies need to support the construction of these learners' habits of mind toward education, the establishment of a community of learning as a lifelong enterprise, and the tacit knowledge necessary to traverse the challenges that lay ahead. A community organization could sponsor a series of mentorships, for example, that emphasized learning from a practicing professional the nature of her activities, her attitudes, and her most important skills on the job. Through such contact, shadowing, and discussion, promising students might come to appreciate the relevance of how they think about themselves and their futures as a state of becoming, a state over which they have some control. Such organizations also could provide internships in business, politics, education, and science and engineering that would provide on-the-job apprenticeships for students to get real-world experience in these professions.

In the educational world, policies and systems also need to be established as the role of talent development is a shared one by society at large and educational institutions in particular. A national educational policy that targets promising students from poverty for special value-added funding for specialized programs and services would be a strong catalyst for states to follow suit. Such funding could be targeted for personalized service options for this population such as tutoring, mentoring, and counseling with the student and his family. Legislation on teacher quality could earmark special funding for the preparation of teachers who could specialize in working with these kinds of learners. Research agendas could be encouraged through governmental agencies to focus on these learners in a more overt way. Teacher certification could acknowledge the competencies needed to be successful with high-end learners from poverty. Professional development plans for teachers could include reflections on how to advance the talent development of students in their schools through planned optimal match experiences, goal-setting, and modeling a passion for and commitment to learning.

Finally, attention to the social and emotional development of these learners is a critical piece to ensure their successful talent development process across the premium educational years in elementary, high school, and the undergraduate years in college. No other population may be at such a disadvantage in terms of fitting in and finding their niche than these students. Inside, they know they have special qualities that may make them successful but rarely do they have the resources to develop those qualities or know how to access them. If they are extraordinarily good at something, their passion and motivation may carry them beyond their current sphere and open up new opportunities through competitions, educational enrichment opportunities, and personalized learning contexts. Fitting in has to do with finding where your aptitudes, interests, and values converge and the environments that support these. As we know from research (see Achter, Benbow, & Lubinski, 1996), many students from age 12 have a cluster of possible careers that they might consider, based on their profile data. Yet for students from poverty, such information often is not available nor are the follow-up mechanisms in place to access the efficient pathway to these careers (Olszewski-Kubilius, 2007). The finding of self, identity development, and social skill development are all integrally related to the quest for career niche as well (Moon, 2008).

Freud once suggested that love and work were the two qualities that made life worth living. Too often promising students from poverty seek love in the absence of work as the secret to life's happiness and meaning in their lives. For example, having a boyfriend or husband and having a baby often are presented as the primary goals for girls in underprivileged circumstances. Family connections are overemphasized to keep the larger world at bay while containing the aspirations of its members. Only strong and consistent external opportunities that provide an alternate view of life's possibilities can counter the strength of these forces and channel energy that too often can explode in rage and socially inappropriate behaviors. Thus identity development must extend beyond gender, family, and ethnic group membership in order to reflect the true self.

Thus the capital investment in promising students from poverty has to be approached from multiple levels—national, state, regional, and local. It also has to be approached from various perspectives—the need for fiscal support, the need for social connection and modeling, the need for educational opportunities matched to talent areas, and the need for career planning. Making a difference in the lives of these learners will require the personal involvement of many people over time as well as the policy levers of government to target resources to this area of social need.

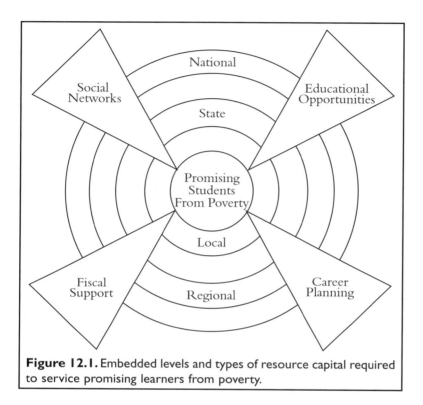

Figure 12.1. Embedded levels and types of resource capital required to service promising learners from poverty.

Figure 12.1 depicts the interplay of the levels of service required in order to leverage the capital necessary to make a real difference in the lives of these learners.

Lingering Concerns

Michael Piechowski (1994) wrote a powerful article called "The Self Victorious: Personal Strengths, Chance, and Co-Incidence," which chronicled the lives of eminent women from poverty who rose above their circumstances to accomplish important work in their world although that work was not paradigm-shifting. His premise was that these women all had internal strength of character and ambition that overcame external obstacles that got in their way. In other words, the power of the individual transcended the power of the societal influences that shaped her world. In today's world, this notion seems somehow antiquated. Psychological explanation has given way to sociological argument—we are the way we are because of how we have been nurtured or thwarted in our developmental path, not because of our own predispositions, will, and determination to make things work.

Yet, examples are all around us of people who charted their own course, despite others who may have doubted their capacity or the strength of their intentions. In the recent Olympic competition in Beijing, Michael Phelps took eight gold medals for his swimming, the most in history. Consistently in interviews, he maintained this had been his dream that he had worked on for years. Was society responsible for his accomplishment in some way because there is an Olympics and an infrastructure to help prepare American athletes, because he had a supportive mother and family around him, and because school people got out of his way so that he could devote more time to practice? I find it troubling that anyone would think that such a human and singular accomplishment could be done just because of the societal structures that were in place and that provided a modicum of favorable support.

And what of the collaborative spirit that fueled the wins in three races that were team relays? Michael gave much credit to his teammates in helping him gain the accolades he received for the medal count. However, could the American relay team have done it without him and his record times for individual legs of the race? Although much can be accomplished in a collaborative way, the desire to persevere and prevail in challenging circumstances must come from within. This will is related to the belief in self, belief in one's power to personally change, to control and overcome circumstances, resiliency, and optimism. In the dark hours of the night and early morning, it is the individual spirit that must be motivated to accomplish what no one has done before. Just as Michael proved his mettle in the Olympic Games, so too must all promising learners from adverse circumstances find their own idiosyncratic pathway to success. Although nurturance at key stages of life may help, in the end it is an individual decision to delay gratification, to develop self-discipline, to continue with education, to resist temptations, to rebound from setbacks, and to find and make a commitment to a niche area.

Thus my concern rests with helping promising learners of poverty understand that they are in charge of their lives and must chart the course, whatever it may be. Ironically, the road out of poverty may be better defined if one has an impossible dream, an area of defined talent or ability, and a desire to work hard to achieve a modicum of success. Seeing oneself as an artist in life's creation is the mindset that may make the vital difference to these individuals over time as it frees them from a faulty belief system based on a predestined fixed sense of fate control or a blind faith that can easily dissipate the drive needed to excel in an area (Olenchak, 2008).

Secondly, promising learners from poverty must carefully consider how family may both facilitate and impede their progress on the road of talent development. The parental model that has been most facilitative for high-level performance has been the self-sacrificing one—mothers like Pablo Casal's who take their sons to study with the great masters, even though it means deserting the rest of the family (Bloom, 1985). Yet, most parents living in poverty cannot do these things, even if they knew it was crucial to their child's development at a certain stage of life. They have financial obligations that preclude such decisions. Single mothers often have several children, and no one to leave them with even for short periods of time. More critical, however, is the lack of understanding in most families, particularly where the child will be a first-generation college student, that academic success requires the development of skills and attitudes associated with a professional world of which parents are not a part. Resentment over a child's opportunities not given to or attained by the parent can impede development as can family routines that focus on group social activities, eating up time that such students need to be spending on more solitary talent-developing pursuits. Parents have a difficult role in talent development under the best of circumstances—how much to help, push, or encourage, which areas of interest to foster, and what aspects of talent development to support with additional resources (Rogers, 2002). In families of poverty, these finer grained decisions are not even thought about, let alone discussed and acted upon. For these students to succeed, they must put their family in perspective and in the process grow away from them in crucial ways. Programs like A Better Chance operate on this premise, that students from poverty will be more successful in a boarding school atmosphere where they can learn the alternative social and intellectual culture of the society that will be the stepping-stone to the Ivy League university. Our specialized residential schools also serve a similar purpose for these students—removal from the day-to-day family routines that focus on survival to experience another world where ideas are the currency of time spent (Coleman, 2005).

Thirdly, poverty must be seen as the overarching problem in raising achievement levels for all in this country. Ethnic group membership, while an important variable, is not the central one in raising aspiration levels, achievement, or accomplishment. Rather it is helping poor children from all races reach a threshold level of competence and unleashing potential to individuate even further. President Barack Obama has made the point that his daughters do not deserve special consideration in programs or scholarships or affirmative action services because they are Black. Rather, he argues, children of poverty should be the recipients of such opportunities due to real disadvantagement that can squander their future. In absolute numbers, there are many more White children living in poverty than Black, all of whom require attention to these needs. Yet poverty and race comingle in insidious ways that call attention to the fact that a majority of Blacks and Hispanics in this country also are poor. When we examine the literature on at-risk populations, the factors of single parent status, racial minority status, poverty, second language learning of English, and education level of the mother all become critical factors in the picture of educational disadvantagement (McDill, Natriello, & Pallas, 1986). That same literature suggests that educational attainment is the best predictor of adult success. Because we cannot control for many aspects of a child's background, we can attempt to moderate the effects of poverty such that educational mobility to the highest levels becomes a reality for the promising poor.

Fourthly, we must tackle the question of "Why not help all of the poor children?" Because we have some evidence that suggests gifted programs, services, and materials are good for all learners, then why not see the importance of upgrading education for all rather than influence the lives of a few? This question is integrally linked to the issue of developing individuals rather than groups in society, and in providing support at propitious times and in critical areas for those who demonstrate promise in a talent development area. Resources have been available for some time at the federal level to students who are poor, ethnically diverse, and underperforming. Yet similar resources have not been forthcoming to poor students who are performing at average and above-average levels. Title I funds and NCLB funds have been targeted to low-performing learners. Thus with the limited funding from the Javits program and some foundations such as Jack Kent Cooke, promising learners from poverty can be targeted for services for the first time. It behooves us to use these funds well to ensure that these learners can specifically benefit from them as other sources are not available. No state currently has targeted gifted funding for this population either, even those states that have a high percentage of such learners. In many respects, this population represents the most efficient and cost effective way to address the achievement gap because it already is showing academic promise. It is less costly to raise the achievement levels for these learners than to focus on low-achieving children from poverty who may make limited progress, even with vast amounts of resources available to them.

As services are found to be propitious for the promising poor, we then can begin to diffuse what works to these other populations. Our research to date suggests that all Title I students can benefit from a high-powered curriculum, delivered by teachers trained in differentiation practices (see VanTassel-Baska, Bracken, Feng, & Brown, in press). This finding bodes well for a diffusion plan that tests alternative services for the gifted from poverty and then extends the services to all who may benefit.

Conclusion

This book has been about presenting the case for children from poverty who show promise academically in one or more areas. It suggests that these students may best be found through a combination of traditional and nontraditional measures that emphasize areas of strength and reveal hidden abilities that can be nurtured through careful attention to the information in their profiles. It also suggests that such learners require ongoing services rather than limited ones at only one stage of development. We need to consider carefully the importance of targeting resource capital at all levels of the society to unearth these learners and develop their talents. Only then can we say that gifted education has made a contribution to the larger society by finding and serving the invisible talent that resides in our school districts, untapped and unsupported by the mechanisms of home, school, and community.

References

Achter, J. A., Benbow, C. P., & Lubinski, D. (1996). Multipotentiality among the gifted: Is it a pervasive problem? *Gifted Child Quarterly, 41*, 2–12.

Bloom, B. S. (1985). *Developing talent in young people.* New York: Ballantine Books.

Coleman, L. (2005). *Nurturing talent in high school: Life in the fast lane.* New York: Teachers College Press.

Hodgkinson, H. (2007). Leaving too many children behind: A demographer's view on the neglect of America's youngest children. In J. VanTassel-Baska & T. Stambaugh (Eds.), *Overlooked gems: A national perspective on low-income promising learners* (pp. 7–22). Washington, DC: National Association for Gifted Children.

McDill, E. L., Natriello, G., & Pallas, A. M. (1986). A population at risk: Potential consequences of tougher school standards for student dropouts. *American Journal of Education, 94*, 135–181.

Moon, S. (2008). Theories to guide affective curriculum development. In J. L. VanTassel-Baska, T. L. Cross, & R. F. Olenchak (Eds.), *Social-emotional curriculum with gifted and talented students* (pp. 11–40). Waco, TX: Prufrock Press.

Olenchak, R. (2008). Creating a life: Orchestrating a symphony of self, a work always in progress. In J. L. VanTassel-Baska, T. L. Cross, & R. F. Olenchak (Eds.), *Social-emotional curriculum with gifted and talented students* (pp. 41–78). Waco, TX: Prufrock Press.

Olszewski-Kubilius, P. (2007). The role of summer programs in developing the talents of gifted students. In J. L. VanTassel-Baska (Ed.),

Serving gifted learners beyond the traditional classroom (pp. 13–32). Waco, TX: Prufrock Press.

Piechowski, M. (1994). The self victorious: Personal strengths, chance, and co-incidence. *Roeper Review, 20,* 191–198.

Rogers, K. B. (2002). *Re-forming gifted education: Matching the program to the child.* Scottsdale, AZ: Gifted Potential Press.

VanTassel-Baska, J., Bracken, B., Feng, A., & Brown, E. (in press). A longitudinal study of reading comprehension and reasoning ability of students in elementary Title I schools. *Journal for the Education of the Gifted.*

Wyner, J., Bridgeland, J., & Dilulio, J. J., Jr. (2007). *Achievementrap: How America is failing milions of high-achieving students from low-income families.* Lansdowne, VA: Jack Kent Cooke Foundation.

About the Editor

Joyce VanTassel-Baska is the Jody and Layton Smith Professor of Education and Executive Director of the Center for Gifted Education at The College of William and Mary in Virginia, where she has developed a graduate program and a research and development center in gifted education. Formerly, she initiated and directed the Center for Talent Development at Northwestern University, and has served as a state director of gifted programs, a district coordinator, and a teacher of high school students. Dr. VanTassel-Baska has published widely including 27 books and more than 500 refereed journal articles, book chapters, and scholarly reports. She is the editor of the Equity and Excellence in Gifted Education Series, of which this is the fourth volume. Dr. VanTassel-Baska is the past-president of the National Association for Gifted Children. During her tenure as NAGC president she oversaw the adoption of the new teacher standards for gifted education, and organized and chaired the National Leadership Conference on Promising and Low-Income Learners. Her major research interests are on the talent development process and effective curricular interventions with the gifted. She has served as principal investigator on 60 grants and contracts totaling over $15 million, including eight from the United States Department of Education

(USDOE). Currently, she is co-principal investigator of Project Clarion, a science concept attainment study for Title I students in grades K–3. She holds her bachelor's, master's, and doctoral degrees from the University of Toledo where she also received a Distinguished Achievement Alumna Award in 2003.

About the Authors

Annie Xuemei Feng is a behavioral scientist, a SAIC Frederick Contractor, supporting the Behavioral Research Program of the Division of Cancer Control and Population Sciences at the National Cancer Institute (NCI). Annie is a member of the NCI evaluation team of transdisciplinary initiatives. Previously, Annie was the Director of Research and Evaluation at the Center for Gifted Education at The College of William and Mary. She has served as the research director of two federal grants from the U.S. Department of Education, examining the impact of curricular and instructional interventions on the academic achievement of disadvantaged learners in Title I school settings. Annie is also a co-principal investigator of the International Studies of Academic Olympiads, where she joined a group of educational researchers and psychologists studying the talent development process and career trajectory of mathematicians and scientists. She received her bachelor's degree from Jilin University in China and her doctorate in education from St. John's University in New York.

Margie Kitano serves as associate dean of the College of Education and professor of special education at San Diego State University (SDSU). She codeveloped and works with the San

Diego Unified School District collaborative certificate in gifted education. The program combines current theory and research with best practices to support services to gifted students, with special attention to underrepresented populations. Her current research and publications focus on improving services to culturally and linguistically diverse gifted learners. She also consults with institutions of higher education on multicultural course transformation.

E. Wayne Lord is department chair and assistant professor in the Department of Educational Leadership, Counseling, and Special Education at Augusta State University in Augusta, GA. He spent 14 years in the Office of Curriculum and Standards at the South Carolina State Department of Education. During his last 8 years there, he coordinated gifted programs for the state, guided two major revisions to state gifted policy, directed a 3-year Javits grant, secured research studies to understand the impact of regulation changes on gifted programs, and collaborated to strengthen the relationship of the department with the state affiliate, district coordinators, and higher education. Recently, Wayne coauthored a guide to state policy in gifted education and is presently coinvestigator on a follow-up study on gifted learners identified through performance assessment in South Carolina.

Bronwyn MacFarlane is assistant professor of gifted education in the Department of Educational Leadership at the University of Arkansas at Little Rock. She teaches graduate-level courses in gifted education and works with the UALR Center for Gifted Education. With professional experiences as a classroom teacher, teacher of gifted students, administrator of gifted programs, professional development consultant, and university faculty responsibilities, Dr. MacFarlane is actively involved with new research initiatives, reviewing school programs, and developing curriculum. She received the 2008 NAGC Outstanding Doctoral Award; the 2008 College of William and Mary School of Education Dean's Award for Excellence; the 2007 College of William and Mary Excellence in Gifted Education Doctoral Award; and the 2007 International P.E.O. Scholar Award. Dr.

MacFarlane is coeditor of *Leading Change in Gifted Education: The Festschrift of Dr. Joyce VanTassel-Baska* (2009).

Paula Olszewski-Kubilius is currently director of the Center for Talent Development at Northwestern University and a professor in the School of Education and Social Policy. Over the past 25 years, she has created programs for all kinds of gifted learners and written more than 80 articles or book chapters on issues of talent development. Dr. Olszewski-Kubilius has served as the editor of *Gifted Child Quarterly*, coeditor of the *Journal of Secondary Gifted Education,* and on the editorial review boards of *Gifted and Talented International, The Roeper Review,* and *Gifted Child Today*. She also serves on the board of trustees of the Illinois Mathematics and Science Academy and the Illinois Association for the Gifted. She currently is Governance Secretary for the National Association for Gifted Children.

Tamra Stambaugh is the research assistant professor of special education and director of programs for talented youth at Vanderbilt University. She is the coauthor/editor of *Comprehensive Curriculum for Gifted Learners, Overlooked Gems: A National Perspective on Low-Income Promising Students,* and the *Jacob's Ladder Reading Comprehension Program* (all with Dr. Joyce VanTassel-Baska). In addition, Stambaugh has authored or coauthored journal articles and book chapters on a variety of topics in gifted education. Her current research interests include the impact of accelerated curriculum on student achievement, teacher effectiveness, and talent development factors—especially for students of poverty. Stambaugh was the recipient of the NAGC doctoral student award, the Center for Gifted Education doctoral student award, and the Margaret The Lady Thatcher Medallion for scholarship, service, and character. Prior to her work at Vanderbilt, she was Director of Grants and Special Projects at The College of William and Mary's Center for Gifted Education.

Julie Dingle Swanson is a researcher and associate professor in gifted education in the Department of Teacher Education at the College of Charleston. Since the early 1980s, Swanson has worked in the field of gifted education as a GT teacher, district GT coordinator, and as director of two Javits demonstration projects designed to improve services for gifted students in high-poverty South Carolina Schools. Swanson's research interests focus on underrepresented gifted learners, gifted education policy, and teacher development in gifted education.

Frank C. Worrell is a professor at the University of California, Berkeley, where he also is director of the School Psychology program and faculty director of the Academic Talent Development Program. He serves as director for research and development for the California College Preparatory Academy, a charter school partnership involving UC Berkeley and Aspire Public Schools. His research interests include academic talent development, at-risk youth, scale development and validation, and teacher effectiveness.